THE DENT ATLAS OF
BRITISH HISTORY

Second edition

Martin Gilbert

Fellow of Merton College, Oxford

JM Dent

© 1968 and 1993 Martin Gilbert

First published 1968
Second edition 1993

The right of Martin Gilbert to be identified as the author of this
work has been asserted by him in accordance with the Copyright,
Designs and Patents Act 1988.

Printed and bound in Great Britain by
Butler & Tanner Ltd, Frome and London

J M Dent Ltd
The Orion Publishing Group
Orion House
5 Upper St Martin's Lane
London WC2H 9EA

British Library Cataloguing-in-Publication Data

A catalogue record for this book is available from the British Library.

ISBN 0 460 861794 (hardcover)
ISBN 0 460 861808 (paperback)

THE DENT ATLAS OF BRITISH HISTORY

OTHER BOOKS BY MARTIN GILBERT

Preface

The maps in this atlas are intended to provide a visual introduction to British history. I have used the word 'British' in its widest sense, including when relevant England, Scotland, Ireland and Wales, the changing overseas empire, the wars and treaties in which Britain engaged, the alliances in time of peace, the growth of industry and trade, and, on five of the maps, famine and plague.

The story of the British Isles forms the central theme. I have included maps to illustrate economic, social and political problems as well as territorial and military ones. I hope this atlas will help to show that there is more to British history than Hastings and Crécy, Blenheim and Waterloo, Passchendaele and Dunkirk, all of which moments of glory I have tried to put in their wider, and no less important, contexts.

For the maps covering the period before the Norman Conquest the sources are often conflicting on specific details. I have therefore drawn these maps on the basis of probability. In many instances precise knowledge of early frontiers is lacking. I have tried nevertheless to give a clear if also, of necessity, an approximate picture.

As British history advances from wattle huts to timber mansions, and thence on to steel and concrete, so too do the number and variety of facts available to the historian. This is reflected in the maps themselves. I have tried to avoid too complex or too cluttered a page; but a map cannot always satisfy all the demands made upon it, and only the reader can judge where clarity of design and sufficiency of information have been successfully combined.

I am under an obligation of gratitude to those historians and colleagues who kindly scrutinised my draft maps at an early stage, and who made many suggestions for their scope and improvement; in particular Dr J. M. Wallace-Hadrill, Dr Roger Highfield, Mr Ralph Davis, Mr T. F. R. G. Braun, Dr C. C. Davies and Miss Barbara Malament. When the maps were more completed, they were checked by Mr Adrian Scheps, Mr Edmund Ranallo, Mrs Elizabeth Goold, Mr Tony Lawdham and Mrs Jean Kelly, to all of whom my thanks are due.

Twenty-five years have passed since the first edition of this atlas. Within a year of its publication, violence in Northern Ireland re-emerged at the centre of the political stage: I have drawn three new maps to reflect this. The evolution of the European Community has led to growing British participation in Europe, culminating in the Maastricht Treaty of February 1992 and the Edinburgh Summit of December 1992, both of which are a part of the new maps. The Falkland Islands and Persian Gulf wars are included, as are the natural and man-made disasters of the past forty years. Also mapped are many of the problems and challenges of the 1990s, among them asylum, charity, homelessness, unemployment, trade, education, religious diversity, and ethnic minorities. Britain's oil and gas resources are a new feature, as is the most recent phase of the reduction of British overseas possessions, her dwindling military and naval commitments world wide, and her new overseas responsibilities.

The first 118 maps were produced for this atlas by Arthur Banks and his team of cartographers, including Terry Bicknell. The new maps in this edition were produced by Tim Aspden and Robert Bradbrook; I have been helped considerably in the task of compiling them by Abe Eisenstat and Kay Thomson. For their help in providing material for this volume, I would also like to thank the Information Officer, Private Secretary's Office, Buckingham Palace; the Board of Deputies of British Jews, Central Information Desk; the Building Societies Association Press Office; the Lesotho High Commission; the Race Relations Commission; the Refugee Arrivals Project, London Airport; and the Royal Ulster Constabulary Press Office, Belfast.

24 June 1993

MARTIN GILBERT
Merton College, Oxford

Maps

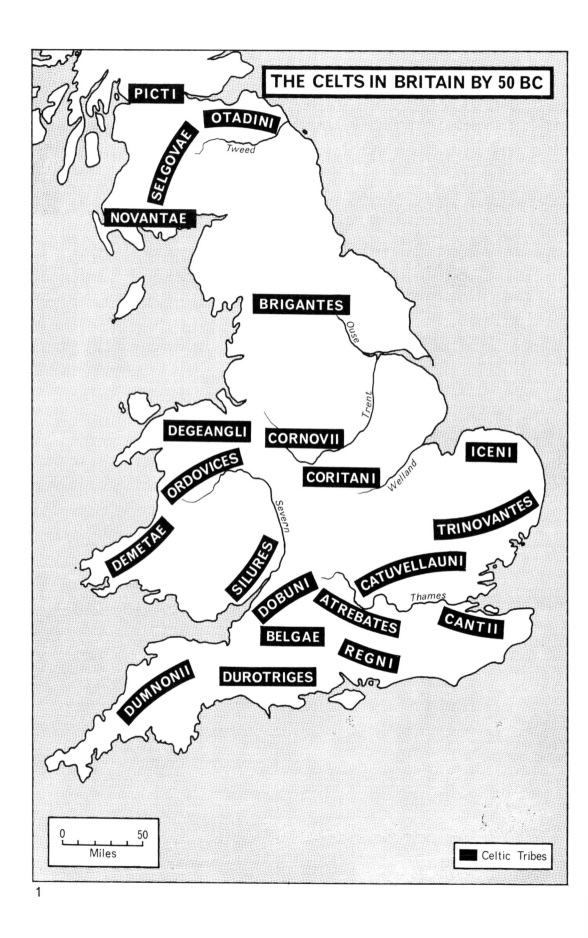

THE CELTS IN BRITAIN BY 50 BC

PICTI

OTADINI

Tweed

SELGOVAE

NOVANTAE

BRIGANTES

Ouse

Trent

DEGEANGLI

CORNOVII

ICENI

ORDOVICES

CORITANI

Welland

Severn

TRINOVANTES

DEMETAE

CATUVELLAUNI

SILURES

DOBUNI

ATREBATES

Thames

BELGAE

CANTII

REGNI

DUMNONII

DUROTRIGES

0 — 50
Miles

■ Celtic Tribes

1

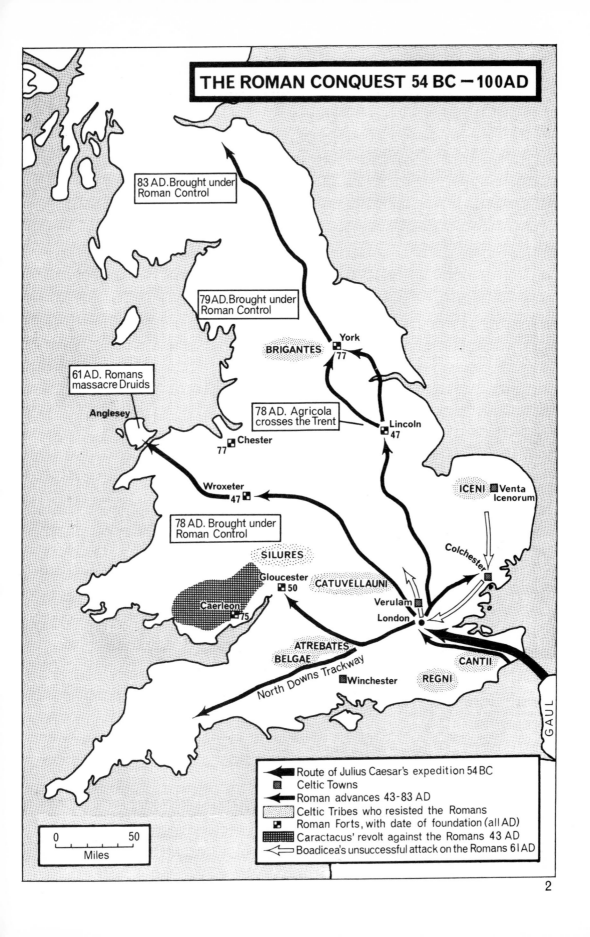

THE ROMAN CONQUEST 54 BC – 100AD

83 AD. Brought under Roman Control

79 AD. Brought under Roman Control

61 AD. Romans massacre Druids

BRIGANTES

York
77

78 AD. Agricola crosses the Trent

Anglesey

77 ■ Chester

Lincoln
47

Wroxeter
47 ■

ICENI ■ Venta Icenorum

78 AD. Brought under Roman Control

SILURES

Colchester

Gloucester
■ 50

CATUVELLAUNI

Caerleon
■ 75

Verulam

London

ATREBATES

BELGAE

CANTII

North Downs Trackway

■ Winchester

REGNI

GAUL

Legend:

- Route of Julius Caesar's expedition 54 BC
- ■ Celtic Towns
- Roman advances 43-83 AD
- Celtic Tribes who resisted the Romans
- ■ Roman Forts, with date of foundation (all AD)
- Caractacus' revolt against the Romans 43 AD
- ⇐ Boadicea's unsuccessful attack on the Romans 61 AD

0 ____ 50
Miles

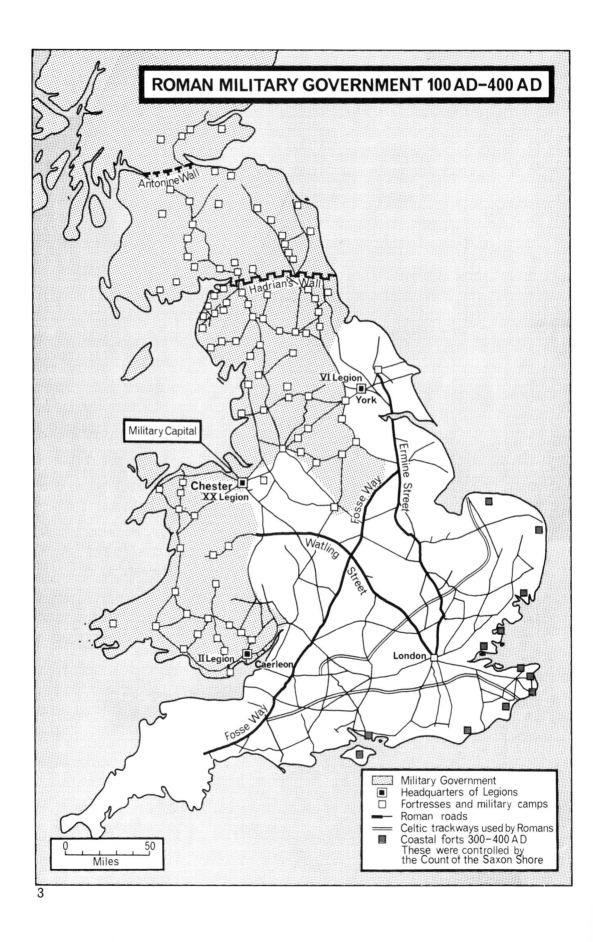

ROMAN MILITARY GOVERNMENT 100 AD–400 AD

Antonine Wall

Hadrian's Wall

VI Legion
York

Military Capital

Chester
XX Legion

Fosse Way

Ermine Street

Watling Street

II Legion
Caerleon

Fosse Way

London

	Military Government
■	Headquarters of Legions
□	Fortresses and military camps
━	Roman roads
═	Celtic trackways used by Romans
▤	Coastal forts 300–400 AD

These were controlled by
the Count of the Saxon Shore

0   50
Miles

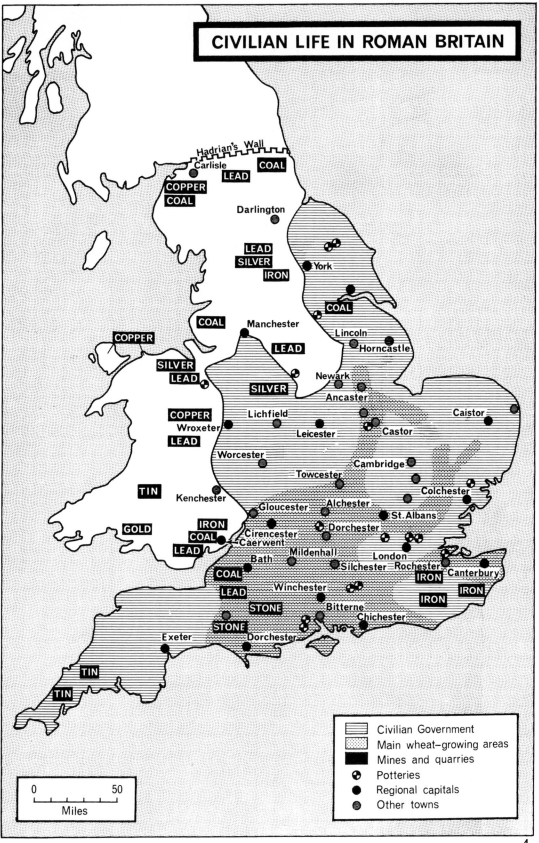

CIVILIAN LIFE IN ROMAN BRITAIN

Hadrian's Wall

Carlisle

COAL
LEAD

COPPER
COAL

Darlington

LEAD
SILVER
IRON

York

COAL

COAL

Manchester

LEAD

Lincoln

Horncastle

COPPER

SILVER
LEAD

SILVER

Newark

Ancaster

COPPER
Wroxeter
LEAD

Lichfield

Leicester

Castor

Caistor

Worcester

Cambridge

Towcester

Colchester

TIN
Kenchester

Alchester

GOLD

IRON
COAL
Cirencester
LEAD
Caerwent

Gloucester

Dorchester

St. Albans

London

Mildenhall

Silchester

Rochester

IRON
Canterbury

IRON

Bath

COAL
LEAD

Winchester

IRON

STONE

Bitterne

Chichester

STONE

Exeter

Dorchester

TIN

TIN

	Civilian Government
	Main wheat-growing areas
	Mines and quarries
☿	Potteries
●	Regional capitals
◉	Other towns

0   50
Miles

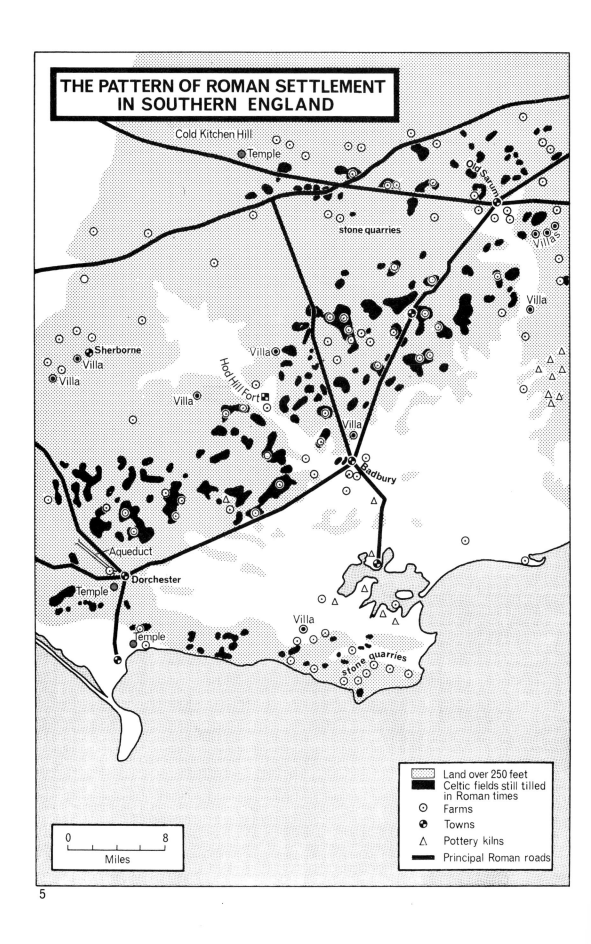

THE PATTERN OF ROMAN SETTLEMENT IN SOUTHERN ENGLAND

Cold Kitchen Hill

Temple

Old Sarum

stone quarries

Villas

Villa

Sherborne

Villa

Villa

Hod Hill Fort

Villa

Villa

Villa

Villa

Badbury

Aqueduct

Dorchester

Temple

Temple

Villa

stone quarries

Land over 250 feet
Celtic fields still tilled
in Roman times
⊙ Farms
❂ Towns
△ Pottery kilns
━ Principal Roman roads

0   8
Miles

5

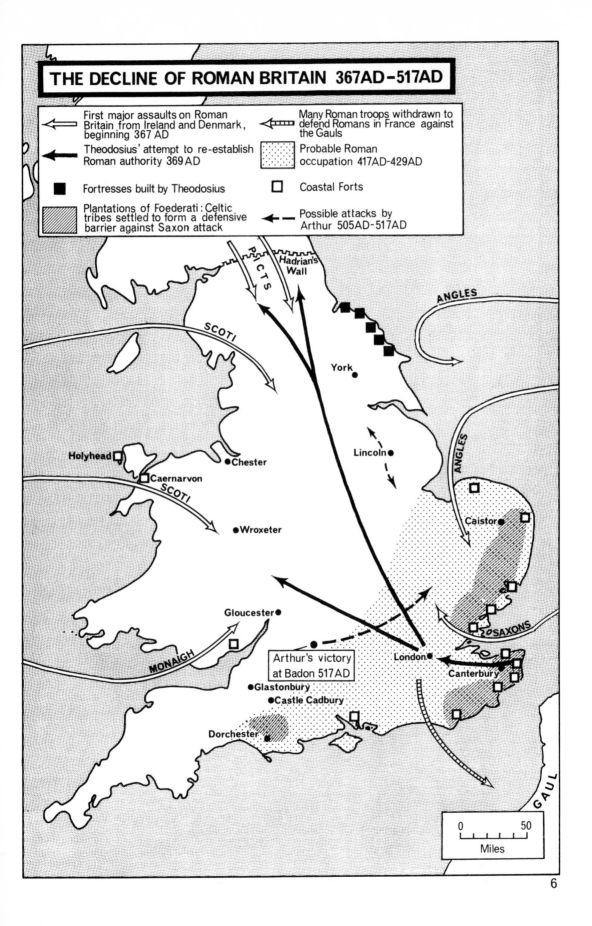

THE DECLINE OF ROMAN BRITAIN 367AD–517AD

First major assaults on Roman Britain from Ireland and Denmark, beginning 367 AD

Theodosius' attempt to re-establish Roman authority 369 AD

Fortresses built by Theodosius

Plantations of Foederati: Celtic tribes settled to form a defensive barrier against Saxon attack

Many Roman troops withdrawn to defend Romans in France against the Gauls

Probable Roman occupation 417AD–429AD

Coastal Forts

Possible attacks by Arthur 505AD–517AD

PICTS

Hadrian's Wall

ANGLES

SCOTI

York

ANGLES

Holyhead

Chester

Caernarvon

SCOTI

Lincoln

Caistor

Wroxeter

SAXONS

Gloucester

MONAIGH

London

Arthur's victory at Badon 517AD

Canterbury

Glastonbury

Castle Cadbury

Dorchester

GAUL

0   50
Miles

6

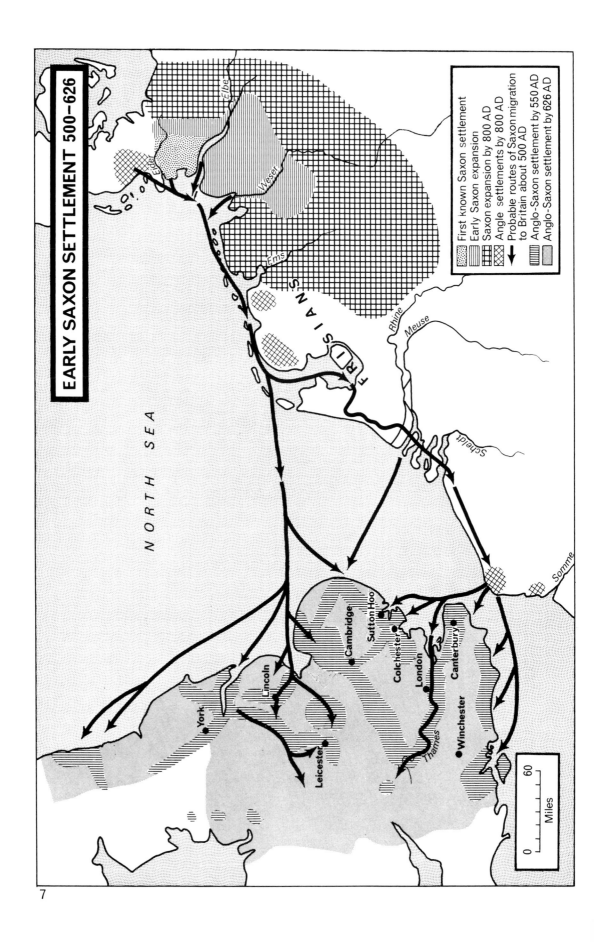

EARLY SAXON SETTLEMENT 500-626

Legend:
- First known Saxon settlement
- Early Saxon expansion
- Saxon expansion by 800 AD
- Angle settlements by 800 AD
- Probable routes of Saxon migration to Britain about 500 AD
- Anglo-Saxon settlement by 550 AD
- Anglo-Saxon settlement by 626 AD

NORTH SEA

FRISIANS

Rivers: Elbe, Weser, Ems, Rhine, Meuse, Scheldt, Somme, Thames

Places: York, Lincoln, Leicester, Cambridge, Sutton Hoo, Colchester, London, Canterbury, Winchester

0   60
Miles

7

SAXON KINGDOMS AND BRETWALDASHIPS 630-829

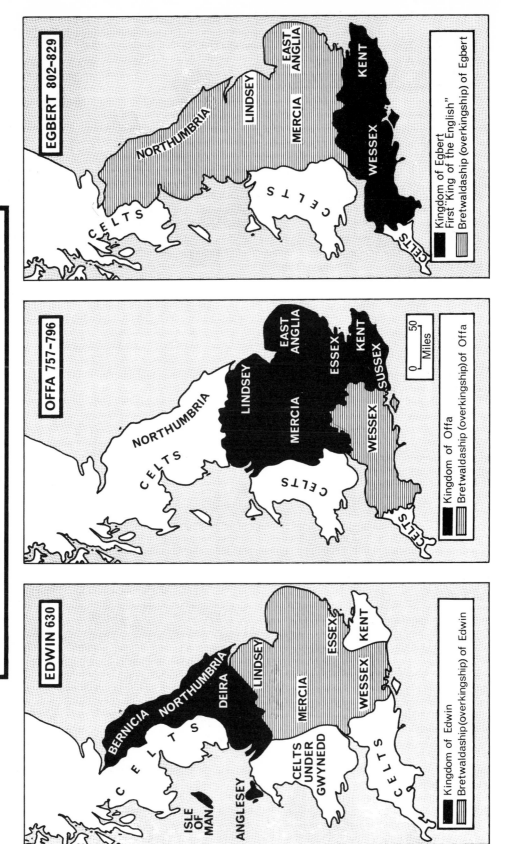

EDWIN 630

BERNICIA
NORTHUMBRIA
DEIRA
LINDSEY
MERCIA
CELTS UNDER GWYNEDD
ESSEX
WESSEX
KENT
CELTS
ISLE OF MAN
ANGLESEY
CELTS

■ Kingdom of Edwin
▥ Bretwaldaship (overkingship) of Edwin

OFFA 757-796

NORTHUMBRIA
CELTS
LINDSEY
MERCIA
EAST ANGLIA
ESSEX
KENT
SUSSEX
WESSEX
CELTS
CELTS

0 50 Miles

■ Kingdom of Offa
▥ Bretwaldaship (overkingship) of Offa

EGBERT 802-829

CELTS
NORTHUMBRIA
LINDSEY
MERCIA
EAST ANGLIA
KENT
WESSEX
CELTS
CELTS

■ Kingdom of Egbert First "King of the English"
▥ Bretwaldaship (overkingship) of Egbert

THE CHURCH 700–850

† Abercorn
Coldingham
Lindisfarne
† Melrose
Coquet Island

L I N D I S F A R N E

WHITHORN

† Tynemouth
† Jarrow
Hexham † † Monkwearmouth

HEXHAM

† Whithorn

Hartlepool

†Gainford
Gilling † Sockburn
Lastingham † Whitby
Hackness†
† Ripon
York

L
O
R
K

Barrow †
Syddensis Civitas
(site not known)

LINDSEY

LICHFIELD

Repton ⊕ † Breedon
Lichfield

Elmham
ELMHAM

Peterborough †
Leicester †Oundle Ely

† Brixworth

LEICESTER

Dunwich
† Bury St.
Edmunds
DUNWICH

HEREFORD

Worcester

WORCESTER

Hereford

DORCHESTER

LONDON

† Malmesbury
Abingdon
Dorchester
Barking ⊕
London

Reculver

ROCH-
ESTER
Minster
Canterbury
CANTER-
BURY Dover
Folkestone
Lyminge

WINCHESTER
Woking

Glastonbury †
Sherborne
†Tisbury
Winchester
SELSEY
Selsey

SHERBORNE
Exeter†
Nursling †
Wimborne†

Miles
0   50

† Religious houses founded by 850

⊕ Double houses where monks and
   nuns lived under the rule of an
   abbess

── Approximate diocesan boundaries

● Diocesan seats

▨ Archbishoprics

9

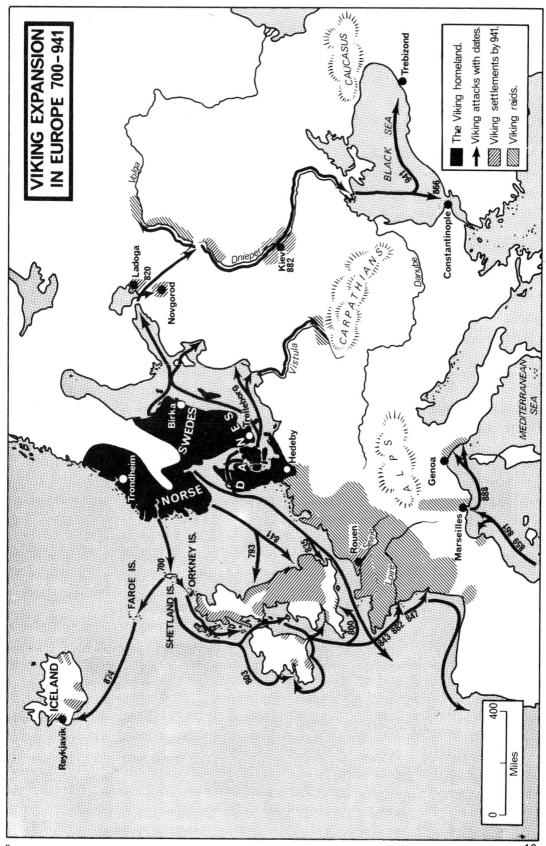

VIKING EXPANSION IN EUROPE 700–941

The Viking homeland.
Viking attacks with dates.
Viking settlements by 941.
Viking raids.

CAUCASUS

Trebizond

BLACK SEA

941

866

Constantinople

Danube

CARPATHIANS

Volga

Dnieper

Ladoga
820

Kiev
882

Novgorod

Vistula

Birka

SWEDES

Trelleborg

D A N E S

Hedeby

MEDITERRANEAN SEA

A L P S

Genoa

Marseilles

888

859

Trondheim

NORSE

Rouen

Seine

Loire

FAROE IS.

SHETLAND IS.

ORKNEY IS.

700

793

878

800

843 802 847

902

ICELAND

Reykjavik

874

0   400

Miles

B

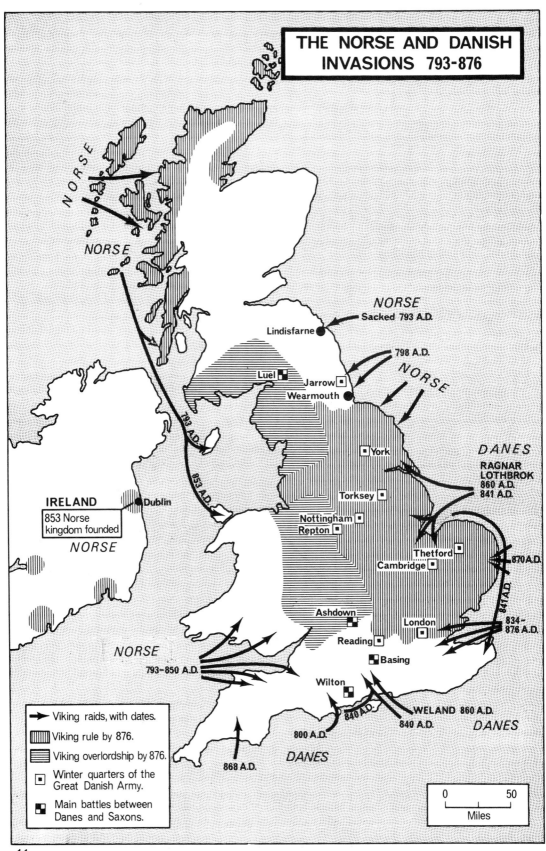

THE NORSE AND DANISH
INVASIONS 793-876

NORSE

NORSE

NORSE

NORSE
Sacked 793 A.D.

Lindisfarne

798 A.D.

Luel

Jarrow

Wearmouth

NORSE

York

DANES

RAGNAR
LOTHBROK
860 A.D.
841 A.D.

Torksey

IRELAND

Dublin

853 Norse
kingdom founded

NORSE

Nottingham
Repton

Thetford

Cambridge

870 A.D.

841 A.D.

Ashdown

London

834–
876 A.D.

Reading

NORSE

Basing

793–850 A.D.

Wilton

WELAND 860 A.D.

840 A.D.

840 A.D.

DANES

800 A.D.

Viking raids, with dates.

Viking rule by 876.

Viking overlordship by 876.

Winter quarters of the
Great Danish Army.

Main battles between
Danes and Saxons.

DANES

868 A.D.

0   50
Miles

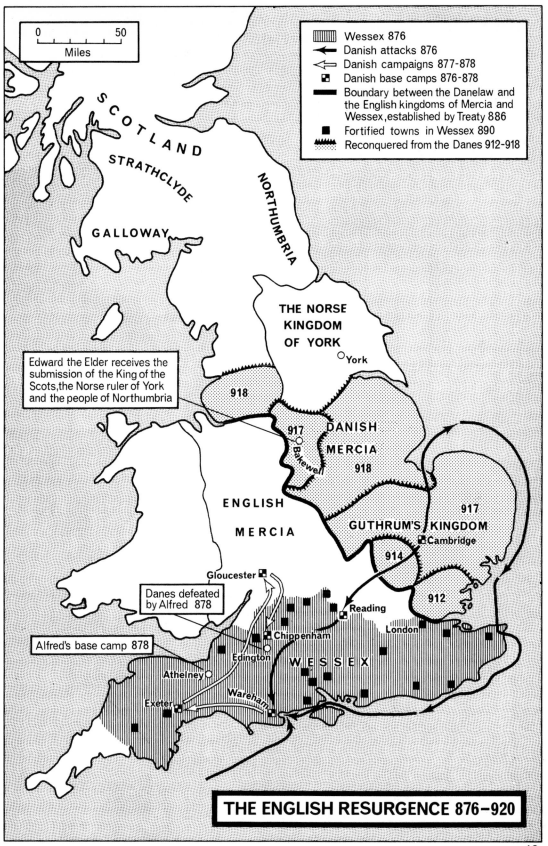

Legend

‖‖‖	Wessex 876
←	Danish attacks 876
⇐	Danish campaigns 877-878
⊡	Danish base camps 876-878
▬	Boundary between the Danelaw and the English kingdoms of Mercia and Wessex, established by Treaty 886
■	Fortified towns in Wessex 890
∿∿∿	Reconquered from the Danes 912-918

SCOTLAND

STRATHCLYDE

GALLOWAY

NORTHUMBRIA

THE NORSE KINGDOM OF YORK

○ York

Edward the Elder receives the submission of the King of the Scots, the Norse ruler of York and the people of Northumbria

918

917

○ Bakewell

DANISH MERCIA

918

ENGLISH MERCIA

GUTHRUM'S KINGDOM

917

■ Cambridge

914

912

Gloucester ■

Danes defeated by Alfred 878

Reading ⊡

London

Alfred's base camp 878

Chippenham ⊡

WESSEX

Edington ○

Athelney ○

Wareham

Exeter ⊡

THE ENGLISH RESURGENCE 876-920

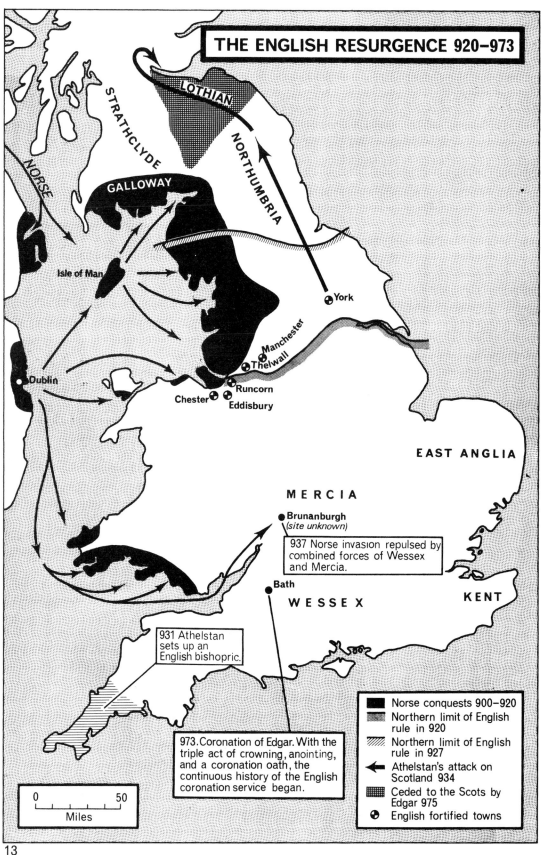

THE ENGLISH RESURGENCE 920–973

STRATHCLYDE

NORSE

LOTHIAN

NORTHUMBRIA

GALLOWAY

Isle of Man

York

Manchester
Thelwall

Dublin

Runcorn
Chester
Eddisbury

EAST ANGLIA

MERCIA

● Brunanburgh
(site unknown)

937 Norse invasion repulsed by combined forces of Wessex and Mercia.

● Bath

WESSEX

KENT

931 Athelstan sets up an English bishopric.

973. Coronation of Edgar. With the triple act of crowning, anointing, and a coronation oath, the continuous history of the English coronation service began.

0 ⊢⊢⊢⊢⊢⊢⊢ 50
Miles

■ Norse conquests 900–920
▨ Northern limit of English rule in 920
▨ Northern limit of English rule in 927
◄ Athelstan's attack on Scotland 934
▨ Ceded to the Scots by Edgar 975
◑ English fortified towns

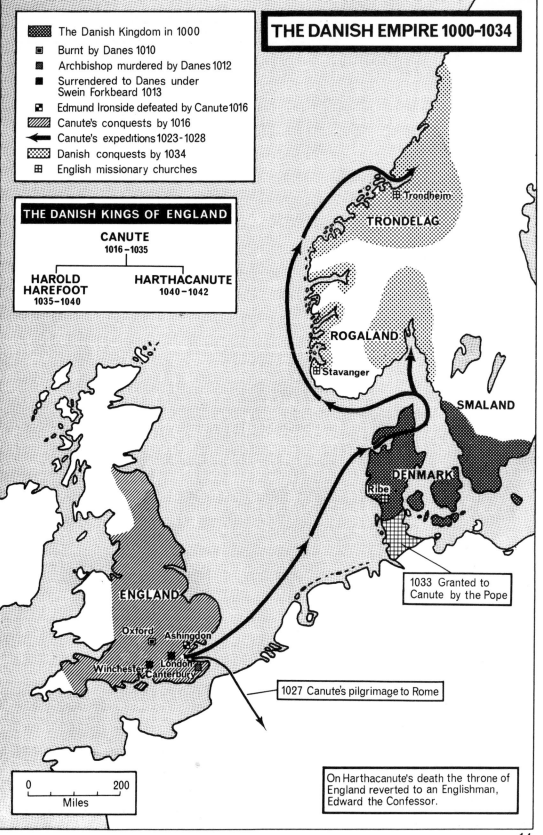

THE DANISH EMPIRE 1000-1034

Legend:
- The Danish Kingdom in 1000
- Burnt by Danes 1010
- Archbishop murdered by Danes 1012
- Surrendered to Danes under Swein Forkbeard 1013
- Edmund Ironside defeated by Canute 1016
- Canute's conquests by 1016
- Canute's expeditions 1023-1028
- Danish conquests by 1034
- English missionary churches

THE DANISH KINGS OF ENGLAND

CANUTE
1016-1035

HAROLD HAREFOOT
1035-1040

HARTHACANUTE
1040-1042

Trondheim

TRONDELAG

ROGALAND

Stavanger

SMALAND

DENMARK

Ribe

1033 Granted to Canute by the Pope

ENGLAND

Oxford
Ashingdon

Winchester London
Canterbury

1027 Canute's pilgrimage to Rome

On Harthacanute's death the throne of England reverted to an Englishman, Edward the Confessor.

0   200
Miles

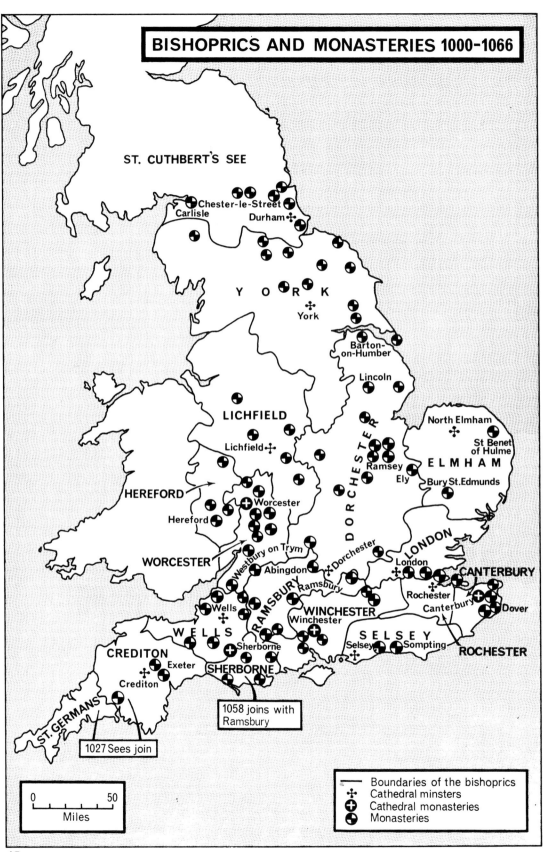

BISHOPRICS AND MONASTERIES 1000-1066

ST. CUTHBERT'S SEE

Chester-le-Street

Carlisle

Durham ✠

Y O R K

York ✠

Barton-on-Humber

Lincoln

LICHFIELD

Lichfield ✠

North Elmham ✠

St Benet of Hulme

E L M H A M

Ramsey

Ely

Bury St.Edmunds

HEREFORD

Worcester

Hereford

WORCESTER

D O R C H E S T E R

Westbury on Trym

Abingdon

Dorchester ✠

Ramsbury

L O N D O N

London

CANTERBURY

Rochester ✠

Canterbury

Dover

Wells

R A M S B U R Y

WINCHESTER

Winchester

SELSEY

Selsey ✠

Sompting

ROCHESTER

W E L L S

Sherborne

CREDITON

Exeter

SHERBORNE

Crediton ✠

ST.GERMANS

1058 joins with Ramsbury

1027 Sees join

———	Boundaries of the bishoprics
✠	Cathedral minsters
⊕	Cathedral monasteries
◓	Monasteries

0 ——— 50
Miles

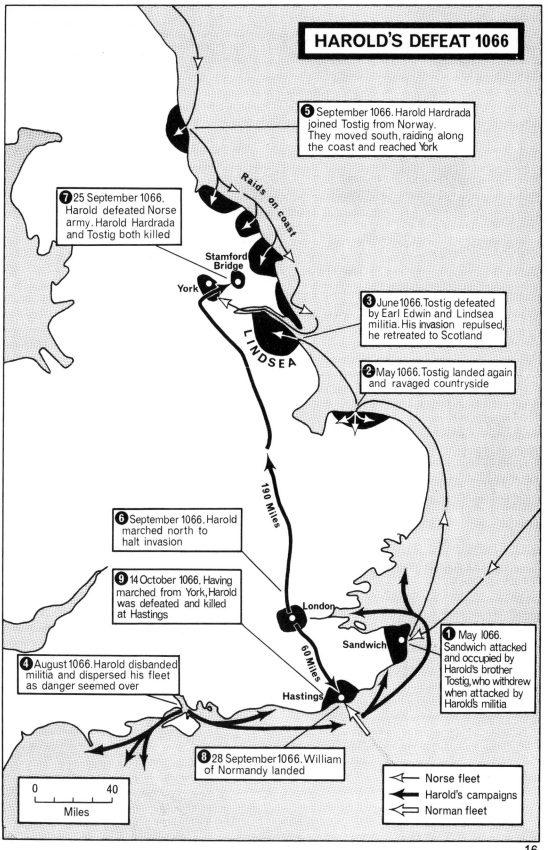

HAROLD'S DEFEAT 1066

⑤ September 1066. Harold Hardrada joined Tostig from Norway. They moved south, raiding along the coast and reached York

⑦ 25 September 1066. Harold defeated Norse army. Harold Hardrada and Tostig both killed

Raids on coast

Stamford Bridge

York

LINDSEA

③ June 1066. Tostig defeated by Earl Edwin and Lindsea militia. His invasion repulsed, he retreated to Scotland

② May 1066. Tostig landed again and ravaged countryside

190 Miles

⑥ September 1066. Harold marched north to halt invasion

⑨ 14 October 1066. Having marched from York, Harold was defeated and killed at Hastings

London

60 Miles

Sandwich

① May 1066. Sandwich attacked and occupied by Harold's brother Tostig, who withdrew when attacked by Harold's militia

④ August 1066. Harold disbanded militia and dispersed his fleet as danger seemed over

Hastings

⑧ 28 September 1066. William of Normandy landed

0   40

Miles

▷ Norse fleet
► Harold's campaigns
▷ Norman fleet

16

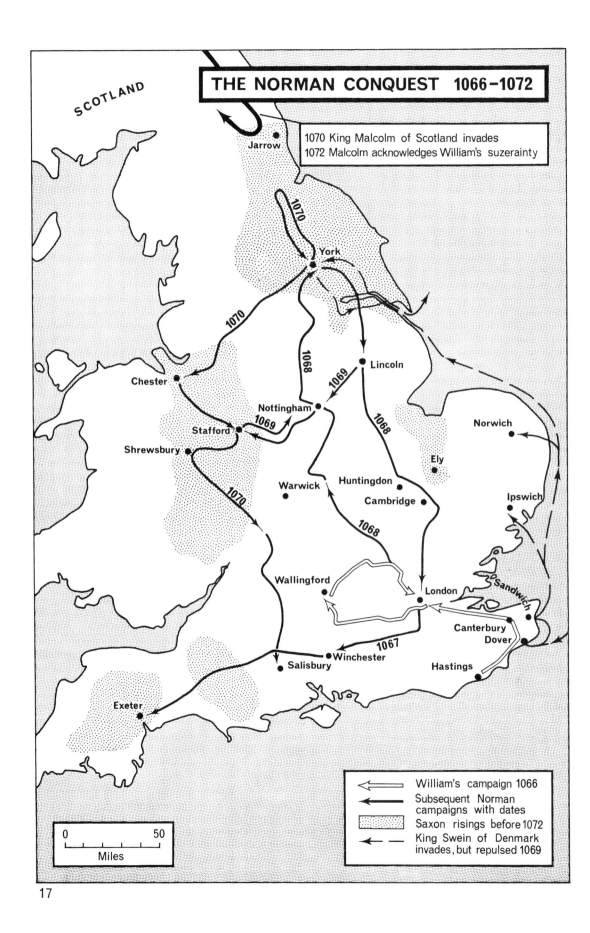

THE NORMAN CONQUEST 1066–1072

SCOTLAND

1070 King Malcolm of Scotland invades
1072 Malcolm acknowledges William's suzerainty

Jarrow

1070

York

1070

1068

1069

Lincoln

Chester

Nottingham

1069

1068

Norwich

Stafford

Shrewsbury

Ely

1070

Warwick

Huntingdon

Ipswich

Cambridge

1068

Wallingford

London

Sandwich

Canterbury
Dover

1067

Winchester

Salisbury

Hastings

Exeter

William's campaign 1066
Subsequent Norman
campaigns with dates
Saxon risings before 1072
King Swein of Denmark
invades, but repulsed 1069

0   50
Miles

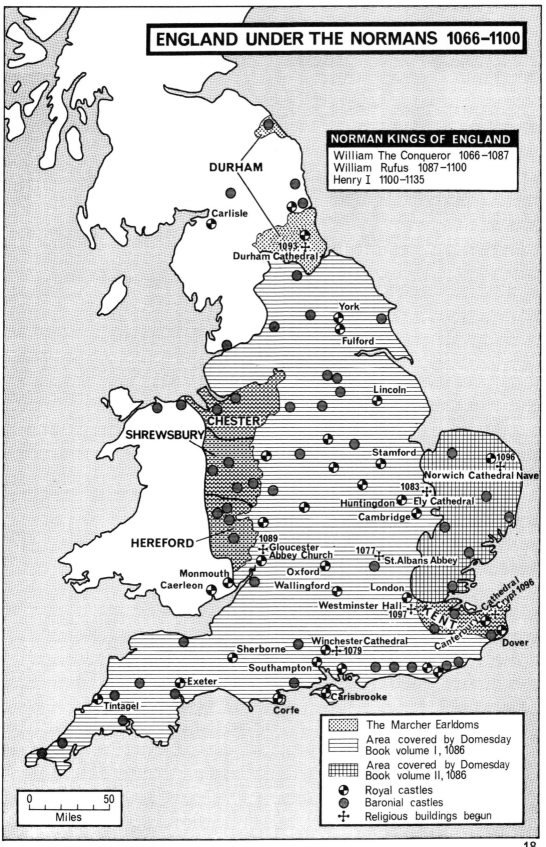

ENGLAND UNDER THE NORMANS 1066–1100

NORMAN KINGS OF ENGLAND
William The Conqueror 1066–1087
William Rufus 1087–1100
Henry I 1100–1135

DURHAM

Carlisle

1093 ✝
Durham Cathedral

York

Fulford

Lincoln

CHESTER

SHREWSBURY

Stamford

1096
Norwich Cathedral Nave

1083 ✝
Ely Cathedral

Huntingdon

Cambridge

HEREFORD

1089
✝ Gloucester
Abbey Church

1077
✝ St.Albans Abbey

Monmouth
Caerleon

Oxford

Wallingford

London

Westminster Hall
1097

KENT

Canterbury Cathedral
Crypt 1096

Dover

Winchester Cathedral
✝ 1079

Sherborne

Southampton

Exeter

Carisbrooke

Tintagel

Corfe

	The Marcher Earldoms
	Area covered by Domesday Book volume I, 1086
	Area covered by Domesday Book volume II, 1086
◑	Royal castles
●	Baronial castles
✝	Religious buildings begun

0   50
Miles

18

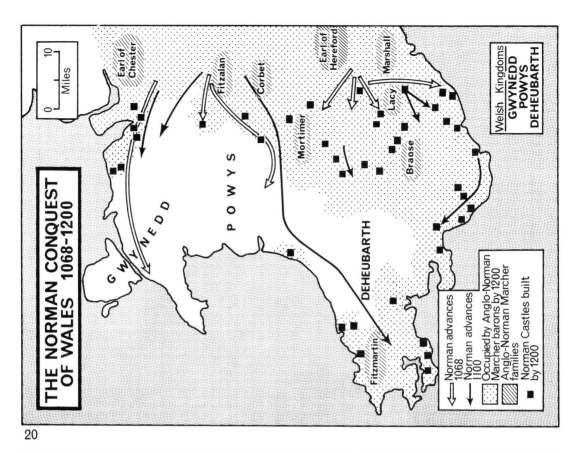

THE NORMAN CONQUEST OF WALES 1068-1200

Welsh Kingdoms
GWYNEDD
POWYS
DEHEUBARTH

Earl of Chester

Fitzalan

Corbet

Earl of Hereford

Marshall

Mortimer

Lacy

Braose

GWYNEDD

POWYS

DEHEUBARTH

Fitzmartin

Miles
0   10

Norman advances 1068
Norman advances 1100
Occupied by Anglo-Norman Marcher barons by 1200
Anglo-Norman Marcher families
Norman Castles built by 1200

20

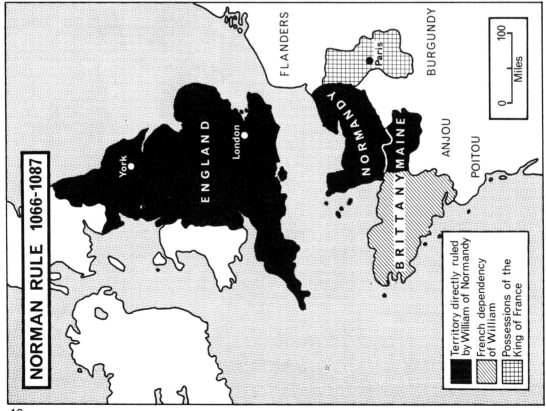

NORMAN RULE 1066-1087

FLANDERS

BURGUNDY

Paris

ENGLAND

York

London

NORMANDY

MAINE

BRITTANY

ANJOU

POITOU

Miles
0   100

Territory directly ruled by William of Normandy
French dependency of William
Possessions of the King of France

19

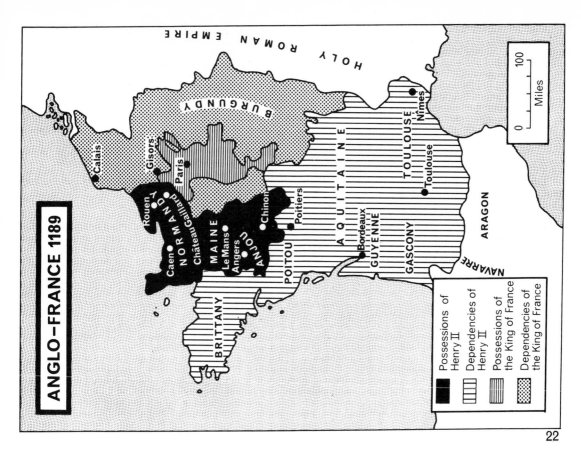

ANGLO-FRANCE 1189

HOLY ROMAN EMPIRE

BURGUNDY

Calais

Gisors
Paris
Rouen
NORMANDY
Château Gaillard
Caen
MAINE
Le Mans
Angers
ANJOU
Chinon
Poitiers

BRITTANY

POITOU

Bordeaux
GUYENNE
AQUITAINE
GASCONY

TOULOUSE
Toulouse
Nîmes

ARAGON

NAVARRE

0   100
Miles

Possessions of Henry II

Dependencies of Henry II

Possessions of the King of France

Dependencies of the King of France

22

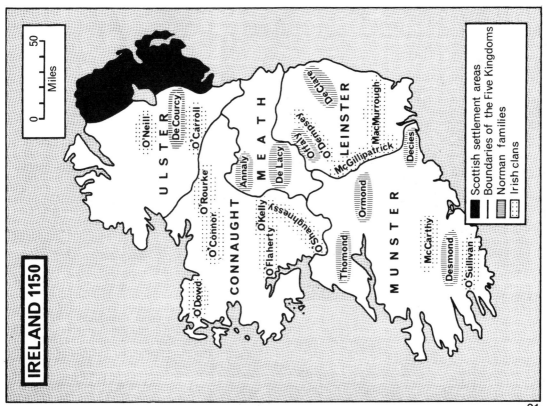

IRELAND 1150

0   50
Miles

ULSTER

O'Neill
De Courcy
O'Carroll

CONNAUGHT

O'Dowd
O'Connor
O'Rourke
O'Flaherty
O'Kelly
O'Shaughnessy

MEATH

Annaly
De Lacy

LEINSTER

Offaly
O'Dempsey
McGillipatrick
MacMurrough
Decies

MUNSTER

Thomond
Ormond
McCarthy
Desmond
O'Sullivan

Scottish settlement areas

Boundaries of the Five Kingdoms

Norman families

Irish clans

21

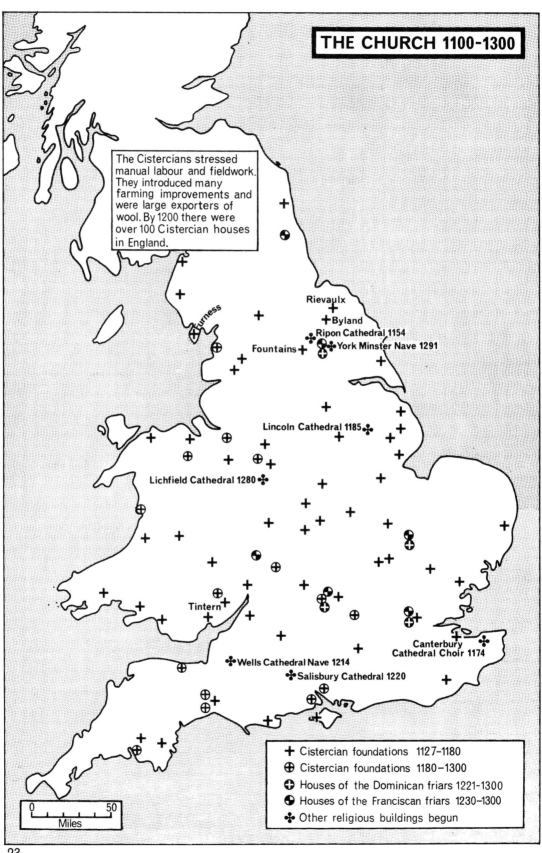

THE CHURCH 1100-1300

The Cistercians stressed manual labour and fieldwork. They introduced many farming improvements and were large exporters of wool. By 1200 there were over 100 Cistercian houses in England.

Rievaulx

Byland

Ripon Cathedral 1154

Furness

Fountains

York Minster Nave 1291

Lincoln Cathedral 1185

Lichfield Cathedral 1280

Tintern

Canterbury
Cathedral Choir 1174

Wells Cathedral Nave 1214

Salisbury Cathedral 1220

0   50
Miles

+ Cistercian foundations 1127-1180
⊕ Cistercian foundations 1180-1300
✚ Houses of the Dominican friars 1221-1300
◐ Houses of the Franciscan friars 1230-1300
♣ Other religious buildings begun

23

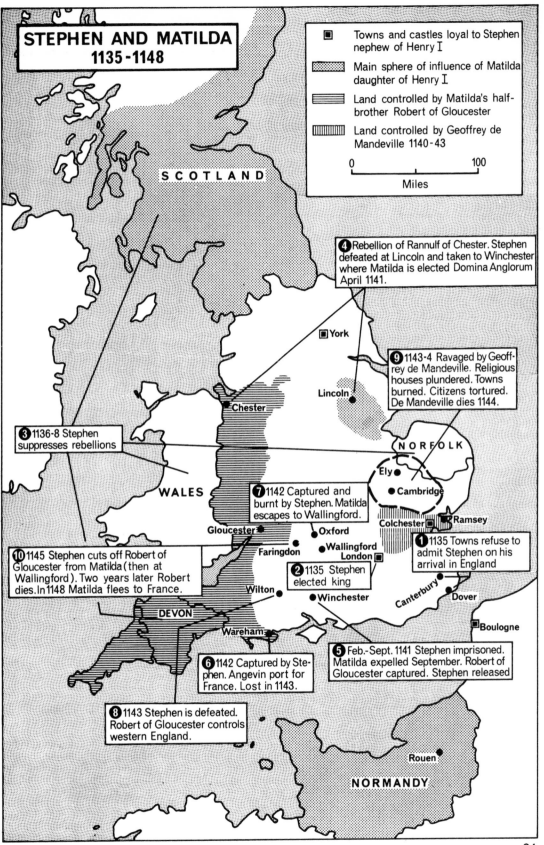

STEPHEN AND MATILDA
1135-1148

■ Towns and castles loyal to Stephen
nephew of Henry I

Main sphere of influence of Matilda
daughter of Henry I

Land controlled by Matilda's half-
brother Robert of Gloucester

Land controlled by Geoffrey de
Mandeville 1140-43

0   100

Miles

SCOTLAND

❹Rebellion of Rannulf of Chester. Stephen
defeated at Lincoln and taken to Winchester
where Matilda is elected Domina Anglorum
April 1141.

■York

❾1143-4 Ravaged by Geoff-
rey de Mandeville. Religious
houses plundered. Towns
burned. Citizens tortured.
De Mandeville dies 1144.

Lincoln ●

■Chester

❸1136-8 Stephen
suppresses rebellions

NORFOLK

Ely ●

● Cambridge

WALES

❼1142 Captured and
burnt by Stephen. Matilda
escapes to Wallingford.

Colchester ■   ■Ramsey

Gloucester ●

● Oxford

❶1135 Towns refuse to
admit Stephen on his
arrival in England

Faringdon ●   ●Wallingford
London ■

❿1145 Stephen cuts off Robert of
Gloucester from Matilda (then at
Wallingford). Two years later Robert
dies. In 1148 Matilda flees to France.

❷1135 Stephen
elected king

Canterbury   ● Dover

Wilton ●

● Winchester

DEVON

■Boulogne

Wareham ●

❻1142 Captured by Ste-
phen. Angevin port for
France. Lost in 1143.

❺Feb.-Sept. 1141 Stephen imprisoned.
Matilda expelled September. Robert of
Gloucester captured. Stephen released

❽1143 Stephen is defeated.
Robert of Gloucester controls
western England.

Rouen ●

NORMANDY

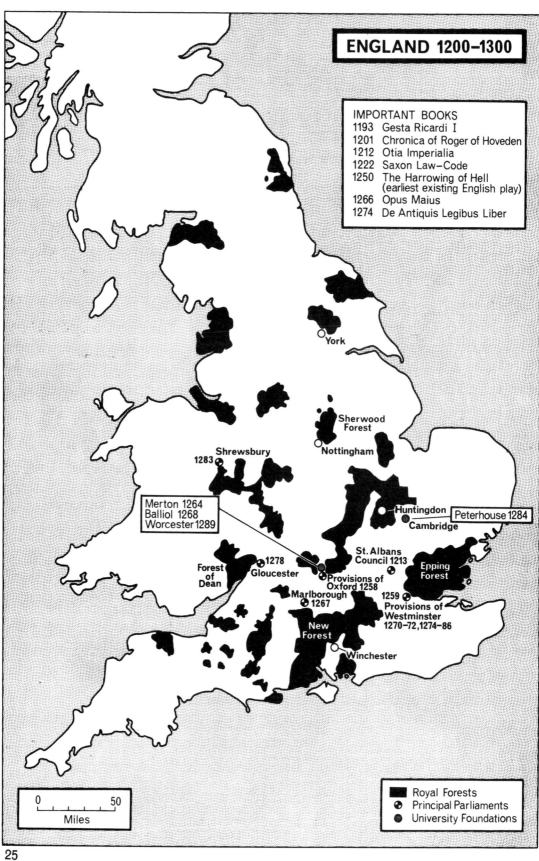

ENGLAND 1200–1300

IMPORTANT BOOKS
1193 Gesta Ricardi I
1201 Chronica of Roger of Hoveden
1212 Otia Imperialia
1222 Saxon Law–Code
1250 The Harrowing of Hell
(earliest existing English play)
1266 Opus Maius
1274 De Antiquis Legibus Liber

York

Sherwood
Forest

Shrewsbury
1283

Nottingham

Merton 1264
Balliol 1268
Worcester 1289

Huntingdon
Cambridge

Peterhouse 1284

1278
Gloucester

Forest
of
Dean

St. Albans
Council 1213

Epping
Forest

Provisions of
Oxford 1258

Marlborough
1267

1259
Provisions of
Westminster
1270–72, 1274–86

New
Forest

Winchester

```
0          50
    Miles
```

◼ Royal Forests
⊕ Principal Parliaments
⊛ University Foundations

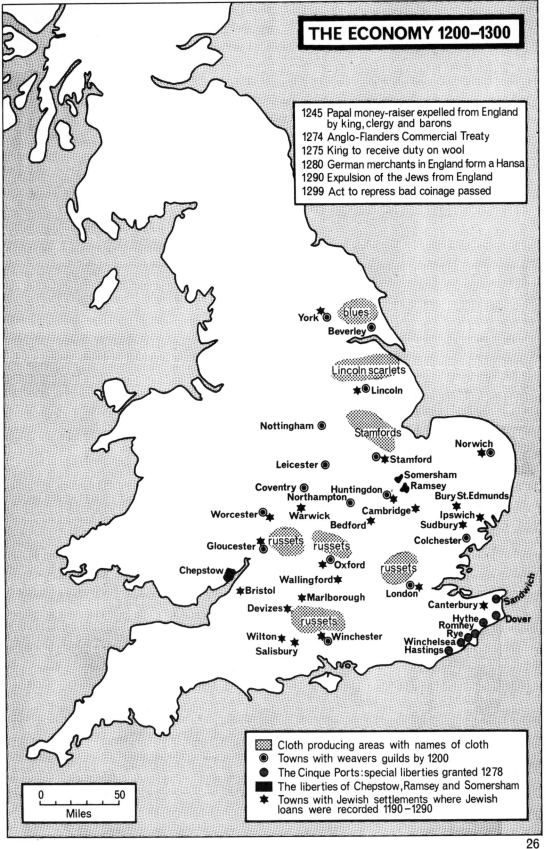

THE ECONOMY 1200–1300

1245 Papal money-raiser expelled from England by king, clergy and barons
1274 Anglo-Flanders Commercial Treaty
1275 King to receive duty on wool
1280 German merchants in England form a Hansa
1290 Expulsion of the Jews from England
1299 Act to repress bad coinage passed

York
blues
Beverley

Lincoln scarlets
Lincoln

Nottingham
Stamfords
Norwich

Leicester
Stamford

Coventry
Somersham
Huntingdon
Ramsey
Bury St.Edmunds

Worcester
Northampton
Cambridge
Ipswich

Warwick
Bedford
Sudbury

Gloucester
russets
russets
Colchester

Chepstow
Oxford
russets

Bristol
Wallingford
London

Marlborough
Canterbury
Sandwich

Devizes
russets
Hythe
Dover

Wilton
Winchester
Romney
Rye

Salisbury
Winchelsea
Hastings

▦ Cloth producing areas with names of cloth
◉ Towns with weavers guilds by 1200
● The Cinque Ports: special liberties granted 1278
◼ The liberties of Chepstow, Ramsey and Somersham
★ Towns with Jewish settlements where Jewish loans were recorded 1190–1290

0 — 50
Miles

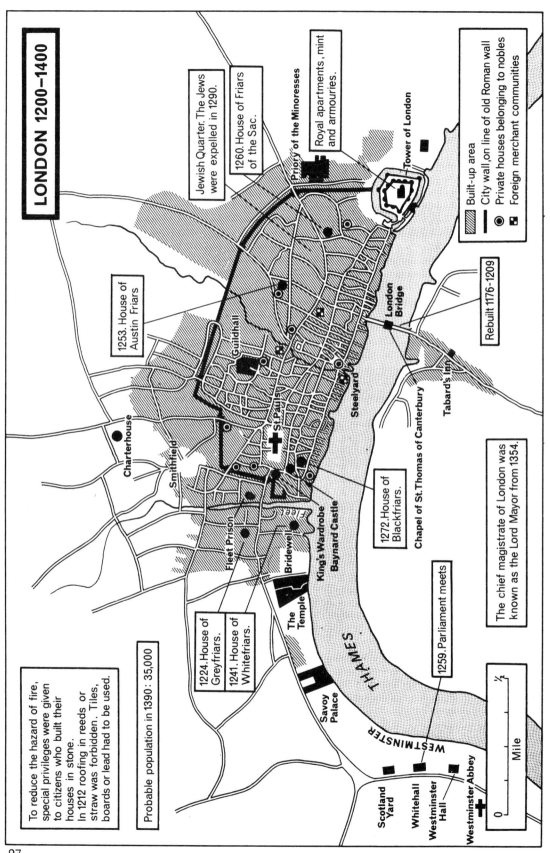

LONDON 1200–1400

Priory of the Minoresses

Jewish Quarter. The Jews were expelled in 1290.

1260. House of Friars of the Sac.

Royal apartments, mint and armouries.

Tower of London

Built-up area

City wall, on line of old Roman wall

Private houses belonging to nobles

Foreign merchant communities

1253. House of Austin Friars

Guildhall

London Bridge

Rebuilt 1176-1209

Charterhouse

Smithfield

St. Paul's

Steelyard

Tabard's Inn

Fleet

1272.House of Blackfriars.

Chapel of St.Thomas of Canterbury

Fleet Prison

Bridewell

King's Wardrobe
Baynard Castle

1259. Parliament meets

The chief magistrate of London was known as the Lord Mayor from 1354.

1224.House of Greyfriars.

1241. House of Whitefriars.

The Temple

THAMES

WESTMINSTER

Savoy Palace

To reduce the hazard of fire, special privileges were given to citizens who built their houses in stone.
In 1212 roofing in reeds or straw was forbidden. Tiles, boards or lead had to be used.

Probable population in 1390 : 35,000

Scotland Yard

Whitehall

Westminster Hall

Westminster Abbey

0   ½   Mile

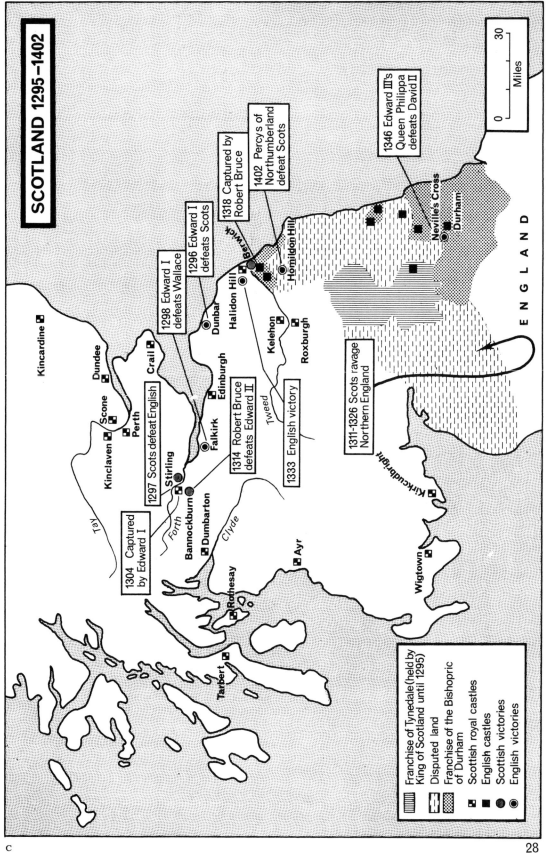

SCOTLAND 1295–1402

1402 Percys of Northumberland defeat Scots

1346 Edward III's Queen Philippa defeats David II

1318 Captured by Robert Bruce

1296 Edward I defeats Scots

1298 Edward I defeats Wallace

Neville's Cross
Durham

Homildon Hill

Berwick

Halidon Hill

Dunbar

Kincardine

Dundee

Scone

Perth

Crail

Kelehon

Roxburgh

Edinburgh

Kinclaven

Tweed

1311–1326 Scots ravage Northern England

Falkirk

1297 Scots defeat English

Stirling

1314 Robert Bruce defeats Edward II

1333 English victory

1304 Captured by Edward I

Forth

Bannockburn

Dumbarton

Clyde

Tay

Ayr

Rothesay

Kirkcudbright

Wigtown

Tarbert

ENGLAND

Miles
0   30

Franchise of Tynedale (held by King of Scotland until 1295)
Disputed land
Franchise of the Bishopric of Durham
Scottish royal castles
English castles
Scottish victories
English victories

c

28

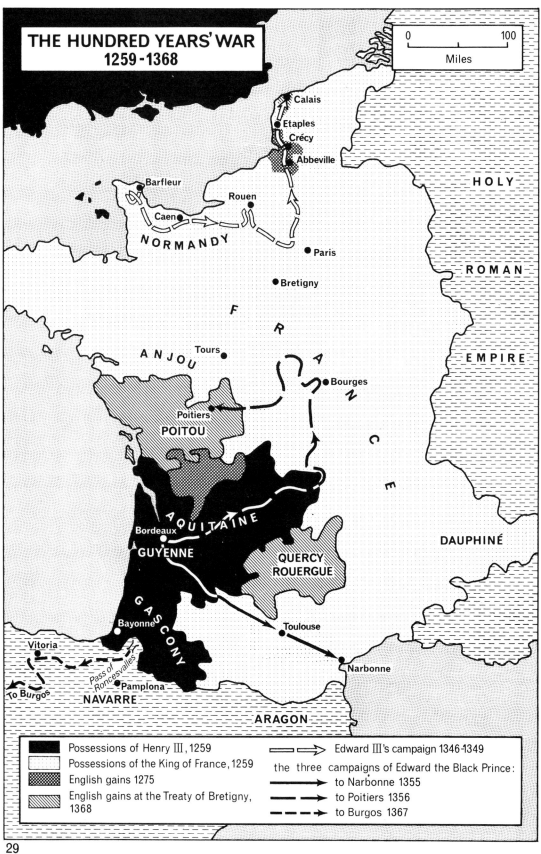

THE HUNDRED YEARS' WAR
1259-1368

Miles
0   100

Calais
Etaples
Crécy
Abbeville

HOLY

Barfleur
Rouen
Caen
NORMANDY
Paris
ROMAN

Bretigny

F
R
A
N
C
E

ANJOU
Tours
Bourges
EMPIRE

Poitiers
POITOU

AQUITAINE
Bordeaux
GUYENNE
QUERCY
ROUERGUE
DAUPHINÉ

GASCONY
Bayonne
Toulouse

Vitoria
Pass of Roncesvalles
Narbonne
To Burgos
Pamplona
NAVARRE
ARAGON

■	Possessions of Henry III, 1259	Edward III's campaign 1346-1349
▒	Possessions of the King of France, 1259	the three campaigns of Edward the Black Prince:
▓	English gains 1275	to Narbonne 1355
▨	English gains at the Treaty of Bretigny, 1368	to Poitiers 1356
		to Burgos 1367

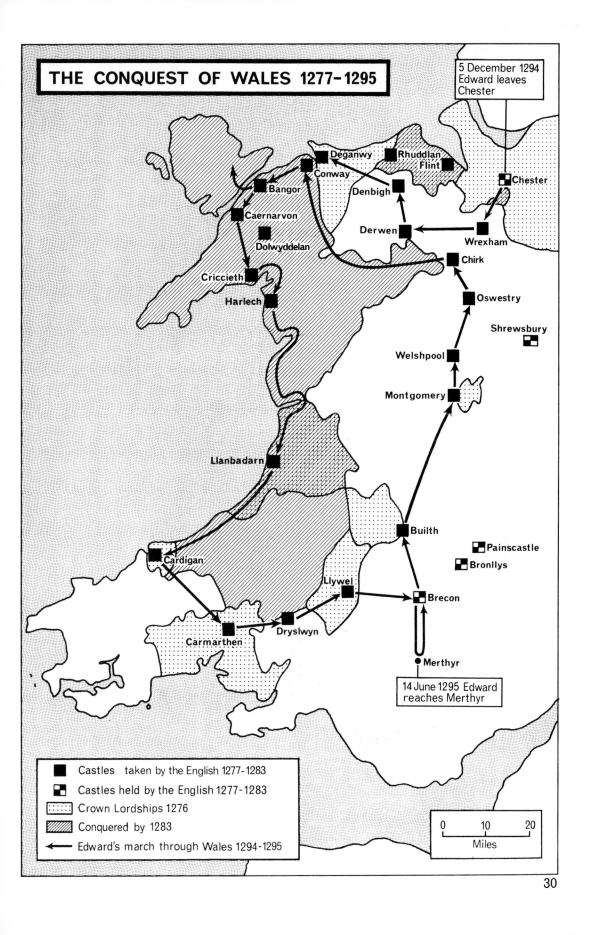

THE CONQUEST OF WALES 1277–1295

5 December 1294
Edward leaves
Chester

Deganwy
Rhuddlan
Flint
Conway
Chester
Bangor
Denbigh
Caernarvon
Derwen
Wrexham
Dolwyddelan
Chirk
Criccieth
Oswestry
Harlech
Shrewsbury
Welshpool
Montgomery
Llanbadarn
Builth
Painscastle
Bronllys
Cardigan
Llywel
Dryslwyn
Brecon
Carmarthen
Merthyr

14 June 1295 Edward
reaches Merthyr

■ Castles taken by the English 1277-1283
◧ Castles held by the English 1277-1283
░ Crown Lordships 1276
▨ Conquered by 1283
← Edward's march through Wales 1294-1295

0   10   20
Miles

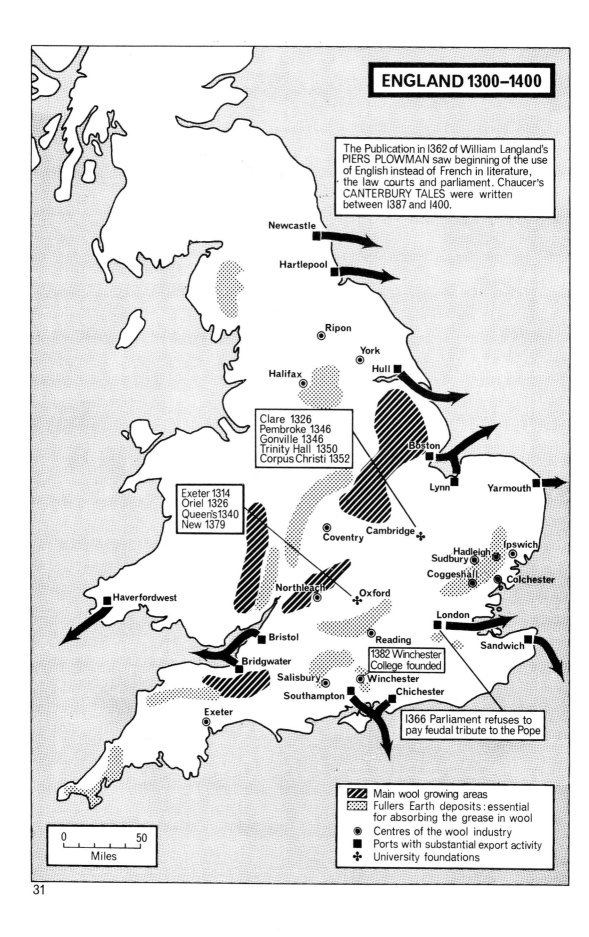

ENGLAND 1300–1400

The Publication in 1362 of William Langland's PIERS PLOWMAN saw beginning of the use of English instead of French in literature, the law courts and parliament. Chaucer's CANTERBURY TALES were written between 1387 and 1400.

Newcastle

Hartlepool

Ripon

York

Hull

Halifax

Clare 1326
Pembroke 1346
Gonville 1346
Trinity Hall 1350
Corpus Christi 1352

Boston

Lynn

Yarmouth

Exeter 1314
Oriel 1326
Queen's 1340
New 1379

Coventry

Cambridge

Hadleigh

Ipswich

Sudbury

Coggeshall

Colchester

Northleach

Oxford

Haverfordwest

London

Bristol

Reading

Sandwich

Bridgwater

1382 Winchester
College founded

Salisbury

Winchester

Southampton

Chichester

Exeter

1366 Parliament refuses to
pay feudal tribute to the Pope

▨ Main wool growing areas
▨ Fullers Earth deposits: essential
for absorbing the grease in wool
◉ Centres of the wool industry
■ Ports with substantial export activity
♣ University foundations

0   50
Miles

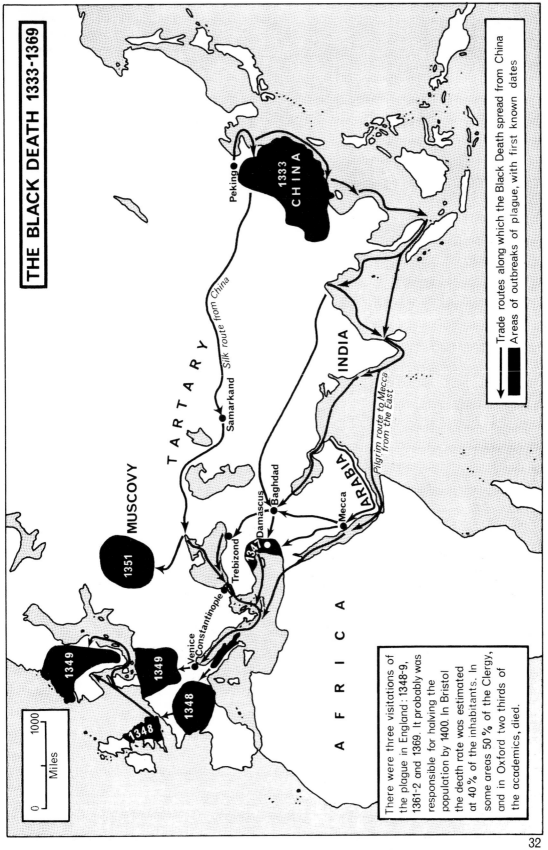

THE BLACK DEATH 1333-1369

CHINA

1333

Peking

TARTARY

Silk route from China

Samarkand

MUSCOVY

1351

INDIA

Trebizond

Damascus

1347

Baghdad

Pilgrim route to Mecca from the East

Mecca

ARABIA

Constantinople

Venice

1349

1349

1348

1348

AFRICA

→ Trade routes along which the Black Death spread from China

■ Areas of outbreaks of plague, with first known dates

There were three visitations of the plague in England: 1348-9, 1361-2 and 1369. It probably was responsible for halving the population by 1400. In Bristol the death rate was estimated at 40% of the inhabitants. In some areas 50% of the Clergy, and in Oxford two thirds of the academics, died.

Miles

0   1000

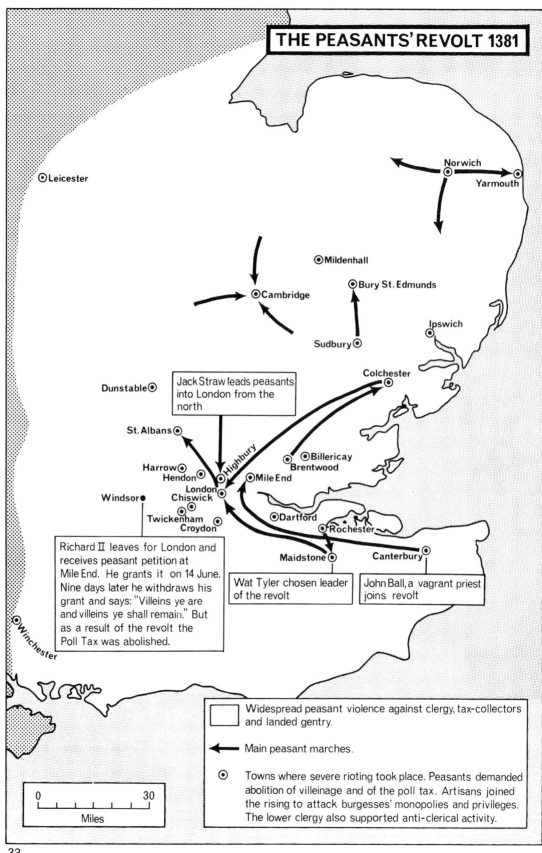

THE PEASANTS' REVOLT 1381

Leicester

Norwich

Yarmouth

Mildenhall

Bury St. Edmunds

Cambridge

Ipswich

Sudbury

Dunstable

Jack Straw leads peasants into London from the north

Colchester

St. Albans

Billericay
Brentwood

Harrow
Hendon

Highbury

Mile End

London
Chiswick

Windsor

Twickenham
Croydon

Dartford

Rochester

Richard II leaves for London and receives peasant petition at Mile End. He grants it on 14 June. Nine days later he withdraws his grant and says: "Villeins ye are and villeins ye shall remain." But as a result of the revolt the Poll Tax was abolished.

Maidstone

Canterbury

Wat Tyler chosen leader of the revolt

John Ball, a vagrant priest joins revolt

Winchester

Widespread peasant violence against clergy, tax-collectors and landed gentry.

Main peasant marches.

Towns where severe rioting took place. Peasants demanded abolition of villeinage and of the poll tax. Artisans joined the rising to attack burgesses' monopolies and privileges. The lower clergy also supported anti-clerical activity.

0   30
Miles

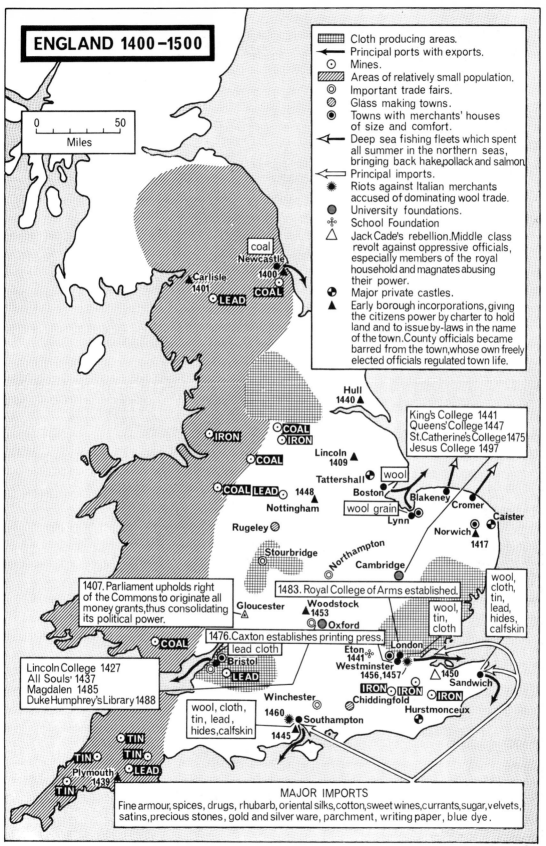

ENGLAND 1400–1500

Legend:
- ▦ Cloth producing areas.
- ← Principal ports with exports.
- ⊙ Mines.
- ▨ Areas of relatively small population.
- ◎ Important trade fairs.
- ⊘ Glass making towns.
- ◉ Towns with merchants' houses of size and comfort.
- ⇐ Deep sea fishing fleets which spent all summer in the northern seas, bringing back hake, pollack and salmon.
- ⇐ Principal imports.
- ✳ Riots against Italian merchants accused of dominating wool trade.
- ⊜ University foundations.
- ⚬ School Foundation
- △ Jack Cade's rebellion. Middle class revolt against oppressive officials, especially members of the royal household and magnates abusing their power.
- ⊕ Major private castles.
- ▲ Early borough incorporations, giving the citizens power by charter to hold land and to issue by-laws in the name of the town. County officials became barred from the town, whose own freely elected officials regulated town life.

coal
Newcastle
1400
COAL

▲ Carlisle
1401
⊙ LEAD

coal

Hull
1440 ▲

King's College 1441
Queens' College 1447
St.Catherine's College 1475
Jesus College 1497

⊙ IRON

⊙ COAL
⊙ IRON

⊙ COAL

Lincoln ▲
1409

Tattershall ⊕   wool

⊙ COAL LEAD ⊙   1448 ▲
Nottingham

Boston
wool grain
Blakeney
Lynn
Cromer
Caister
Norwich ▲
1417

Rugeley ⊘

Stourbridge ⊘

Northampton

Cambridge ⊜

1483. Royal College of Arms established.

1407. Parliament upholds right of the Commons to originate all money grants, thus consolidating its political power.

Gloucester △

Woodstock
▲ 1453
◎ ⊜ Oxford

1476. Caxton establishes printing press.

lead cloth

⊙ COAL

◉ Bristol
⊙ LEAD

Lincoln College 1427
All Souls' 1437
Magdalen 1485
Duke Humphrey's Library 1488

wool,
cloth,
tin,
lead,
hides,
calfskin

wool,
tin,
cloth

Eton ⚬
1441
Westminster
1456, 1457

London

△ 1450
Sandwich

IRON ⊙ IRON
Chiddingfold
Hurstmonceux ⊕

Winchester ◎

wool, cloth,
tin, lead,
hides, calfskin

1460 ✳ ◉ Southampton
1445

⊙ TIN
⊙ TIN
TIN ⊙
⊙ LEAD
Plymouth
1439
⊙ TIN

MAJOR IMPORTS
Fine armour, spices, drugs, rhubarb, oriental silks, cotton, sweet wines, currants, sugar, velvets, satins, precious stones, gold and silver ware, parchment, writing paper, blue dye.

THE DEFEAT OF OWEN GLENDOWER 1405-1412

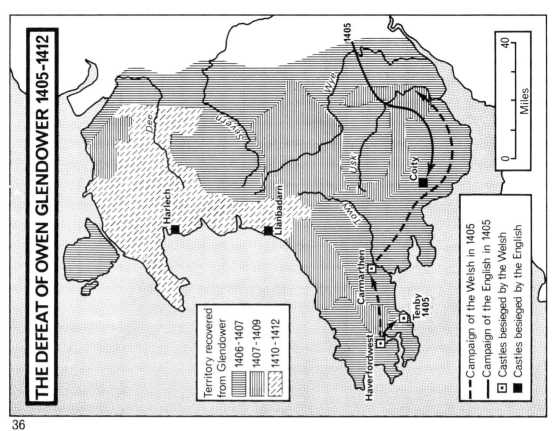

Territory recovered from Glendower
- 1406-1407
- 1407-1409
- 1410-1412

- - - Campaign of the Welsh in 1405
——— Campaign of the English in 1405
◻ Castles besieged by the Welsh
■ Castles besieged by the English

Harlech
Llanbadarn
Carmarthen
Haverfordwest
Tenby 1405
Coity
1405

Dee
Severn
Wye
Usk
Towy

Miles
0   40

36

OWEN GLENDOWER'S REVOLT 1400 – 1405

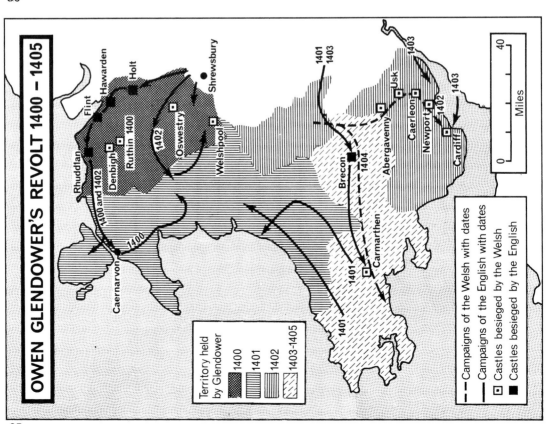

Territory held by Glendower
- 1400
- 1401
- 1402
- 1403-1405

- - - Campaigns of the Welsh with dates
——— Campaigns of the English with dates
◻ Castles besieged by the Welsh
■ Castles besieged by the English

Caernarvon
Rhuddlan
Flint
Hawarden
Holt
Shrewsbury
Denbigh
Ruthin 1400
Oswestry
Welshpool
1402
1400 and 1402
1400
1401
Brecon
1404
Carmarthen
Abergavenny
Usk
Caerleon
Newport
Cardiff
1401
1403
1402
1403
1403
1401
1403

Miles
0   40

35

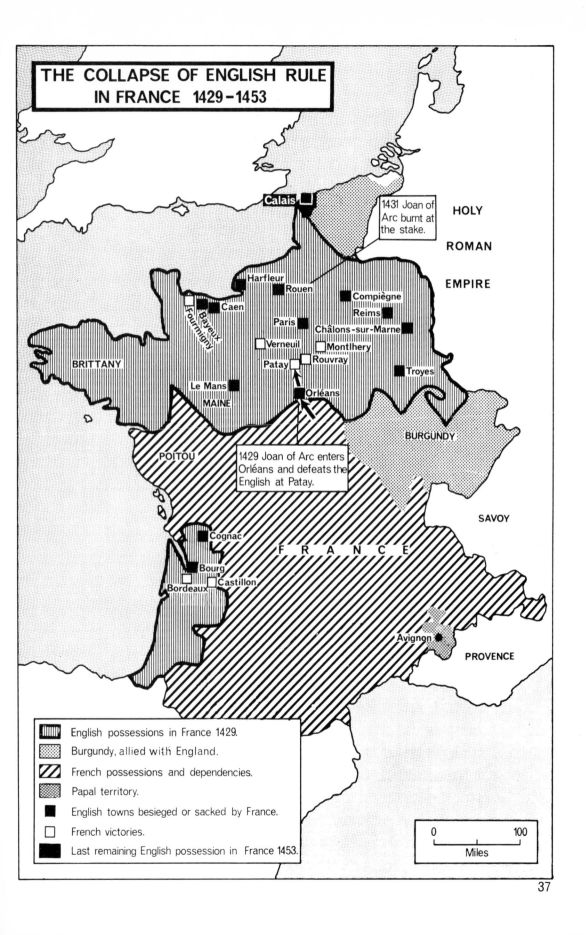

THE COLLAPSE OF ENGLISH RULE IN FRANCE 1429-1453

HOLY ROMAN EMPIRE

Calais

1431 Joan of Arc burnt at the stake.

Harfleur
Rouen
Compiègne
Caen
Reims
Bayeux
Fourmigny
Paris
Châlons-sur-Marne
Verneuil
Montlhery
Patay
Rouvray
Troyes

BRITTANY

Le Mans
MAINE
Orléans

BURGUNDY

1429 Joan of Arc enters Orléans and defeats the English at Patay.

POITOU

SAVOY

F R A N C E

Cognac
Bourg
Bordeaux
Castillon

Avignon

PROVENCE

▥	English possessions in France 1429.
▦	Burgundy, allied with England.
▨	French possessions and dependencies.
▧	Papal territory.
■	English towns besieged or sacked by France.
□	French victories.
■	Last remaining English possession in France 1453.

0   100
Miles

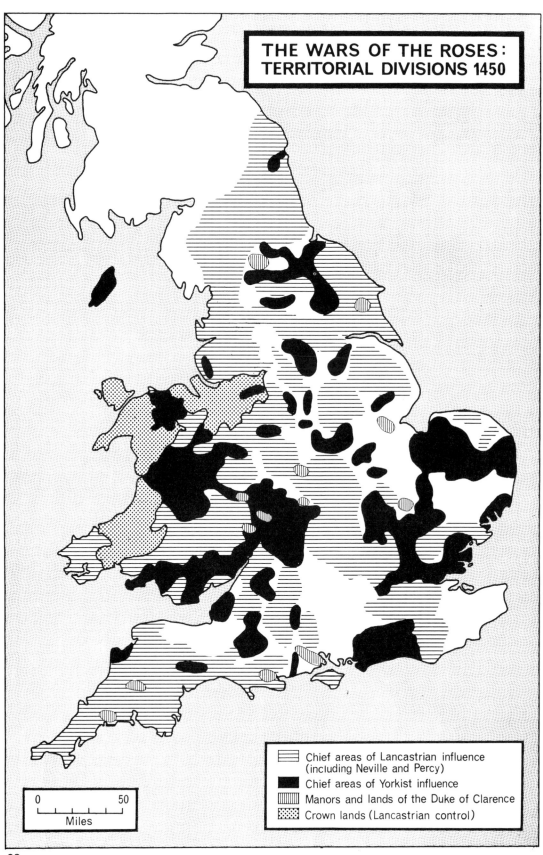

THE WARS OF THE ROSES:
TERRITORIAL DIVISIONS 1450

Chief areas of Lancastrian influence
(including Neville and Percy)

Chief areas of Yorkist influence

Manors and lands of the Duke of Clarence

Crown lands (Lancastrian control)

0   50
Miles

HENRY TUDOR'S DYNASTY

HENRY VII
KING 1485 – 1509

HENRY VIII
KING 1509 – 1547

EDWARD VI
KING 1547 – 1553

ELIZABETH
QUEEN 1558 – 1603

MARY
QUEEN 1553 – 1558

THE WARS OF THE ROSES: CASTLES AND BATTLES 1450 – 1485

Bamburgh
Dunstanburgh
Alnwick
Warkworth
Wark
Newcastle
Hexham 1464
Carlisle
Lumley
Appleby
Raby
Barnard Castle
Skelton
Richmond
Bolton
Middleham
Masham
Knaresborough
Spofforth
Towton 1461
Cawood
Pontefract
Wressell
Wakefield 1460
Conisborough
Sandal
Tickhill
Bolingbroke
Chester
Newark
Conway
Denbigh
Ruthin
Newcastle
Tattershall
Belvoir
Castle Rising
Blore Heath 1459
Tutbury
Caister
Bosworth 1485
Stokesay
Ludlow
Ludford 1459
1461
Kenilworth
Warwick
Wingfield
Mortimers Cross
Grosmont
Skenfrith
1471
1469 Edgcote
1460 Northampton
Framlingham
White Castle
Tewkesbury
St. Davids
Abergavenny
Raglan
St. Albans
Pleshey
Haverfordwest
Kidwelly
Usk
1455 1461
1471 Barnet
Swansea
Milford Haven
Pembroke
Manorbier
Ogmore
Caerphilly
Cardiff
Wallingford
Windsor
Leeds
Dover
Farnham
Reigate
Tiverton
Steyning
Hurstmonceux
Okehampton
Portchester
Pevensey
Compton
Carisbrooke
Corfe

■ Lancastrian castles
▣ Lancastrian victories
⊡ Yorkist castles
▨ Yorkist victories
→ Henry Tudor's march to Bosworth. His victory established the Tudor royal house.

0   50
Miles

39

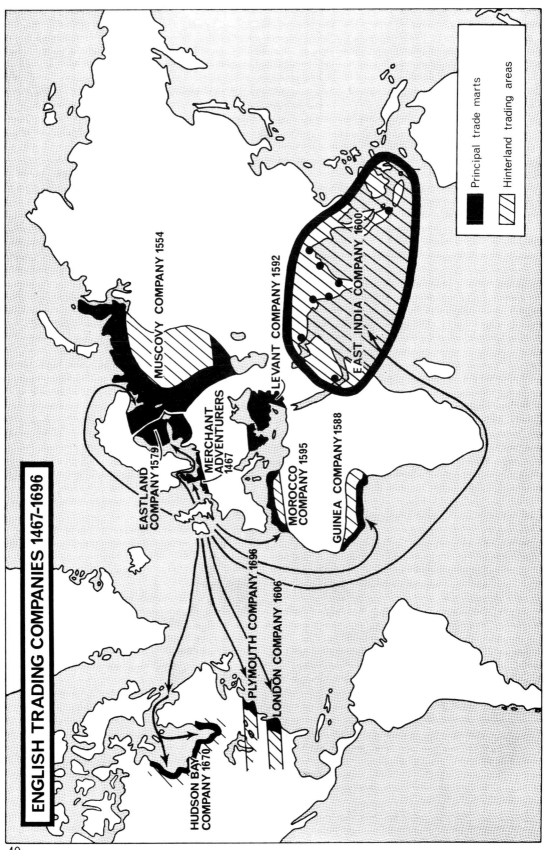

ENGLISH TRADING COMPANIES 1467-1696

MUSCOVY COMPANY 1554

LEVANT COMPANY 1592

EAST INDIA COMPANY 1600

EASTLAND COMPANY 1579

MERCHANT ADVENTURERS 1467

MOROCCO COMPANY 1595

GUINEA COMPANY 1588

PLYMOUTH COMPANY 1696

LONDON COMPANY 1606

HUDSON BAY COMPANY 1670

Principal trade marts

Hinterland trading areas

40

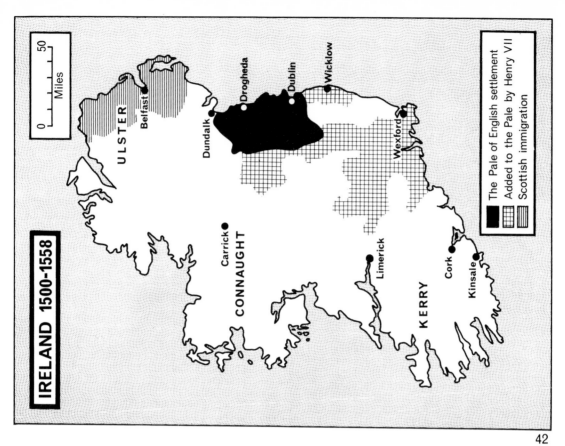

IRELAND 1500-1558

Miles
0 50

ULSTER
Belfast
Dundalk
Drogheda
Dublin
Wicklow
Wexford

Carrick
CONNAUGHT

Limerick

KERRY
Cork
Kinsale

The Pale of English settlement
Added to the Pale by Henry VII
Scottish immigration

42

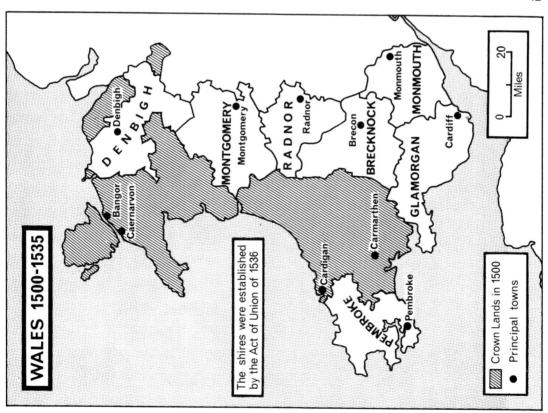

WALES 1500-1535

Denbigh
DENBIGH
Bangor
Caernarvon

MONTGOMERY
Montgomery

RADNOR
Radnor

BRECKNOCK
Brecon

MONMOUTH
Monmouth

Cardigan

Carmarthen

GLAMORGAN
Cardiff

PEMBROKE
Pembroke

The shires were established
by the Act of Union of 1536

Miles
0 20

Crown Lands in 1500
Principal towns

41

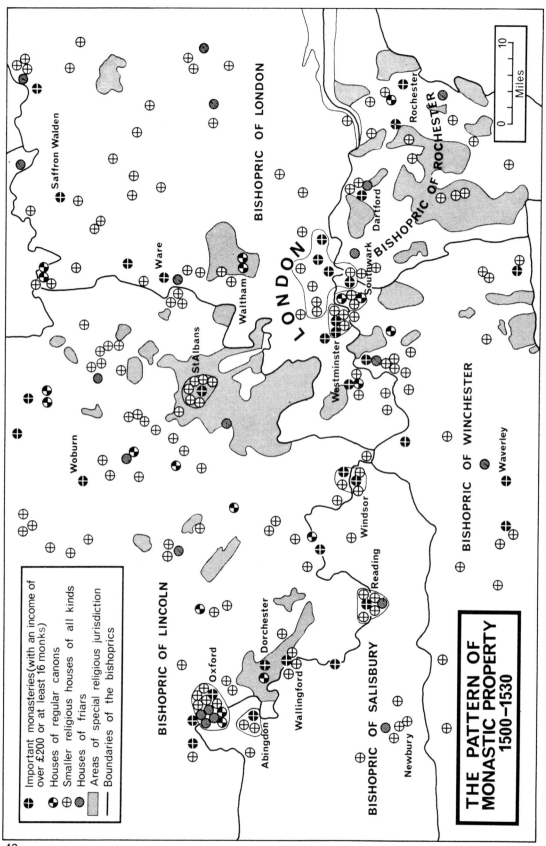

THE PATTERN OF
MONASTIC PROPERTY
1500–1530

Important monasteries (with an income of
over £200 or at least 16 monks)

Houses of regular canons

Smaller religious houses of all kinds

Houses of friars

Areas of special religious jurisdiction

Boundaries of the bishoprics

BISHOPRIC OF LONDON

BISHOPRIC OF ROCHESTER

BISHOPRIC OF WINCHESTER

BISHOPRIC OF LINCOLN

BISHOPRIC OF SALISBURY

LONDON

Saffron Walden

Ware

Waltham

St Albans

Westminster

Southwark

Dartford

Rochester

Woburn

Windsor

Waverley

Reading

Oxford

Dorchester

Wallingford

Abingdon

Newbury

Miles

10

0

THE ENGLISH REFORMATION 1531–1571

1531 Henry VIII recognized as supreme head of the English Church by Parliament
1533 The Pope excommunicates Henry VIII.
1534 Act of Supremacy. Church of England severed itself from Rome.
1535 Sir Thomas More beheaded. Canonised in 1935.
1536 Dissolution of monasteries begun.
1539 Henry VIII issues Six Articles: repealed 1547.
1549 First Act of Uniformity. First Prayer Book.
1552 Second Act of Uniformity. Second Prayer Book.
1554 Reconciliation with Rome under Queen Mary. Roman Catholicism restored.
1559 Queen Elizabeth reintroduced the Act of Supremacy. Catholicism ceased to be the religion of England.
1571 Parliament forbids the import of Papal Bulls into England.

Carlisle

Jervaulx
Bridlington
Fountains
York
Whalley
Pontefract
CHESTER
Doncaster
Louth
Barlings
Lincoln
Kirkstead
Lenton

PETERBOROUGH

OXFORD

Woburn
Colchester
GLOUCESTER
Bishops Ridley and Latimer burnt by Catholics in 1555
Oxford
London
Canterbury
Reading
BRISTOL
Becket's shrine destroyed by protestants in 1538
Glastonbury

Areas affected by the Pilgrimage of Grace 1536-1537
Monasteries whose abbots were executed by Henry VIII.
Bishoprics created by Henry VIII

0   50
Miles

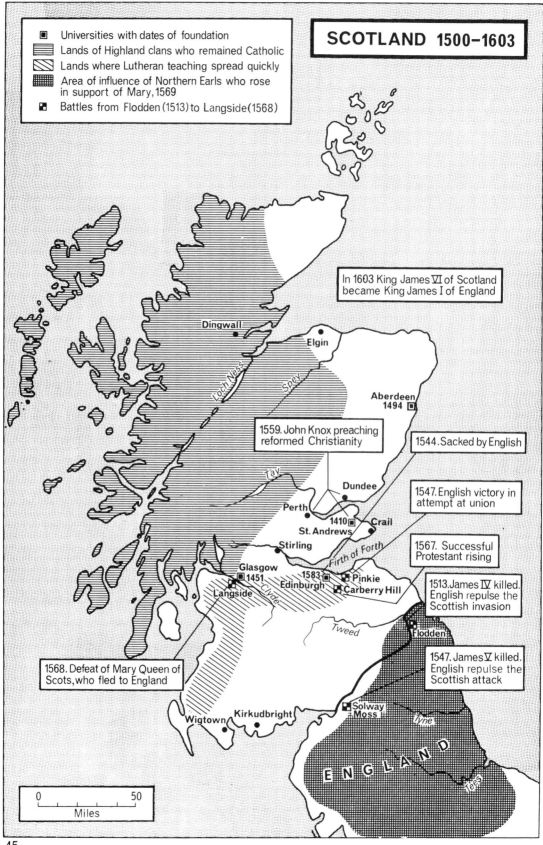

SCOTLAND 1500-1603

Universities with dates of foundation
Lands of Highland clans who remained Catholic
Lands where Lutheran teaching spread quickly
Area of influence of Northern Earls who rose in support of Mary, 1569
Battles from Flodden (1513) to Langside (1568)

In 1603 King James VI of Scotland became King James I of England

1559. John Knox preaching reformed Christianity

1544. Sacked by English

1547. English victory in attempt at union

1567. Successful Protestant rising

1513. James IV killed. English repulse the Scottish invasion

1547. James V killed. English repulse the Scottish attack

1568. Defeat of Mary Queen of Scots, who fled to England

Dingwall

Elgin

Aberdeen 1494

Dundee

Perth

1410 St. Andrews

Crail

Stirling

Glasgow

1451

Edinburgh

1583 Pinkie

Carberry Hill

Langside

Flodden

Solway Moss

Wigtown

Kirkudbright

ENGLAND

Loch Ness

Spey

Tay

Clyde

Firth of Forth

Tweed

Tyne

Tees

0   50
Miles

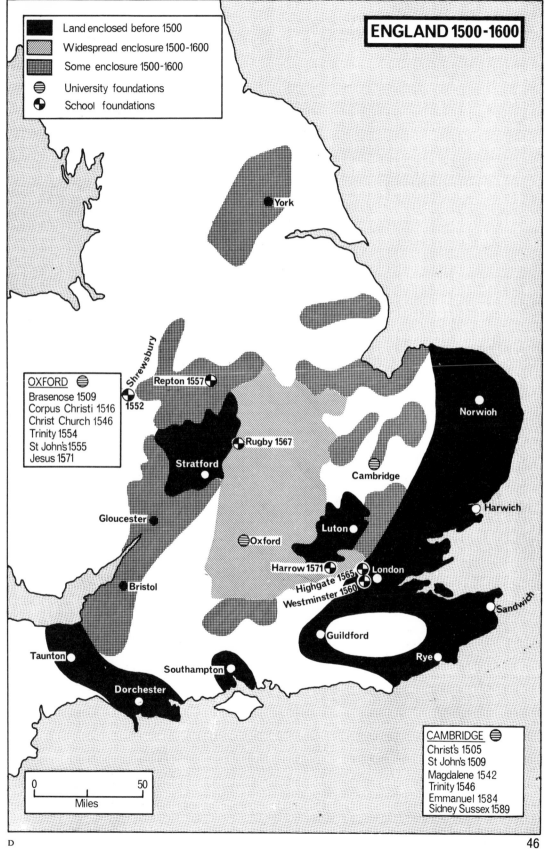

ENGLAND 1500-1600

Land enclosed before 1500

Widespread enclosure 1500-1600

Some enclosure 1500-1600

University foundations

School foundations

OXFORD
Brasenose 1509
Corpus Christi 1516
Christ Church 1546
Trinity 1554
St John's 1555
Jesus 1571

CAMBRIDGE
Christ's 1505
St John's 1509
Magdalene 1542
Trinity 1546
Emmanuel 1584
Sidney Sussex 1589

York

Norwioh

Shrewsbury
1552

Repton 1557

Rugby 1567

Stratford

Cambridge

Harwich

Gloucester

Luton

Oxford

Harrow 1571

Highgate 1565

London

Westminster 1560

Bristol

Sandwich

Guildford

Taunton

Rye

Southampton

Dorchester

0   50
Miles

D

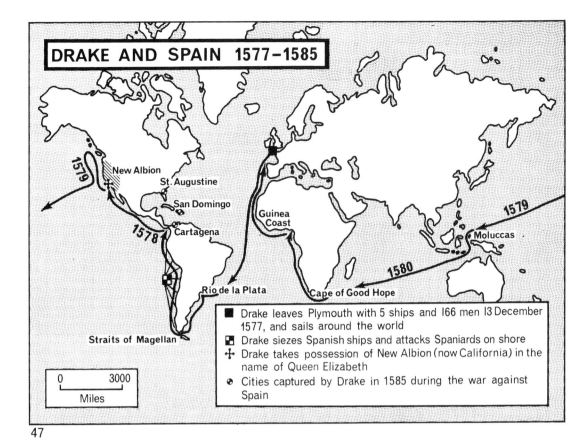

DRAKE AND SPAIN 1577–1585

New Albion
St. Augustine
San Domingo
1579
1578
Cartagena
Guinea Coast
Rio de la Plata
Cape of Good Hope
Straits of Magellan
1579
Moluccas
1580

0   3000
Miles

■ Drake leaves Plymouth with 5 ships and 166 men 13 December 1577, and sails around the world
◪ Drake siezes Spanish ships and attacks Spaniards on shore
✛ Drake takes possession of New Albion (now California) in the name of Queen Elizabeth
◉ Cities captured by Drake in 1585 during the war against Spain

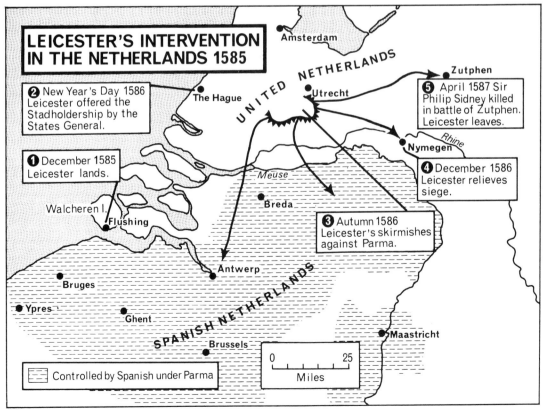

LEICESTER'S INTERVENTION IN THE NETHERLANDS 1585

Amsterdam

UNITED NETHERLANDS

Zutphen

❷ New Year's Day 1586 Leicester offered the Stadholdership by the States General.

The Hague

Utrecht

❺ April 1587 Sir Philip Sidney killed in battle of Zutphen. Leicester leaves.

Nymegen

Rhine

❶ December 1585 Leicester lands.

Meuse

❹ December 1586 Leicester relieves siege.

Walcheren I.
Flushing

Breda

❸ Autumn 1586 Leicester's skirmishes against Parma.

Antwerp

Bruges

SPANISH NETHERLANDS

Ypres

Ghent

Maastricht

Brussels

0   25
Miles

▒ Controlled by Spanish under Parma

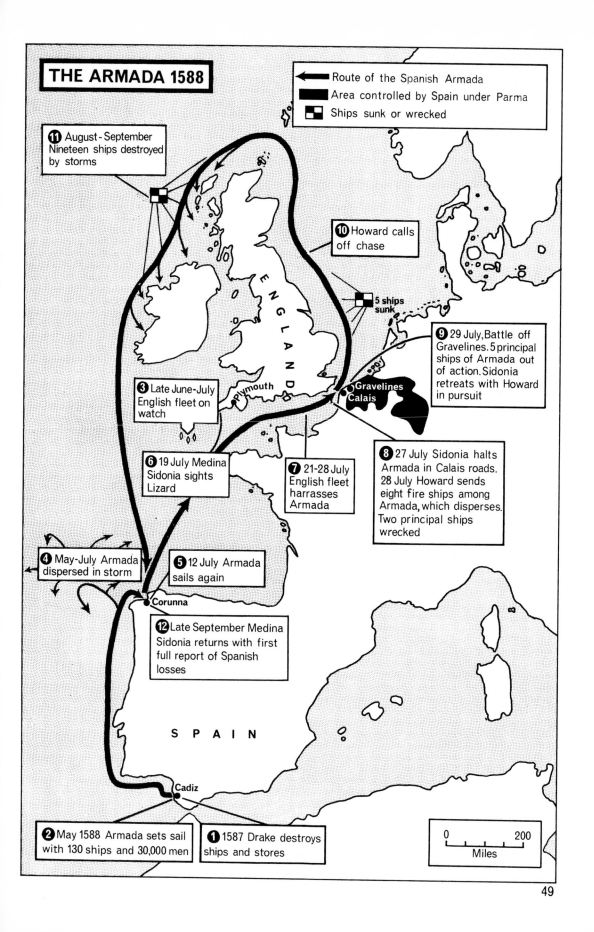

THE ARMADA 1588

⬅️ Route of the Spanish Armada
⬛ Area controlled by Spain under Parma
⬜ Ships sunk or wrecked

11 August - September Nineteen ships destroyed by storms

10 Howard calls off chase

5 ships sunk

9 29 July, Battle off Gravelines. 5 principal ships of Armada out of action. Sidonia retreats with Howard in pursuit

ENGLAND

3 Late June-July English fleet on watch

Plymouth

Gravelines
Calais

8 27 July Sidonia halts Armada in Calais roads. 28 July Howard sends eight fire ships among Armada, which disperses. Two principal ships wrecked

6 19 July Medina Sidonia sights Lizard

7 21-28 July English fleet harrasses Armada

4 May-July Armada dispersed in storm

5 12 July Armada sails again

Corunna

12 Late September Medina Sidonia returns with first full report of Spanish losses

S P A I N

Cadiz

2 May 1588 Armada sets sail with 130 ships and 30,000 men

1 1587 Drake destroys ships and stores

0   200
Miles

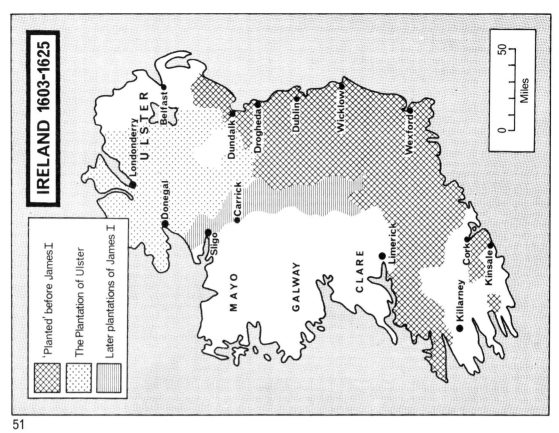

IRELAND 1603-1625

ULSTER

Londonderry
Belfast
Donegal
Dundalk
Drogheda
Dublin
Wicklow
Wexford
Carrick
Sligo

MAYO

GALWAY

CLARE

Limerick
Killarney
Cork
Kinsale

'Planted' before James I

The Plantation of Ulster

Later plantations of James I

0   50
Miles

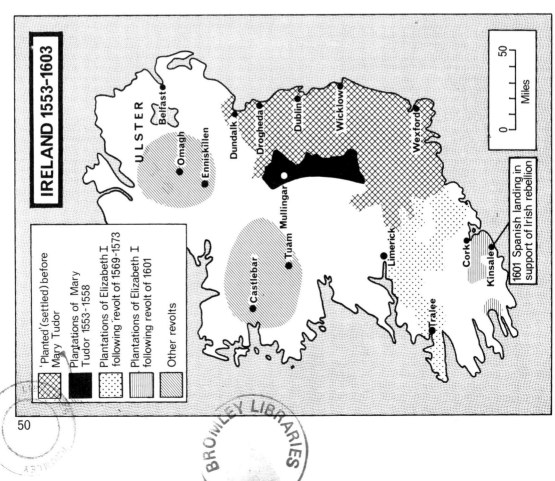

IRELAND 1553-1603

ULSTER

Belfast
Omagh
Enniskillen
Dundalk
Drogheda
Dublin
Wicklow
Wexford
Mullingar
Tuam
Castlebar
Limerick
Tralee
Cork
Kinsale

'Planted' (settled) before
Mary Tudor

Plantations of Mary
Tudor 1553-1558

Plantations of Elizabeth I
following revolt of 1569-1573

Plantations of Elizabeth I
following revolt of 1601

Other revolts

1601 Spanish landing in
support of Irish rebellion

0   50
Miles

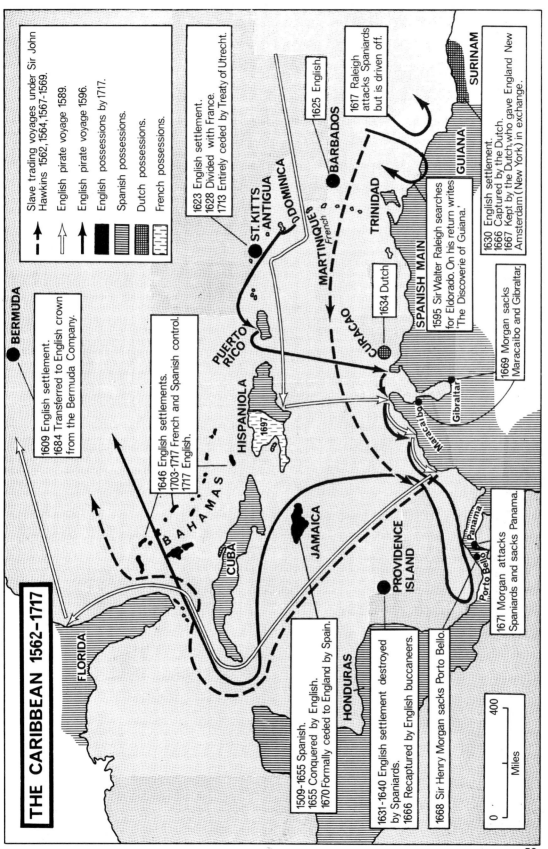

THE CARIBBEAN 1562–1717

Legend:
- Slave trading voyages under Sir John Hawkins 1562, 1564, 1567-1569.
- English pirate voyage 1589.
- English pirate voyage 1596.
- English possessions by1717.
- Spanish possessions.
- Dutch possessions.
- French possessions.

BERMUDA
1609 English settlement.
1684 Transferred to English crown from the Bermuda Company.

ST. KITTS
1623 English settlement.
1628 Divided with France.
1713 Entirely ceded by Treaty of Utrecht.

ANTIGUA

DOMINICA

MARTINIQUE French

BARBADOS
1625 English

TRINIDAD

1617 Raleigh attacks Spaniards but is driven off.

SURINAM

GUIANA
1630 English settlement.
1666 Captured by the Dutch.
1667 Kept by the Dutch, who gave England New Amsterdam (New York) in exchange.

1595 Sir Walter Raleigh searches for Eldorado. On his return writes 'The Discoverie of Guiana.'

SPANISH MAIN

CURACAO
1634 Dutch

PUERTO RICO

HISPANIOLA
1697

BAHAMAS
1646 English settlements.
1703-1717 French and Spanish control.
1717 English.

Maracaibo

Gibraltar

1669 Morgan sacks Maracaibo and Gibraltar.

CUBA

JAMAICA
1509-1655 Spanish.
1655 Conquered by English.
1670 Formally ceded to England by Spain.

PROVIDENCE ISLAND
1631-1640 English settlement destroyed by Spaniards.
1666 Recaptured by English buccaneers.

Porto Bello
1668 Sir Henry Morgan sacks Porto Bello.

Panama
1671 Morgan attacks Spaniards and sacks Panama.

FLORIDA

HONDURAS

0   400
Miles

52

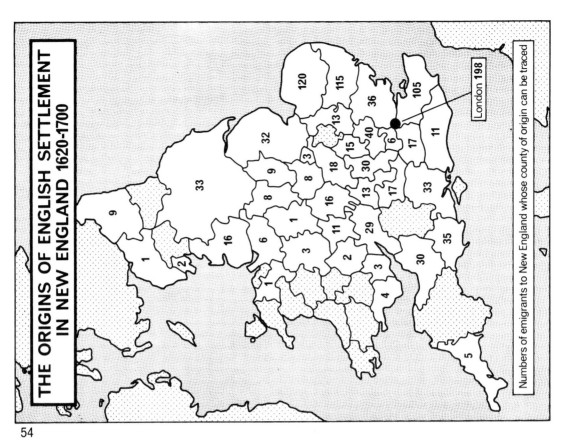

THE ORIGINS OF ENGLISH SETTLEMENT IN NEW ENGLAND 1620-1700

London 198

Numbers of emigrants to New England whose county of origin can be traced

54

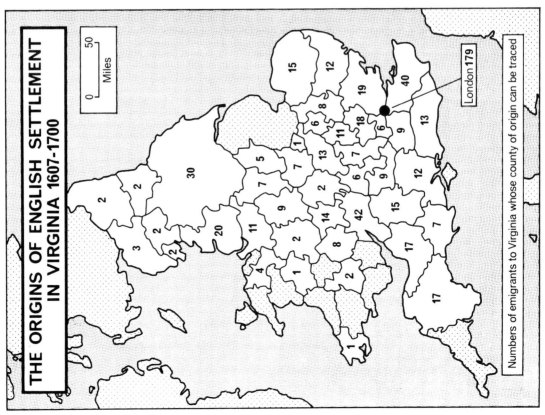

THE ORIGINS OF ENGLISH SETTLEMENT IN VIRGINIA 1607-1700

0 50
Miles

London 179

Numbers of emigrants to Virginia whose county of origin can be traced

53

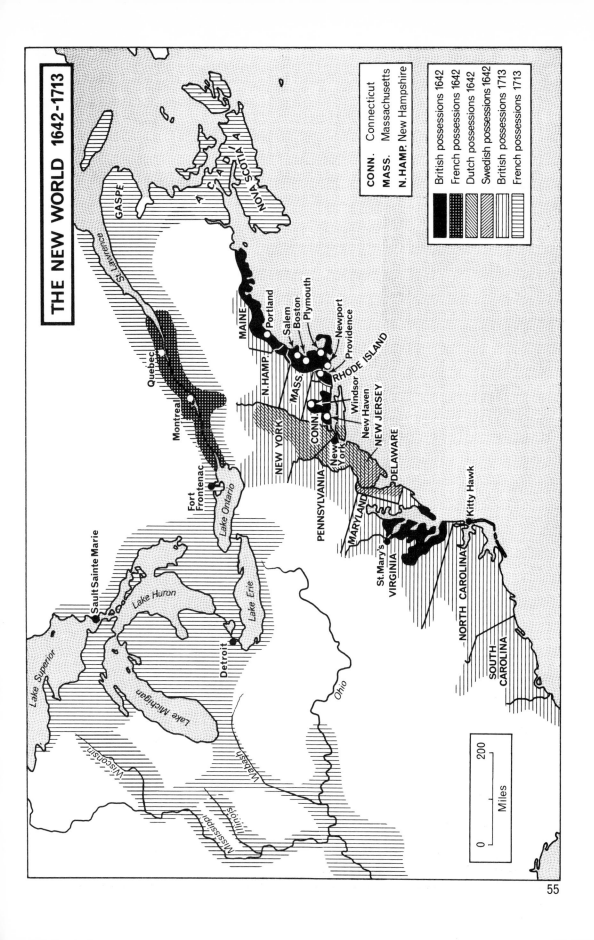

THE NEW WORLD 1642-1713

CONN. Connecticut
MASS. Massachusetts
N.HAMP. New Hampshire

British possessions 1642
French possessions 1642
Dutch possessions 1642
Swedish possessions 1642
British possessions 1713
French possessions 1713

GASPE

NOVA SCOTIA

ACADIA

St. Lawrence

Quebec

Montreal

Fort Frontenac

Lake Ontario

Sault Sainte Marie

Lake Superior

Lake Huron

Lake Michigan

Lake Erie

Detroit

Wisconsin

Mississippi

Illinois

Wabash

Ohio

MAINE

N.HAMP.

MASS.

Portland
Salem
Boston
Plymouth
Newport
Providence

RHODE ISLAND

Windsor
New Haven

CONN.

NEW YORK

New York

NEW JERSEY

DELAWARE

PENNSYLVANIA

MARYLAND

St. Mary's

VIRGINIA

Kitty Hawk

NORTH CAROLINA

SOUTH CAROLINA

0   200
Miles

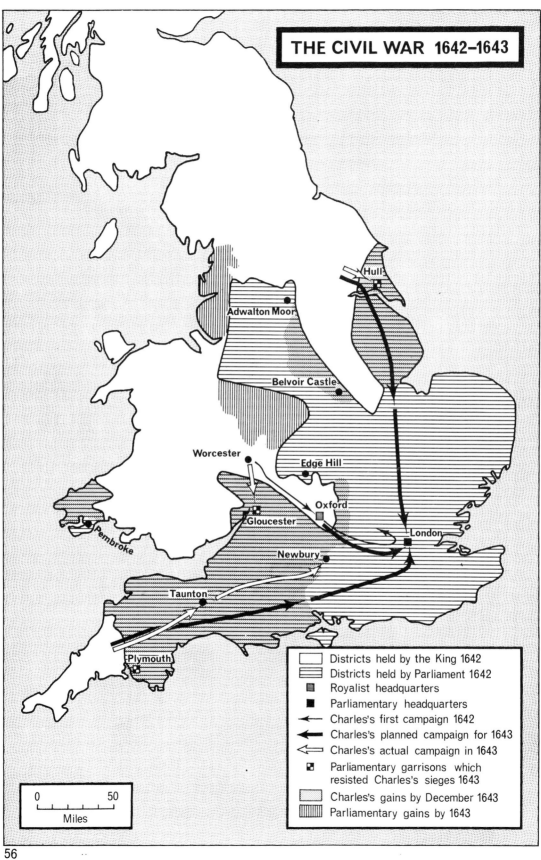

THE CIVIL WAR 1642–1643

Hull

Adwalton Moor

Belvoir Castle

Worcester

Edge Hill

Oxford

Gloucester

Pembroke

London

Newbury

Taunton

Plymouth

☐   Districts held by the King 1642

▤   Districts held by Parliament 1642

▤   Royalist headquarters

■   Parliamentary headquarters

←   Charles's first campaign 1642

⬅   Charles's planned campaign for 1643

⇦   Charles's actual campaign in 1643

▣   Parliamentary garrisons which resisted Charles's sieges 1643

▥   Charles's gains by December 1643

▦   Parliamentary gains by 1643

0   50

Miles

THE CIVIL WAR 1644–1646

In May 1646 King Charles surrendered to the Scottish Army at Newark.
In February 1647 the Scots sold the King to Parliament for £400,000.
He was beheaded on 30 January 1649.

Carlisle

Marston Moor

Hull

Preston
Bolton

Liverpool

Sandal Castle

Stockport

Hulme

Newark

Nantwich

Belvoir Castle

Shrewsbury

Ashby

Lichfield

Naseby

Holmby House

Banbury
Cropredy Bridge

Gloucester

Oxford

Donnington Castle

Bridgewater

Taunton

Lyme Regis

Corfe Castle

Plymouth

The Eastern Association: main recruiting ground for Parliamentary Army 1643

Campaign of Prince Rupert to Marston Moor.

Parliamentary advances to Marston Moor, where the Royalists were defeated 2 July 1644

Area controlled by Parliament in December 1644.

Area gained by Parliament by December 1645.

Districts held by the King in May 1646.

Area gained by Parliament by December 1646.

0   50
Miles

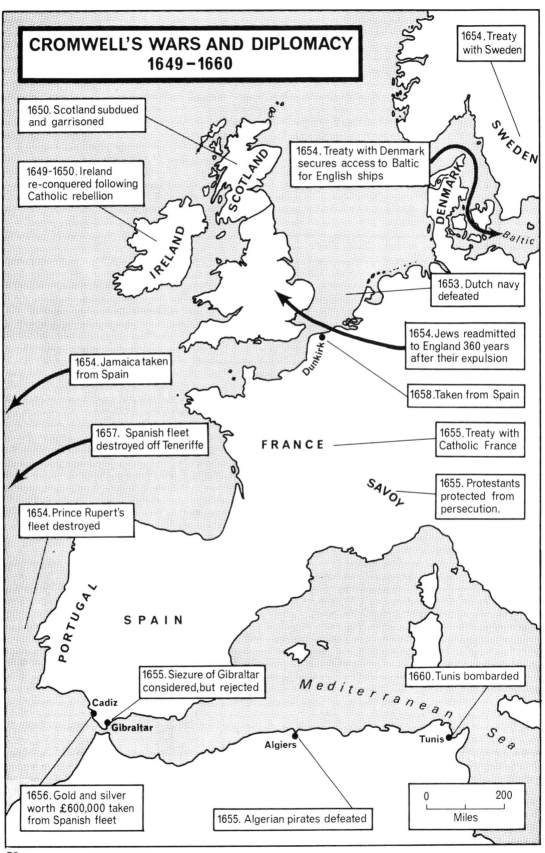

CROMWELL'S WARS AND DIPLOMACY 1649–1660

1654. Treaty with Sweden

1650. Scotland subdued and garrisoned

1654. Treaty with Denmark secures access to Baltic for English ships

1649-1650. Ireland re-conquered following Catholic rebellion

1653. Dutch navy defeated

1654. Jews readmitted to England 360 years after their expulsion

1654. Jamaica taken from Spain

1658. Taken from Spain

1655. Treaty with Catholic France

1657. Spanish fleet destroyed off Teneriffe

1655. Protestants protected from persecution.

1654. Prince Rupert's fleet destroyed

1655. Siezure of Gibraltar considered, but rejected

1660. Tunis bombarded

1656. Gold and silver worth £600,000 taken from Spanish fleet

1655. Algerian pirates defeated

SWEDEN

DENMARK

Baltic

SCOTLAND

IRELAND

Dunkirk

FRANCE

SAVOY

PORTUGAL

SPAIN

Mediterranean Sea

Cadiz

Gibraltar

Algiers

Tunis

0   200
Miles

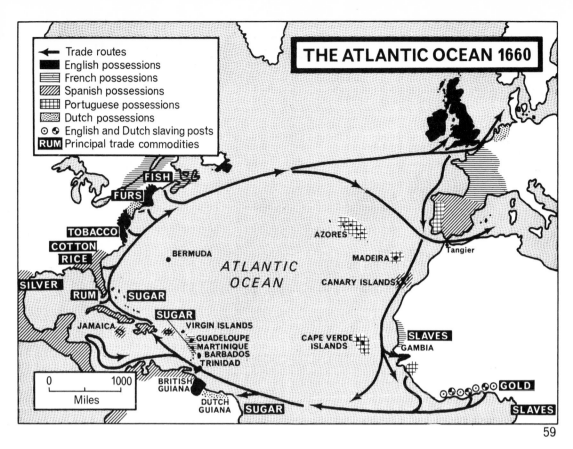

THE ATLANTIC OCEAN 1660

Trade routes
English possessions
French possessions
Spanish possessions
Portuguese possessions
Dutch possessions
English and Dutch slaving posts
RUM Principal trade commodities

FISH
FURS
TOBACCO
COTTON
RICE
SILVER
RUM
SUGAR
SUGAR
BERMUDA
AZORES
MADEIRA
Tangier
ATLANTIC OCEAN
CANARY ISLANDS
JAMAICA
VIRGIN ISLANDS
GUADELOUPE
MARTINIQUE
BARBADOS
TRINIDAD
CAPE VERDE ISLANDS
SLAVES
GAMBIA
0   1000
Miles
BRITISH GUIANA
DUTCH GUIANA
SUGAR
GOLD
SLAVES

59

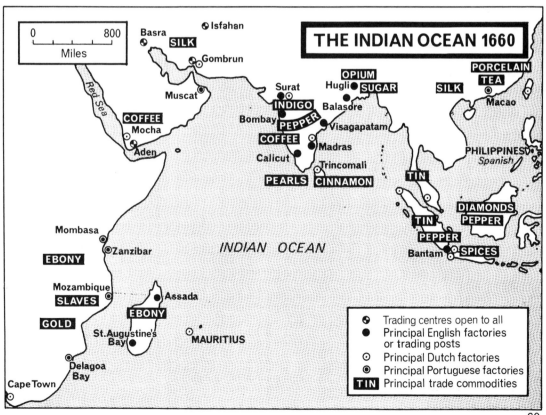

THE INDIAN OCEAN 1660

0   800
Miles

Basra
Isfahan
SILK
Gombrun
PORCELAIN
TEA
Surat
OPIUM
Hugli
SUGAR
Muscat
INDIGO
Balasore
SILK
Macao
COFFEE
Bombay
PEPPER
Mocha
Visagapatam
COFFEE
Madras
Aden
Calicut
PHILIPPINES
Spanish
Trincomali
PEARLS
CINNAMON
TIN
Mombasa
Zanzibar
INDIAN OCEAN
DIAMONDS
PEPPER
TIN
EBONY
PEPPER
Bantam
SPICES
Mozambique
SLAVES
Assada
GOLD
EBONY
St.Augustine's Bay
MAURITIUS
Delagoa Bay
Cape Town

Trading centres open to all
Principal English factories or trading posts
Principal Dutch factories
Principal Portuguese factories
TIN Principal trade commodities

60

THE THREE DUTCH WARS

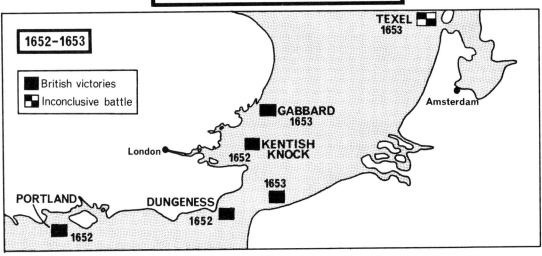

1652-1653

- ■ British victories
- ◧ Inconclusive battle

TEXEL 1653

Amsterdam

GABBARD 1653

London

KENTISH KNOCK 1652

1653

PORTLAND 1652

DUNGENESS 1652

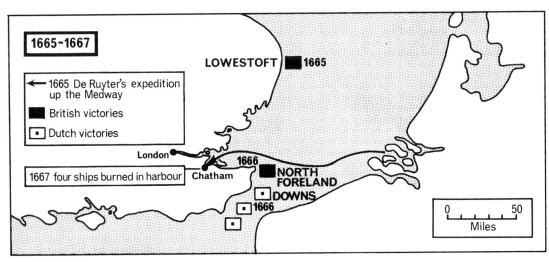

1665-1667

LOWESTOFT ■ 1665

- ← 1665 De Ruyter's expedition up the Medway
- ■ British victories
- ▣ Dutch victories

London

1667 four ships burned in harbour

Chatham

1666

NORTH FORELAND

▣ **DOWNS**

▣ 1666

▣

0   50
Miles

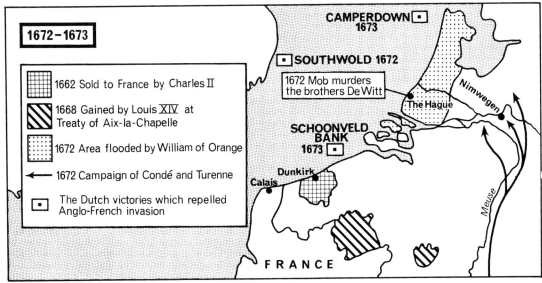

1672-1673

CAMPERDOWN ▣ 1673

▣ **SOUTHWOLD** 1672

1672 Mob murders the brothers De Witt

The Hague

Nimwegen

- ▦ 1662 Sold to France by Charles II
- ▨ 1668 Gained by Louis XIV at Treaty of Aix-la-Chapelle
- ▒ 1672 Area flooded by William of Orange
- ← 1672 Campaign of Condé and Turenne
- ▣ The Dutch victories which repelled Anglo-French invasion

SCHOONVELD BANK 1673 ▣

Dunkirk

Calais

Meuse

F R A N C E

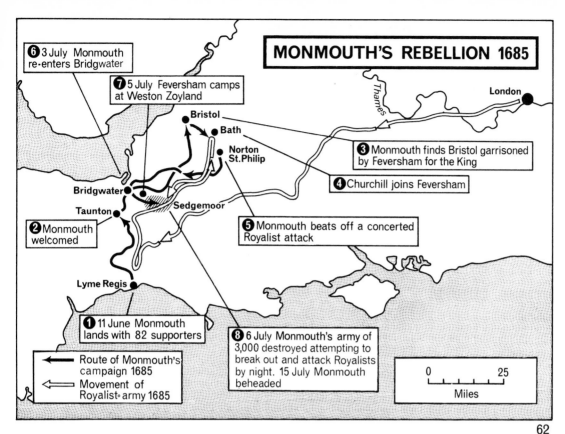

MONMOUTH'S REBELLION 1685

6 3 July Monmouth re-enters Bridgwater

7 5 July Feversham camps at Weston Zoyland

3 Monmouth finds Bristol garrisoned by Feversham for the King

4 Churchill joins Feversham

5 Monmouth beats off a concerted Royalist attack

2 Monmouth welcomed

1 11 June Monmouth lands with 82 supporters

8 6 July Monmouth's army of 3,000 destroyed attempting to break out and attack Royalists by night. 15 July Monmouth beheaded

Route of Monmouth's campaign 1685
Movement of Royalist army 1685

Bristol
Bath
Norton St.Philip
Bridgwater
Taunton
Sedgemoor
Lyme Regis
London
Thames

0   25
Miles

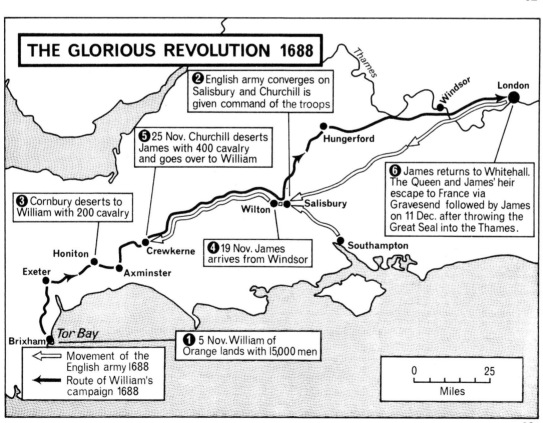

THE GLORIOUS REVOLUTION 1688

2 English army converges on Salisbury and Churchill is given command of the troops

5 25 Nov. Churchill deserts James with 400 cavalry and goes over to William

6 James returns to Whitehall. The Queen and James' heir escape to France via Gravesend followed by James on 11 Dec. after throwing the Great Seal into the Thames.

3 Cornbury deserts to William with 200 cavalry

4 19 Nov. James arrives from Windsor

1 5 Nov. William of Orange lands with 15,000 men

Movement of the English army 1688
Route of William's campaign 1688

Thames
Windsor
London
Hungerford
Wilton
Salisbury
Southampton
Honiton
Crewkerne
Exeter
Axminster
Brixham
Tor Bay

0   25
Miles

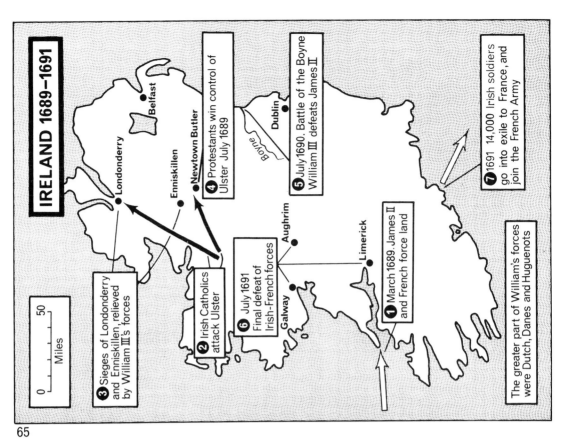

IRELAND 1689–1691

3 Sieges of Londonderry and Enniskillen, relieved by William III's forces

2 Irish Catholics attack Ulster

6 July 1691 Final defeat of Irish-French forces

50

0 Miles

Belfast

Londonderry

Enniskillen

Newtown Butler

4 Protestants win control of Ulster July 1689

Dublin

Boyne

5 July 1690. Battle of the Boyne William III defeats James II

Aughrim

Galway

Limerick

1 March 1689. James II and French force land

7 1691 14,000 Irish soldiers go into exile to France, and join the French Army

The greater part of William's forces were Dutch, Danes and Huguenots

65

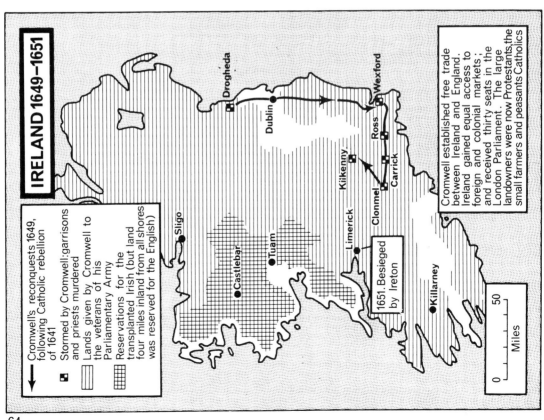

IRELAND 1649–1651

→ Cromwell's reconquests 1649, following Catholic rebellion of 1641

■ Stormed by Cromwell: garrisons and priests murdered

▥ Lands given by Cromwell to the veterans of his Parliamentary Army

▦ Reservations for the transplanted Irish (but land four miles inland from all shores was reserved for the English)

Drogheda

Dublin

Wexford

Ross

Kilkenny

Carrick

Clonmel

Sligo

Castlebar

Tuam

Limerick

1651. Besieged by Ireton

Killarney

Cromwell established free trade between Ireland and England. Ireland gained equal access to foreign and colonial markets; and received thirty seats in the London Parliament. The large landowners were now Protestants; the small farmers and peasants Catholics

50

0 Miles

64

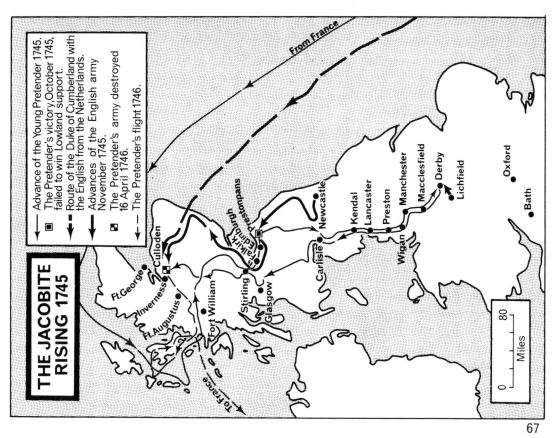

THE JACOBITE RISING 1745

Advance of the Young Pretender 1745.

■ The Pretender's victory, October 1745, failed to win Lowland support.

Route of the Duke of Cumberland with the English from the Netherlands.

Advances of the English army November 1745.

□ The Pretender's army destroyed 16 April 1746.

The Pretender's flight 1746.

From France

To France

Ft.George
Inverness
Culloden
Ft.Augustus
Fort William
Stirling
Glasgow
Edinburgh
Prestonpans
Falkirk
Carlisle
Newcastle
Kendal
Lancaster
Preston
Wigan
Manchester
Macclesfield
Derby
Lichfield
Oxford
Bath

0   80
Miles

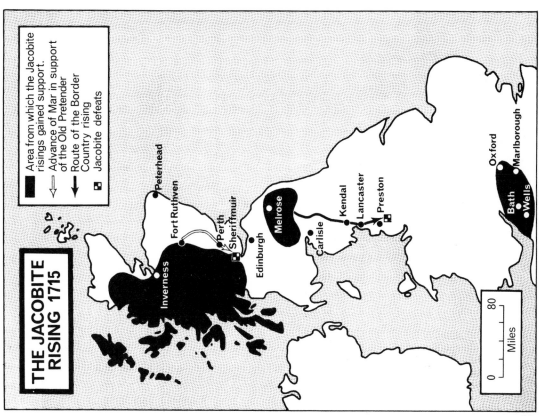

THE JACOBITE RISING 1715

■ Area from which the Jacobite risings gained support.

⇨ Advance of Mar in support of the Old Pretender

→ Route of the Border Country rising

□ Jacobite defeats

Peterhead
Inverness
Fort Ruthven
Perth
Sheriffmuir
Edinburgh
Melrose
Carlisle
Kendal
Lancaster
Preston
Oxford
Bath
Wells
Marlborough

0   80
Miles

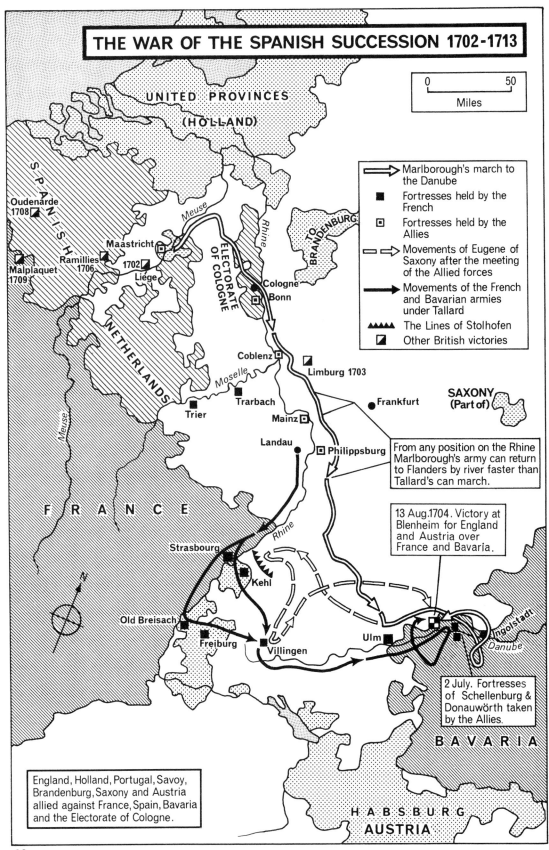

THE WAR OF THE SPANISH SUCCESSION 1702-1713

0   50

Miles

UNITED PROVINCES

(HOLLAND)

SPANISH

Oudenarde
1708

Ramillies
1706

Malplaquet
1709

Maastricht

1702

Liège

NETHERLANDS

Meuse

Meuse

Rhine

ELECTORATE
OF COLOGNE

TO
BRANDENBURG

BRANDENBURG

Cologne
Bonn

Coblenz

Moselle

Limburg 1703

Trarbach

Trier

Mainz

Frankfurt

SAXONY
(Part of)

Landau

Philippsburg

FRANCE

Rhine

Strasbourg

Kehl

Old Breisach

Freiburg

Villingen

Ulm

Ingolstadt

Danube

BAVARIA

Legend:

→ Marlborough's march to the Danube

■ Fortresses held by the French

▣ Fortresses held by the Allies

⇢ Movements of Eugene of Saxony after the meeting of the Allied forces

→ Movements of the French and Bavarian armies under Tallard

▲▲▲▲▲ The Lines of Stolhofen

◪ Other British victories

From any position on the Rhine Marlborough's army can return to Flanders by river faster than Tallard's can march.

13 Aug.1704. Victory at Blenheim for England and Austria over France and Bavaria.

2 July. Fortresses of Schellenburg & Donauwörth taken by the Allies.

England, Holland, Portugal, Savoy, Brandenburg, Saxony and Austria allied against France, Spain, Bavaria and the Electorate of Cologne.

HABSBURG
AUSTRIA

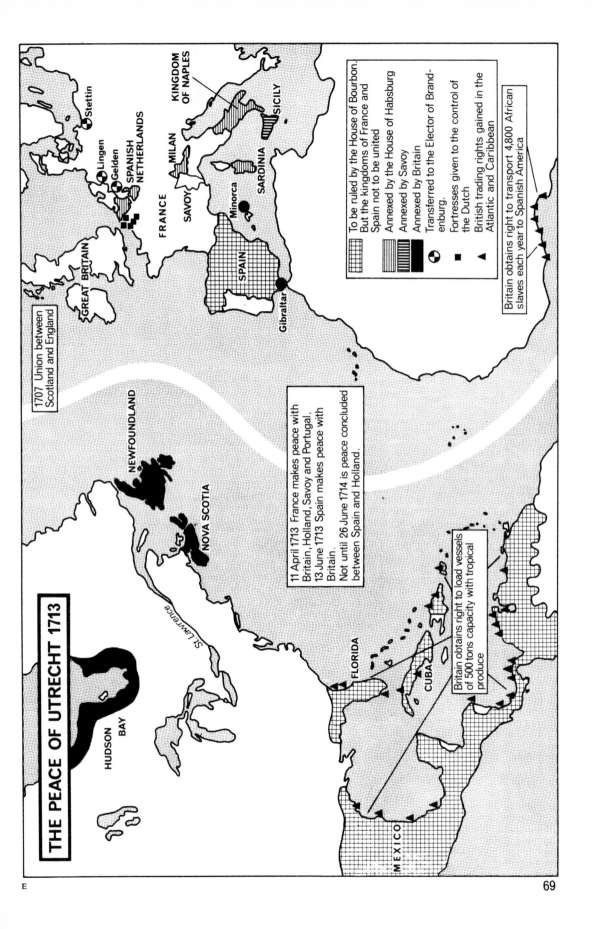

THE PEACE OF UTRECHT 1713

1707 Union between Scotland and England

HUDSON BAY

NEWFOUNDLAND

St.Lawrence

NOVA SCOTIA

FLORIDA

CUBA

MEXICO

11 April 1713 France makes peace with Britain, Holland, Savoy and Portugal.
13 June 1713 Spain makes peace with Britain.
Not until 26 June 1714 is peace concluded between Spain and Holland.

Britain obtains right to load vessels of 500 tons capacity with tropical produce

GREAT BRITAIN

Stettin

Lingen

Gelden

SPANISH NETHERLANDS

FRANCE

MILAN

SAVOY

KINGDOM OF NAPLES

SICILY

SARDINIA

Minorca

SPAIN

Gibraltar

To be ruled by the House of Bourbon. But the kingdoms of France and Spain not to be united

Annexed by the House of Habsburg

Annexed by Savoy

Annexed by Britain

Transferred to the Elector of Brandenburg.

Fortresses given to the control of the Dutch

British trading rights gained in the Atlantic and Caribbean

Britain obtains right to transport 4,800 African slaves each year to Spanish America

E

69

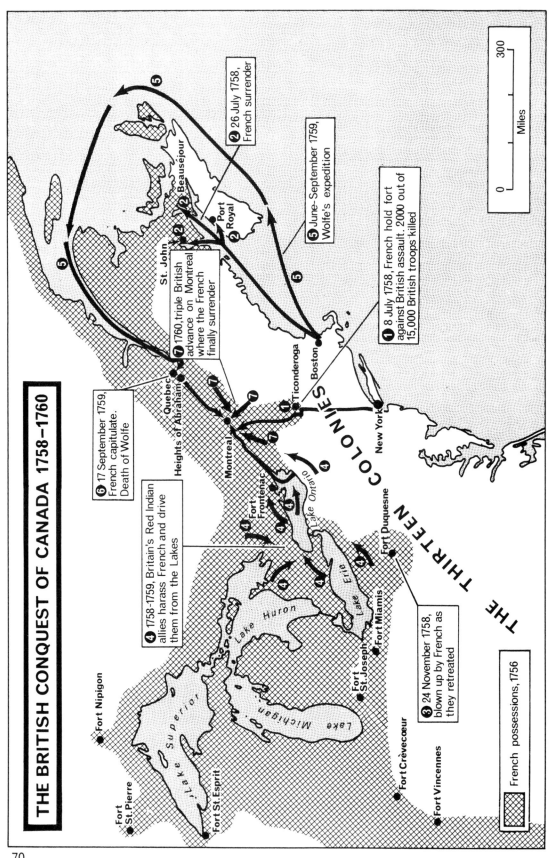

THE BRITISH CONQUEST OF CANADA 1758–1760

⑥ 17 September 1759, French capitulate. Death of Wolfe

④ 1758-1759, Britain's Red Indian allies harass French and drive them from the Lakes

② 26 July 1758, French surrender

⑤ June–September 1759, Wolfe's expedition

① 8 July 1758, French hold fort against British assault. 2000 out of 15,000 British troops killed

⑦ 1760, triple British advance on Montreal where the French finally surrender

③ 24 November 1758, blown up by French as they retreated

Fort St. Pierre

Fort St. Esprit

Fort Nipigon

Lake Superior

Lake Michigan

Lake Huron

Lake Erie

Lake Ontario

Fort St. Joseph

Fort Miamis

Fort Duquesne

Fort Crèvecoeur

Fort Vincennes

THE THIRTEEN COLONIES

New York

Boston

Ticonderoga

Montreal

Fort Frontenac

Quebec

Heights of Abraham

St. John

Beauséjour

Port Royal

French possessions, 1756

0   300

Miles

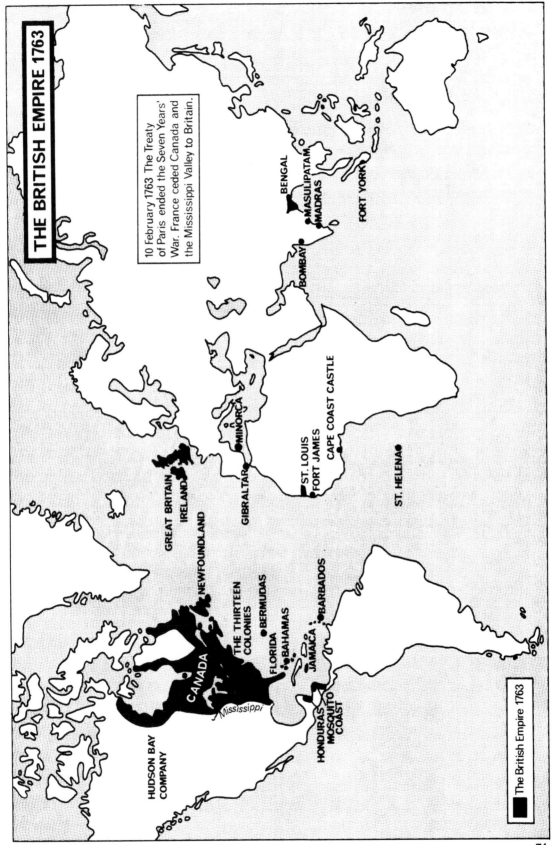

THE BRITISH EMPIRE 1763

10 February 1763 The Treaty of Paris ended the Seven Years' War. France ceded Canada and the Mississippi Valley to Britain.

BENGAL
MASULIPATAM
MADRAS
FORT YORK
BOMBAY

MINORCA
GIBRALTAR
ST. LOUIS
FORT JAMES
CAPE COAST CASTLE
ST. HELENA

GREAT BRITAIN
IRELAND
NEWFOUNDLAND

HUDSON BAY COMPANY
CANADA
Mississippi
THE THIRTEEN COLONIES
BERMUDAS
FLORIDA
BAHAMAS
JAMAICA
BARBADOS
HONDURAS
MOSQUITO COAST

■ The British Empire 1763

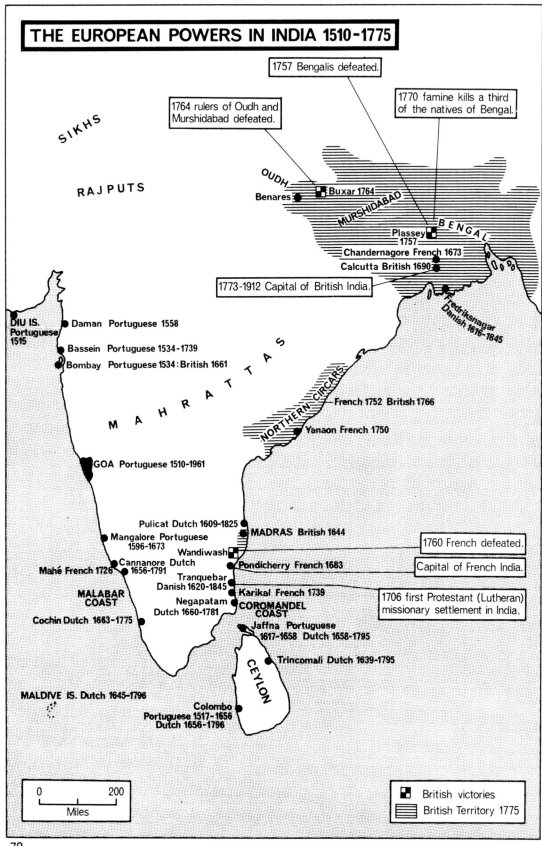

THE EUROPEAN POWERS IN INDIA 1510-1775

1757 Bengalis defeated.

1764 rulers of Oudh and Murshidabad defeated.

1770 famine kills a third of the natives of Bengal.

SIKHS

RAJPUTS

OUDH

Benares ● ☐■ Buxar 1764

MURSHIDABAD

BENGAL

Plassey ■☐ 1757

Chandernagore French 1673

Calcutta British 1690 ●

1773-1912 Capital of British India.

Fredriksnagar Danish 1816-1845

DIU IS. Portuguese 1515

● Daman Portuguese 1558

● Bassein Portuguese 1534-1739

● Bombay Portuguese 1534: British 1661

M A H R A T T A S

NORTHERN CIRCARS

French 1752 British 1766

● Yanaon French 1750

● GOA Portuguese 1510-1961

Pulicat Dutch 1609-1825 ●

☐■ MADRAS British 1644

Mangalore Portuguese 1596-1673 ●

Wandiwash ■

1760 French defeated.

● Pondicherry French 1683

Capital of French India.

Mahé French 1726 ● Cannanore Dutch 1656-1791

Tranquebar Danish 1620-1845

● Karikal French 1739

1706 first Protestant (Lutheran) missionary settlement in India.

MALABAR COAST

Negapatam Dutch 1660-1781

COROMANDEL COAST

Cochin Dutch 1663-1775 ●

Jaffna Portuguese 1617-1658 Dutch 1658-1795

● Trincomali Dutch 1639-1795

MALDIVE IS. Dutch 1645-1796

CEYLON

Colombo Portuguese 1517-1656 Dutch 1656-1796 ●

0   200
Miles

■☐ British victories

≣ British Territory 1775

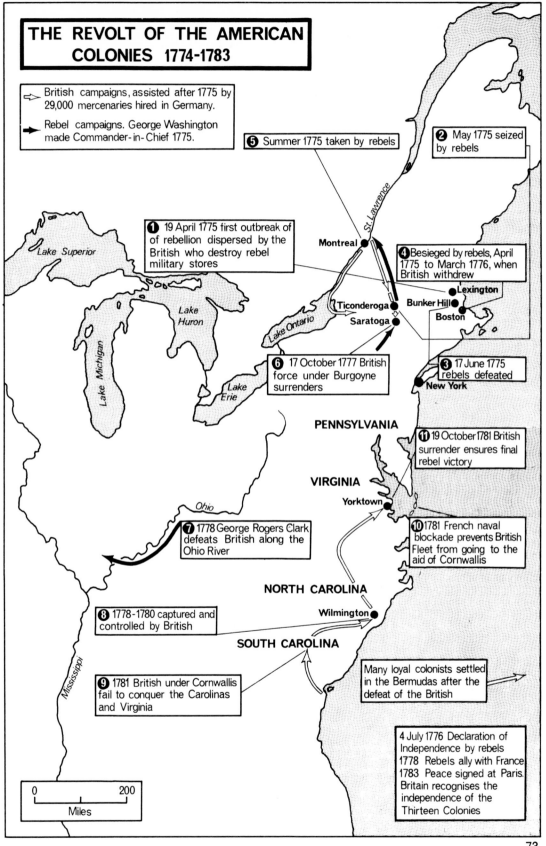

THE REVOLT OF THE AMERICAN COLONIES 1774-1783

⇨ British campaigns, assisted after 1775 by 29,000 mercenaries hired in Germany.

➡ Rebel campaigns. George Washington made Commander-in-Chief 1775.

5 Summer 1775 taken by rebels

2 May 1775 seized by rebels

1 19 April 1775 first outbreak of of rebellion dispersed by the British who destroy rebel military stores

4 Besieged by rebels, April 1775 to March 1776, when British withdrew

6 17 October 1777 British force under Burgoyne surrenders

3 17 June 1775 rebels defeated

11 19 October 1781 British surrender ensures final rebel victory

7 1778 George Rogers Clark defeats British along the Ohio River

10 1781 French naval blockade prevents British Fleet from going to the aid of Cornwallis

8 1778-1780 captured and controlled by British

9 1781 British under Cornwallis fail to conquer the Carolinas and Virginia

Many loyal colonists settled in the Bermudas after the defeat of the British

4 July 1776 Declaration of Independence by rebels
1778 Rebels ally with France
1783 Peace signed at Paris. Britain recognises the independence of the Thirteen Colonies

Lake Superior
Lake Huron
Lake Michigan
Lake Erie
Lake Ontario
St. Lawrence
Montreal
Ticonderoga
Saratoga
Lexington
Bunker Hill
Boston
New York
PENNSYLVANIA
VIRGINIA
Ohio
Yorktown
NORTH CAROLINA
Wilmington
SOUTH CAROLINA
Mississippi

0   200
Miles

73

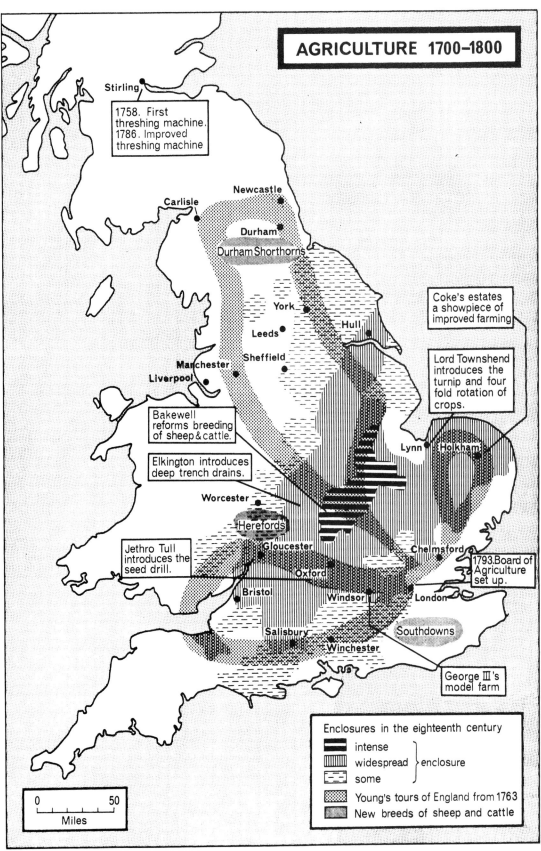

AGRICULTURE 1700–1800

1758. First threshing machine. 1786. Improved threshing machine

Stirling

Carlisle

Newcastle

Durham
Durham Shorthorns

Coke's estates a showpiece of improved farming

York

Hull

Leeds

Sheffield

Lord Townshend introduces the turnip and four fold rotation of crops.

Manchester

Liverpool

Bakewell reforms breeding of sheep & cattle.

Elkington introduces deep trench drains.

Lynn

Holkham

Worcester

Herefords

Gloucester

Chelmsford

1793. Board of Agriculture set up.

Jethro Tull introduces the seed drill.

Oxford

Bristol

Windsor

London

Salisbury

Winchester

Southdowns

George III's model farm

Enclosures in the eighteenth century

▬	intense
▦	widespread } enclosure
▭	some

Young's tours of England from 1763

New breeds of sheep and cattle

0   50
Miles

74

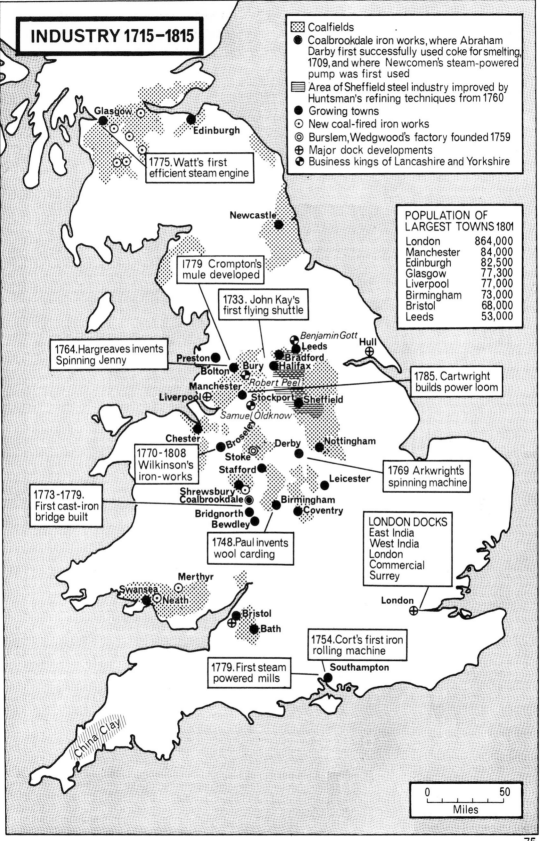

INDUSTRY 1715–1815

Coalfields

● Coalbrookdale iron works, where Abraham Darby first successfully used coke for smelting, 1709, and where Newcomen's steam-powered pump was first used

Area of Sheffield steel industry improved by Huntsman's refining techniques from 1760

● Growing towns

⊙ New coal-fired iron works

◎ Burslem, Wedgwood's factory founded 1759

⊕ Major dock developments

⊕ Business kings of Lancashire and Yorkshire

POPULATION OF LARGEST TOWNS 1801

London	864,000
Manchester	84,000
Edinburgh	82,500
Glasgow	77,300
Liverpool	77,000
Birmingham	73,000
Bristol	68,000
Leeds	53,000

1775. Watt's first efficient steam engine

Glasgow
Edinburgh

Newcastle

1779 Crompton's mule developed

1733. John Kay's first flying shuttle

1764. Hargreaves invents Spinning Jenny

Benjamin Gott
Leeds
Bradford
Halifax
Hull

Preston
Bolton   Bury
Manchester   *Robert Peel*
Liverpool
Stockport   Sheffield

1785. Cartwright builds power loom

Samuel Oldknow

Chester
Broseley   Derby   Nottingham
1770-1808 Wilkinson's iron-works
Stoke
Stafford
Leicester

1769 Arkwright's spinning machine

1773-1779. First cast-iron bridge built

Shrewsbury
Coalbrookdale
Birmingham
Bridgnorth   Coventry
Bewdley

1748. Paul invents wool carding

LONDON DOCKS
East India
West India
London
Commercial
Surrey

Merthyr
Swansea
Neath

Bristol
Bath

1754. Cort's first iron rolling machine

1779. First steam powered mills

London

Southampton

China Clay

0   50
Miles

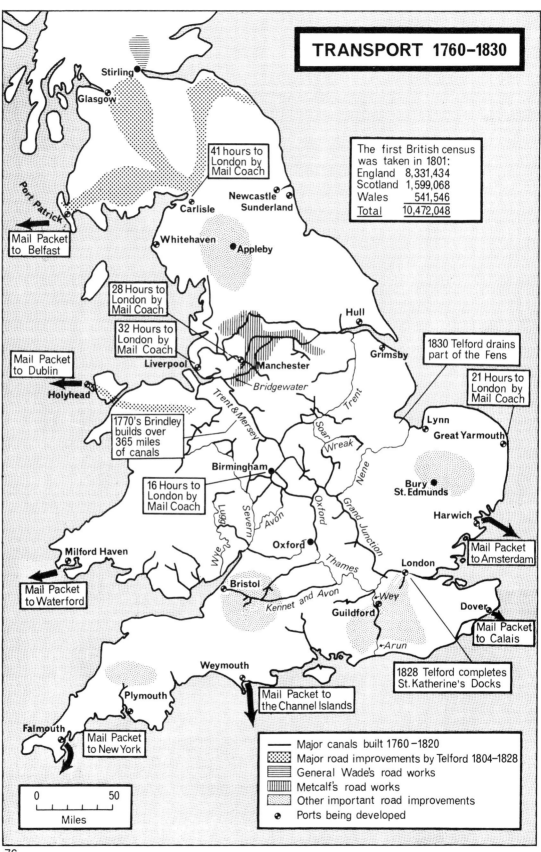

TRANSPORT 1760–1830

Stirling

Glasgow

41 hours to London by Mail Coach

Port Patrick

Mail Packet to Belfast

Carlisle

Newcastle
Sunderland

Whitehaven

Appleby

The first British census was taken in 1801:
England   8,331,434
Scotland 1,599,068
Wales   541,546
Total   10,472,048

28 Hours to London by Mail Coach

32 Hours to London by Mail Coach

Mail Packet to Dublin

Holyhead

Liverpool

Manchester

Bridgewater

Trent & Mersey

Hull

Grimsby

1830 Telford drains part of the Fens

Trent

Soar

Wreak

Nene

Lynn
Great Yarmouth

21 Hours to London by Mail Coach

1770's Brindley builds over 365 miles of canals

Birmingham

16 Hours to London by Mail Coach

Lugg

Wye

Severn

Avon

Oxford

Grand Junction

Bury St. Edmunds

Harwich

Mail Packet to Amsterdam

Oxford

Thames

London

Wey

Milford Haven

Mail Packet to Waterford

Bristol

Kennet and Avon

Guildford

Arun

Dover

Mail Packet to Calais

1828 Telford completes St. Katherine's Docks

Weymouth

Mail Packet to the Channel Islands

Plymouth

Falmouth

Mail Packet to New York

——	Major canals built 1760–1820
	Major road improvements by Telford 1804–1828
	General Wade's road works
	Metcalf's road works
	Other important road improvements
⊕	Ports being developed

0   50
Miles

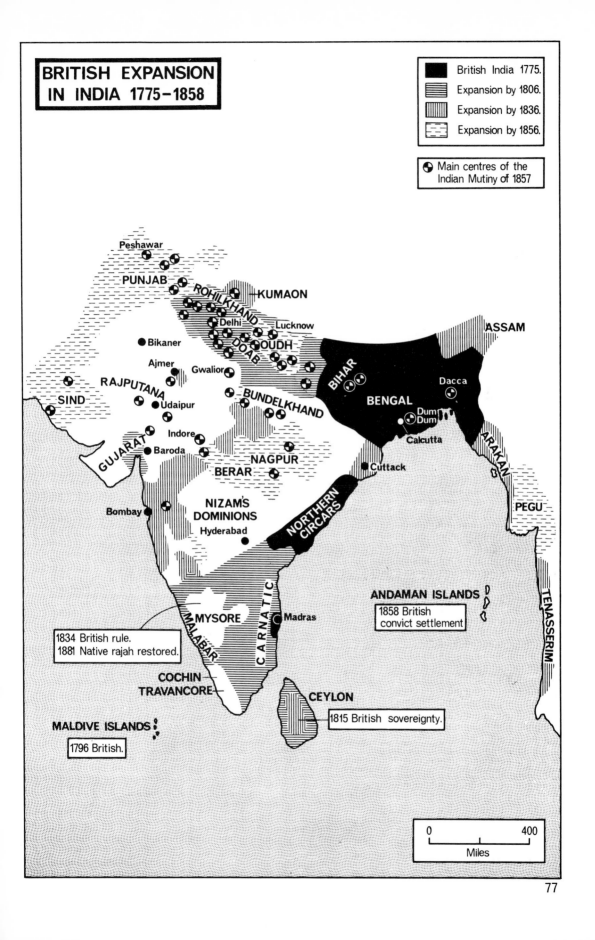

BRITISH EXPANSION IN INDIA 1775–1858

British India 1775.
Expansion by 1806.
Expansion by 1836.
Expansion by 1856.

Main centres of the Indian Mutiny of 1857

Peshawar
PUNJAB
ROHILKHAND
KUMAON
Delhi
Lucknow
OUDH
DOAB
Bikaner
Ajmer
Gwalior
RAJPUTANA
Udaipur
BUNDELKHAND
BIHAR
ASSAM
BENGAL
Dacca
SIND
Indore
GUJARAT
Baroda
NAGPUR
Dum Dum
Calcutta
ARAKAN
BERAR
Cuttack
NIZAM'S DOMINIONS
NORTHERN CIRCARS
PEGU
Bombay
Hyderabad

ANDAMAN ISLANDS
1858 British convict settlement

MYSORE
CARNATIC
Madras

1834 British rule.
1881 Native rajah restored.

MALABAR

TENASSERIM

COCHIN
TRAVANCORE

CEYLON
1815 British sovereignty.

MALDIVE ISLANDS
1796 British.

0   400
Miles

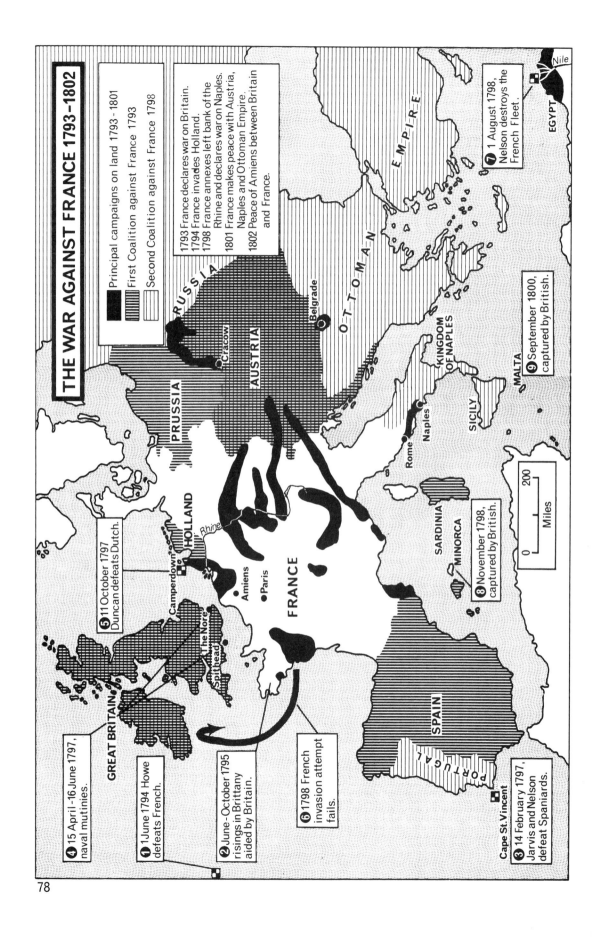

THE WAR AGAINST FRANCE 1793–1802

- ■ Principal campaigns on land 1793 – 1801
- ▤ First Coalition against France 1793
- ▥ Second Coalition against France 1798

1793 France declares war on Britain.
1794 France invades Holland.
1798 France annexes left bank of the Rhine and declares war on Naples.
1801 France makes peace with Austria, Naples and Ottoman Empire.
1802 Peace of Amiens between Britain and France.

7 1 August 1798, Nelson destroys the French Fleet.

Nile

EGYPT

OTTOMAN EMPIRE

RUSSIA

Cracow

AUSTRIA

Belgrade

9 September 1800, captured by British.

MALTA

KINGDOM OF NAPLES

SICILY

Naples

Rome

PRUSSIA

HOLLAND

Camperdown

Rhine

FRANCE

Amiens

Paris

SARDINIA

MINORCA

8 November 1798, captured by British.

0   200
Miles

5 11 October 1797, Duncan defeats Dutch.

The Nore
Spithead

GREAT BRITAIN

4 15 April–16 June 1797, naval mutinies.

1 1 June 1794 Howe defeats French.

2 June–October 1795 risings in Brittany aided by Britain.

6 1798 French invasion attempt fails.

SPAIN

PORTUGAL

Cape St. Vincent

3 14 February 1797, Jarvis and Nelson defeat Spaniards.

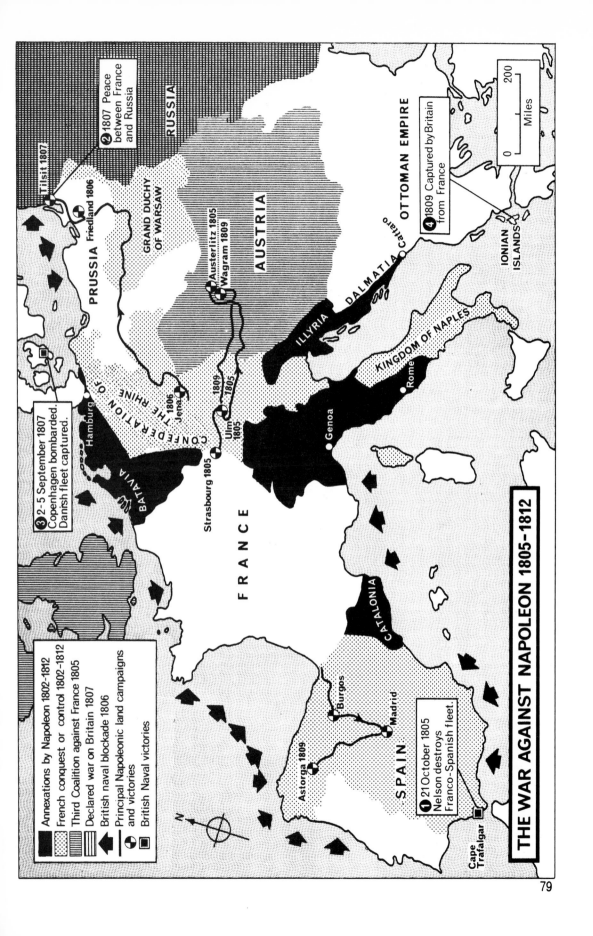

THE WAR AGAINST NAPOLEON 1805–1812

② 1807 Peace between France and Russia

RUSSIA

OTTOMAN EMPIRE

④ 1809 Captured by Britain from France

0   200   Miles

Tilsit 1807

Friedland 1806

PRUSSIA

GRAND DUCHY OF WARSAW

Austerlitz 1805
Wagram 1809

AUSTRIA

DALMATIA

Cattaro

IONIAN ISLANDS

③ 2 – 5 September 1807 Copenhagen bombarded. Danish fleet captured.

Hamburg

Jena 1806

CONFEDERATION OF THE RHINE

1809
1805

Ulm 1805

BATAVIA

ILLYRIA

KINGDOM OF NAPLES

Rome

Strasbourg 1805

Genoa

FRANCE

CATALONIA

Burgos

Madrid

① 21 October 1805 Nelson destroys Franco-Spanish fleet.

Astorga 1809

SPAIN

Cape Trafalgar

- Annexations by Napoleon 1802–1812
- French conquest or control 1802–1812
- Third Coalition against France 1805
- Declared war on Britain 1807
- British naval blockade 1806
- Principal Napoleonic land campaigns and victories
- British Naval victories

N

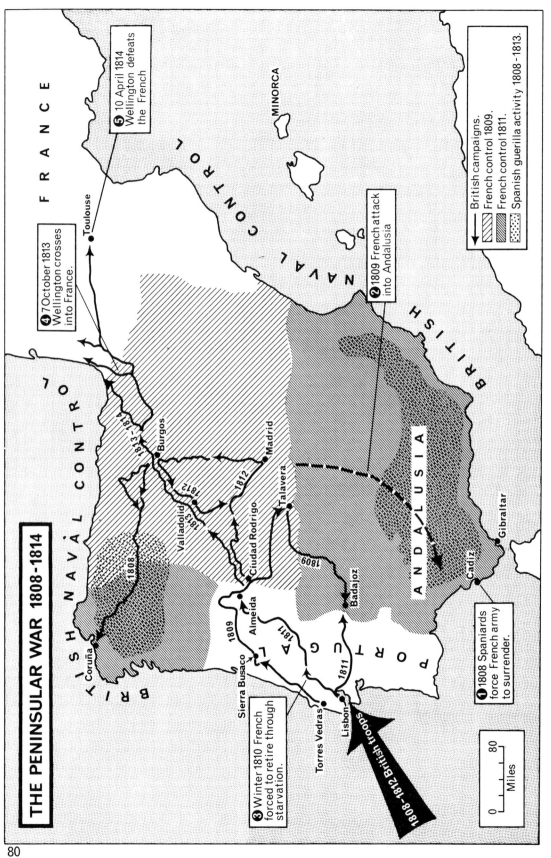

THE PENINSULAR WAR 1808-1814

FRANCE

MINORCA

5 10 April 1814 Wellington defeats the French

Toulouse

4 7 October 1813 Wellington crosses into France.

British campaigns.
French control 1809.
French control 1811.
Spanish guerilla activity 1808 - 1813.

2 1809 French attack into Andalusia

BRITISH NAVAL CONTROL

Burgos

1813-1814

Madrid

Valladolid

1812

1813-

1812

Talavera

Ciudad Rodrigo

1809

ANDALUSIA

Gibraltar

Cadiz

Badajoz

Almeida

1809

1811

PORTUGAL

1811

Sierra Busaco

Torres Vedras

Lisbon

BRITISH NAVAL CONTROL TO

Coruña

1808

3 Winter 1810 French forced to retire through starvation.

1808-1812 British troops

1 1808 Spaniards force French army to surrender.

0   80

Miles

80

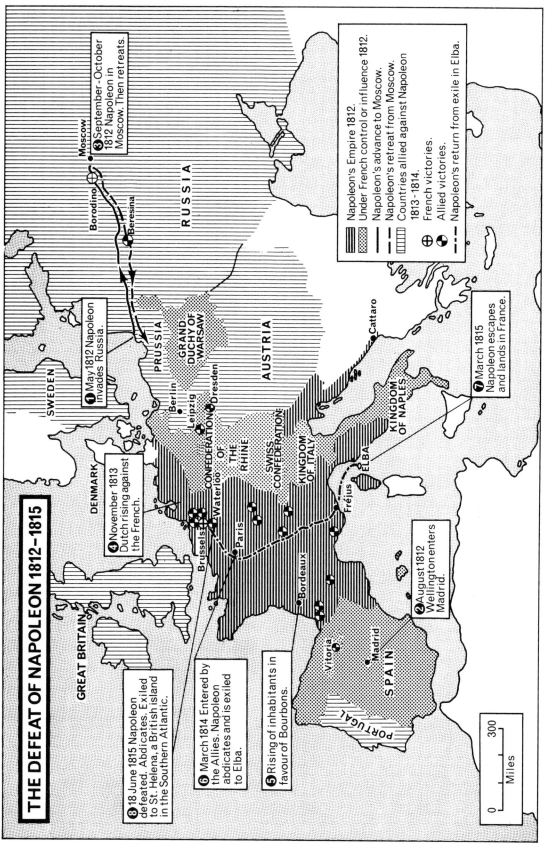

THE DEFEAT OF NAPOLEON 1812–1815

Legend:
- Napoleon's Empire 1812.
- Under French control or influence 1812.
- Napoleon's advance to Moscow.
- Napoleon's retreat from Moscow.
- Countries allied against Napoleon 1813-1814.
- ⊕ French victories.
- ◐ Allied victories.
- Napoleon's return from exile in Elba.

① May 1812 Napoleon invades Russia.

② August 1812 Wellington enters Madrid.

③ September-October 1812 Napoleon in Moscow. Then retreats.

④ November 1813 Dutch rising against the French.

⑤ Rising of inhabitants in favour of Bourbons.

⑥ March 1814 Entered by the Allies. Napoleon abdicates and is exiled to Elba.

⑦ March 1815 Napoleon escapes and lands in France.

⑧ 18 June 1815 Napoleon defeated. Abdicates. Exiled to St. Helena, a British island in the Southern Atlantic.

SWEDEN

RUSSIA

Moscow

Borodino

Beresina

PRUSSIA

GRAND DUCHY OF WARSAW

AUSTRIA

Cattaro

DENMARK

GREAT BRITAIN

Berlin

Leipzig

Dresden

CONFEDERATION OF THE RHINE

SWISS CONFEDERATION

KINGDOM OF ITALY

KINGDOM OF NAPLES

Brussels

Waterloo

Paris

Bordeaux

Fréjus

ELBA

SPAIN

PORTUGAL

Vitoria

Madrid

0   300
Miles

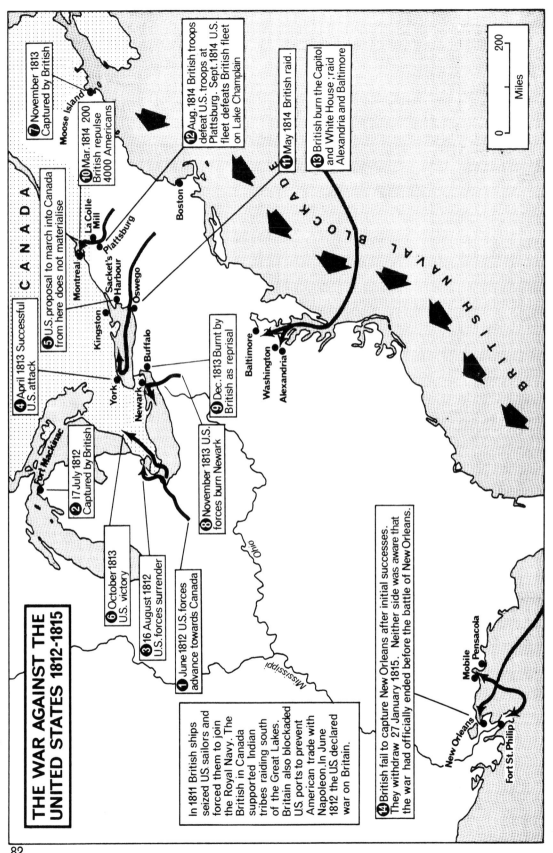

THE WAR AGAINST THE UNITED STATES 1812-1815

CANADA

BLOCKADE

BRITISH NAVAL

In 1811 British ships seized US sailors and forced them to join the Royal Navy. The British in Canada supported Indian tribes raiding south of the Great Lakes. Britain also blockaded US ports to prevent American trade with Napoleon. In June 1812 the US declared war on Britain.

① June 1812 U.S. forces advance towards Canada

② 17 July 1812 Captured by British

③ 16 August 1812 U.S. forces surrender

④ April 1813 Successful U.S. attack

⑤ U.S. proposal to march into Canada from here does not materialise

⑥ October 1813 U.S. victory

⑦ November 1813 Captured by British

⑧ November 1813 U.S. forces burn Newark

⑨ Dec. 1813 Burnt by British as reprisal

⑩ Mar. 1814 200 British repulse 4000 Americans

⑪ May 1814 British raid.

⑫ Aug. 1814 British troops defeat U.S. troops at Plattsburg. Sept. 1814 U.S. fleet defeats British fleet on Lake Champlain

⑬ British burn the Capitol and White House : raid Alexandria and Baltimore

⑭ British fail to capture New Orleans after initial successes. They withdraw 27 January 1815. Neither side was aware that the war had officially ended before the battle of New Orleans.

Moose Island

La Colle Mill

Boston

Montreal

Plattsburg

Sacket's Harbour

Kingston

Oswego

York

Newark

Buffalo

Fort Mackinac

Ohio

Mississippi

Baltimore

Washington

Alexandria

New Orleans

Mobile

Pensacola

Fort St. Philip

Miles

0   200

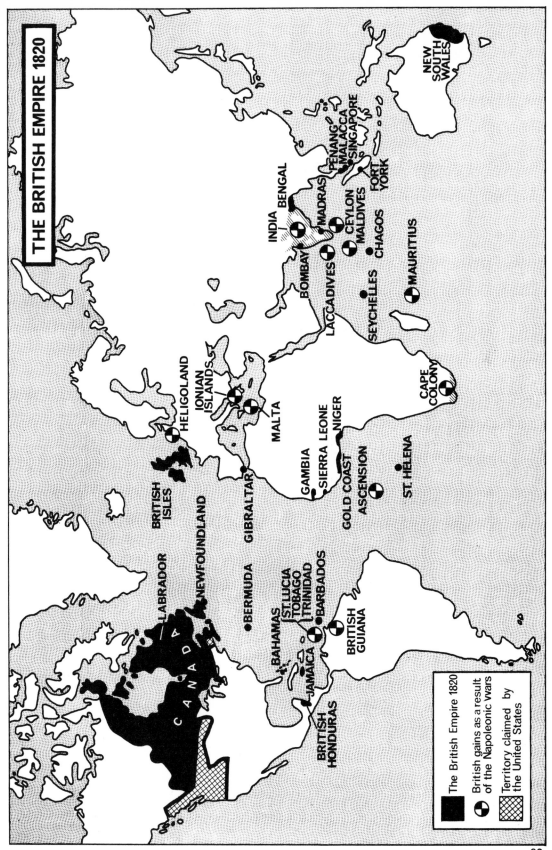

THE BRITISH EMPIRE 1820

NEW SOUTH WALES

PENANG
MALACCA
SINGAPORE
FORT YORK
INDIA
BENGAL
MADRAS
CEYLON
MALDIVES
CHAGOS
BOMBAY
LACCADIVES
SEYCHELLES
MAURITIUS

HELIGOLAND
IONIAN ISLANDS
MALTA
SIERRA LEONE
NIGER
GAMBIA
GOLD COAST
ASCENSION
ST. HELENA
CAPE COLONY

BRITISH ISLES
NEWFOUNDLAND
GIBRALTAR
BERMUDA
BAHAMAS
ST. LUCIA
TOBAGO
TRINIDAD
BARBADOS
JAMAICA
BRITISH GUIANA

LABRADOR
CANADA
BRITISH HONDURAS

The British Empire 1820

British gains as a result
of the Napoleonic wars

Territory claimed by
the United States

83

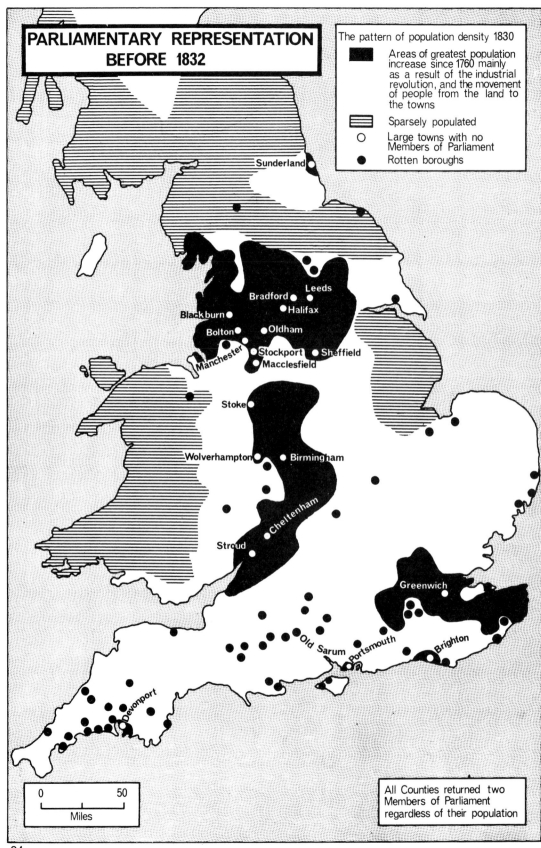

PARLIAMENTARY REPRESENTATION BEFORE 1832

The pattern of population density 1830

Areas of greatest population increase since 1760 mainly as a result of the industrial revolution, and the movement of people from the land to the towns

Sparsely populated

○ Large towns with no Members of Parliament

● Rotten boroughs

Sunderland

Bradford Leeds
Blackburn Halifax
Bolton Oldham
Manchester Stockport Sheffield
Macclesfield

Stoke

Wolverhampton Birmingham

Cheltenham

Stroud

Greenwich

Old Sarum Portsmouth Brighton

Devonport

0   50
Miles

All Counties returned two Members of Parliament regardless of their population

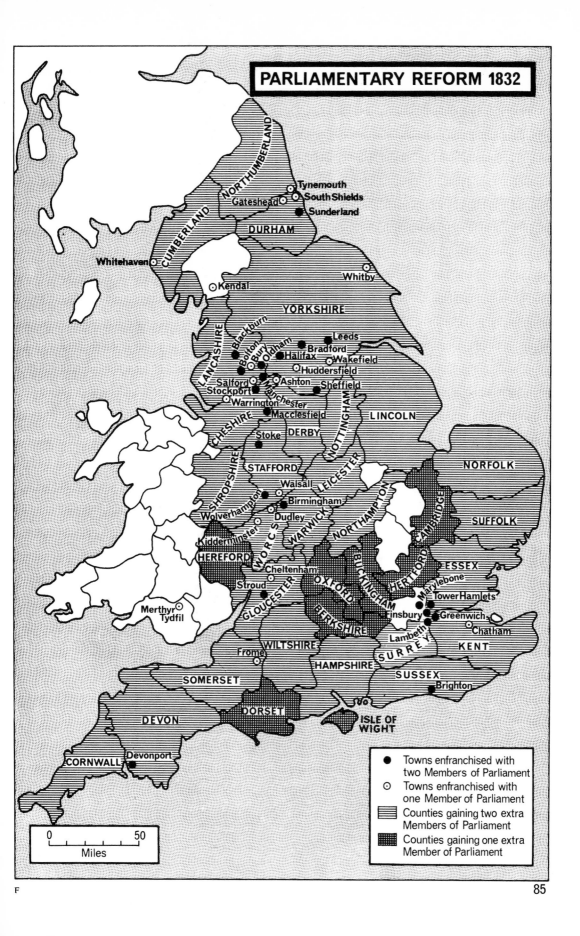

PARLIAMENTARY REFORM 1832

NORTHUMBERLAND
CUMBERLAND
Tynemouth
South Shields
Gateshead
Sunderland
DURHAM
Whitehaven
Kendal
Whitby
YORKSHIRE
LANCASHIRE
Blackburn
Bolton
Bury
Oldham
Leeds
Bradford
Halifax
Wakefield
Huddersfield
Salford
Ashton
Stockport
Manchester
Sheffield
Warrington
LINCOLN
Macclesfield
CHESHIRE
DERBY
Stoke
NOTTINGHAM
SHROPSHIRE
STAFFORD
Walsall
LEICESTER
NORFOLK
Wolverhampton
Birmingham
WARWICK
Dudley
NORTHAMPTON
CAMBRIDGE
SUFFOLK
Kidderminster
HEREFORD
WORCS
Cheltenham
HERTFORD
ESSEX
Stroud
GLOUCESTER
OXFORD
BUCKINGHAM
Marylebone
Tower Hamlets
Merthyr Tydfil
BERKSHIRE
Finsbury
Greenwich
Lambeth
Chatham
Frome
WILTSHIRE
SURREY
KENT
HAMPSHIRE
SOMERSET
SUSSEX
Brighton
DORSET
DEVON
ISLE OF WIGHT
CORNWALL
Devonport

● Towns enfranchised with
  two Members of Parliament
⊙ Towns enfranchised with
  one Member of Parliament
▦ Counties gaining two extra
  Members of Parliament
▦ Counties gaining one extra
  Member of Parliament

0   50
Miles

F

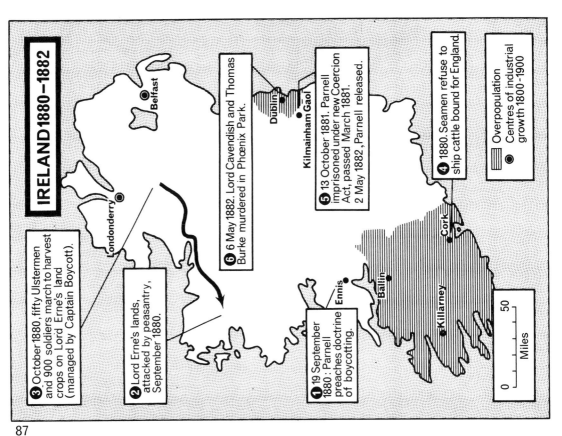

IRELAND 1880–1882

3 October 1880, fifty Ulstermen and 900 soldiers march to harvest crops on Lord Erne's land (managed by Captain Boycott).

2 Lord Erne's lands, attacked by peasantry, September 1880.

6 6 May 1882. Lord Cavendish and Thomas Burke murdered in Phœnix Park.

5 13 October 1881. Parnell imprisoned under new Coercion Act, passed March 1881. 2 May 1882, Parnell released.

4 1880. Seamen refuse to ship cattle bound for England.

1 19 September 1880 : Parnell preaches doctrine of boycotting.

Londonderry

Belfast

Dublin

Kilmainham Gaol

Ennis

Ballin

Cork

Killarney

☐ Overpopulation

◉ Centres of industrial growth 1800-1900

0   50
Miles

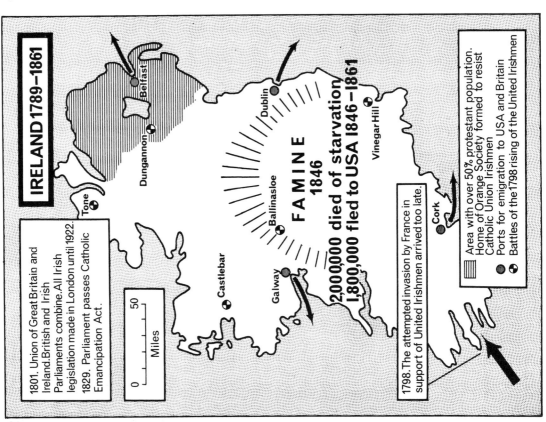

IRELAND 1789–1861

1801. Union of Great Britain and Ireland. British and Irish Parliaments combine. All Irish legislation made in London until 1922.

1829. Parliament passes Catholic Emancipation Act.

Belfast

Dungannon

Tone

Castlebar

Galway

Ballinasloe

F A M I N E 1846

2,000,000 died of starvation 1,800,000 fled to USA 1846–1861

Dublin

Vinegar Hill

Cork

1798. The attempted invasion by France in support of United Irishmen arrived too late.

▥ Area with over 50% protestant population. Home of Orange Society formed to resist Catholic Union Irishmen

◉ Ports for emigration to USA and Britain

✠ Battles of the 1798 rising of the United Irishmen

0   50
Miles

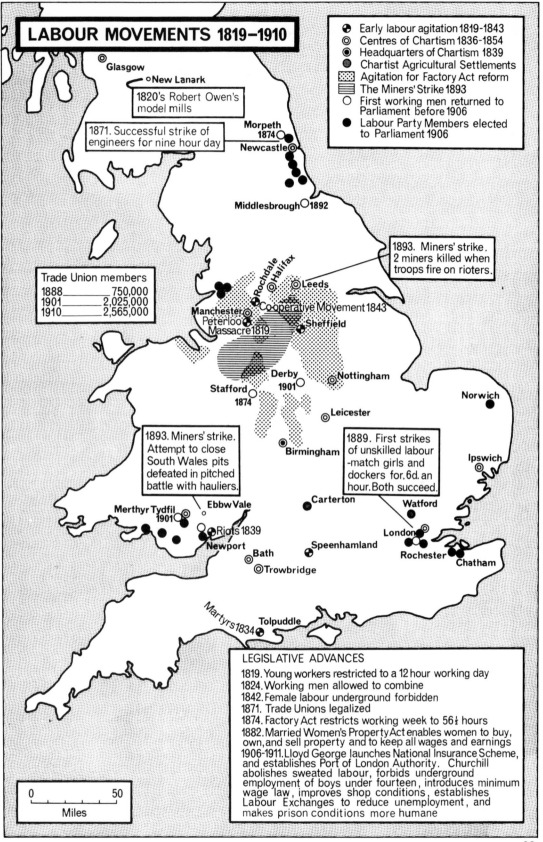

LABOUR MOVEMENTS 1819–1910

Legend:
- ◓ Early labour agitation 1819-1843
- ◎ Centres of Chartism 1836-1854
- ◉ Headquarters of Chartism 1839
- ◒ Chartist Agricultural Settlements
- ▦ Agitation for Factory Act reform
- ▤ The Miners' Strike 1893
- ○ First working men returned to Parliament before 1906
- ● Labour Party Members elected to Parliament 1906

◎ Glasgow

○ New Lanark

1820's Robert Owen's model mills

1871. Successful strike of engineers for nine hour day

Morpeth 1874 ○

Newcastle ◎

Middlesbrough ○ 1892

1893. Miners' strike. 2 miners killed when troops fire on rioters.

Rochdale

Halifax

◎ Leeds

Trade Union members
1888_____750,000
1901_____2,025,000
1910_____2,565,000

Co-operative Movement 1843

Manchester ◎
Peterloo Massacre 1819

✦ Sheffield

Derby 1901 ○

Stafford 1874 ○

▣ Nottingham

Norwich ●

◎ Leicester

1893. Miners' strike. Attempt to close South Wales pits defeated in pitched battle with hauliers.

◉ Birmingham

1889. First strikes of unskilled labour -match girls and dockers for. 6d. an hour. Both succeed.

Ipswich ◎

Merthyr Tydfil 1901

Ebbw Vale ○

Carterton ●

Watford ●

London ●

○ Riots 1839
Newport

Bath ◎

Speenhamland ●

Rochester ●

Chatham ●

○ Trowbridge

Martyrs 1834 ✦ Tolpuddle

LEGISLATIVE ADVANCES

1819. Young workers restricted to a 12 hour working day
1824. Working men allowed to combine
1842. Female labour underground forbidden
1871. Trade Unions legalized
1874. Factory Act restricts working week to 56½ hours
1882. Married Women's Property Act enables women to buy, own, and sell property and to keep all wages and earnings
1906-1911. Lloyd George launches National Insurance Scheme, and establishes Port of London Authority. Churchill abolishes sweated labour, forbids underground employment of boys under fourteen, introduces minimum wage law, improves shop conditions, establishes Labour Exchanges to reduce unemployment, and makes prison conditions more humane

0 _____ 50
Miles

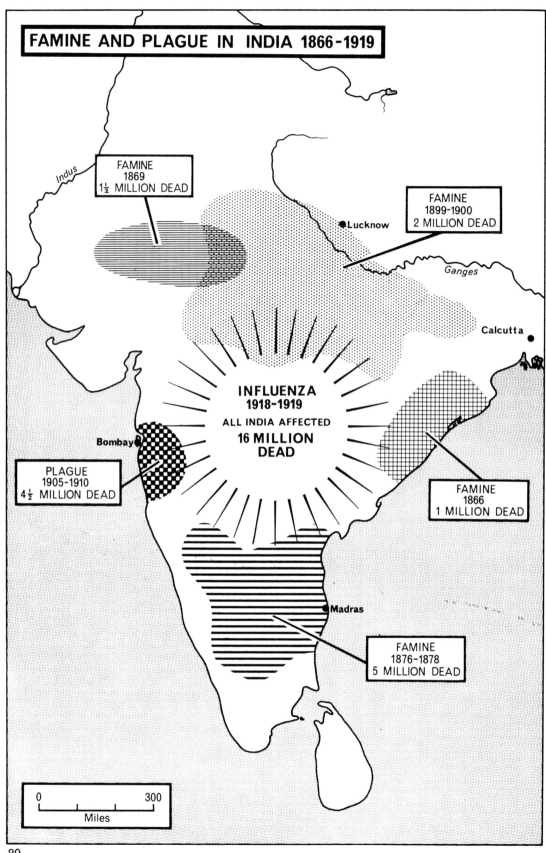

FAMINE AND PLAGUE IN INDIA 1866-1919

FAMINE
1869
1½ MILLION DEAD

FAMINE
1899-1900
2 MILLION DEAD

Lucknow

Indus

Ganges

Calcutta

INFLUENZA
1918-1919
ALL INDIA AFFECTED
16 MILLION
DEAD

Bombay

PLAGUE
1905-1910
4½ MILLION DEAD

FAMINE
1866
1 MILLION DEAD

Madras

FAMINE
1876-1878
5 MILLION DEAD

```
0            300
|__|__|__|__|__|
     Miles
```

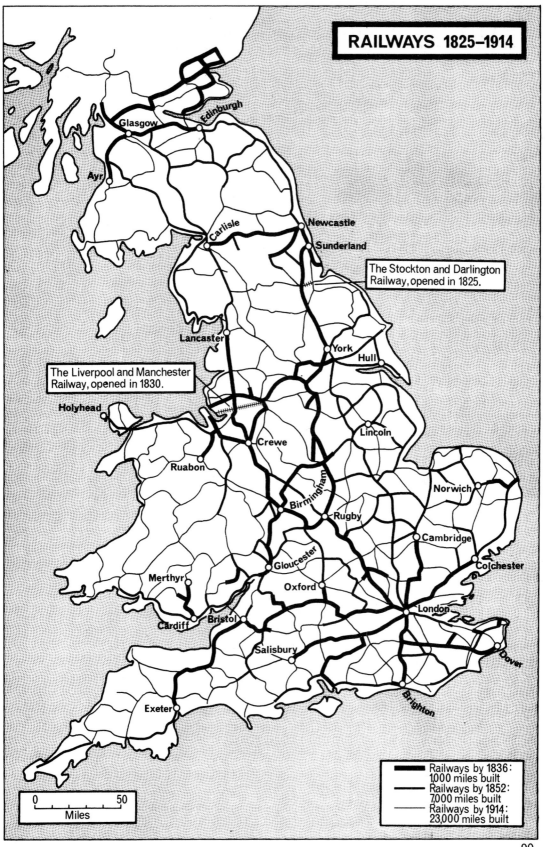

RAILWAYS 1825–1914

The Stockton and Darlington Railway, opened in 1825.

The Liverpool and Manchester Railway, opened in 1830.

Glasgow

Edinburgh

Ayr

Carlisle

Newcastle

Sunderland

Lancaster

York

Hull

Holyhead

Crewe

Lincoln

Ruabon

Norwich

Birmingham

Rugby

Cambridge

Gloucester

Colchester

Merthyr

Oxford

Cardiff

Bristol

London

Salisbury

Dover

Brighton

Exeter

	Railways by 1836: 1000 miles built
	Railways by 1852: 7000 miles built
	Railways by 1914: 23,000 miles built

0 ___ 50
Miles

90

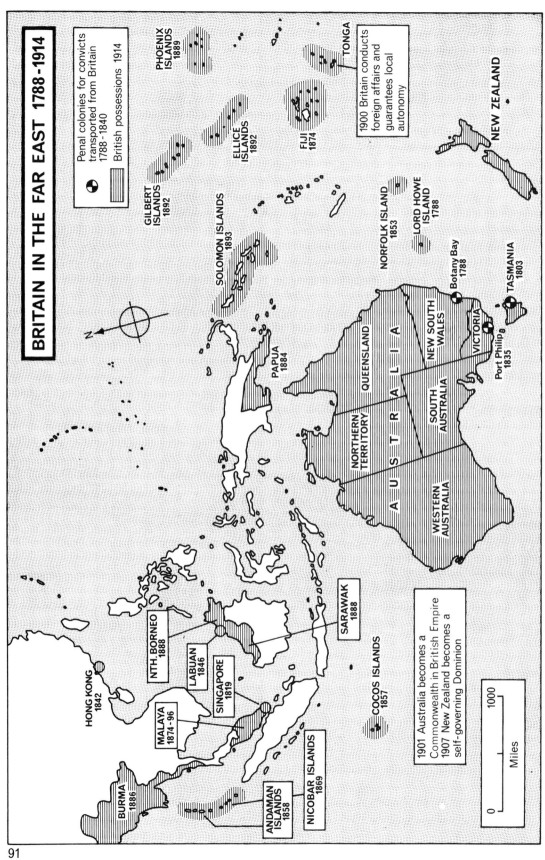

BRITAIN IN THE FAR EAST 1788-1914

Penal colonies for convicts transported from Britain 1788-1840

British possessions 1914

PHOENIX ISLANDS 1889

TONGA

1900 Britain conducts foreign affairs and guarantees local autonomy

GILBERT ISLANDS 1892

ELLICE ISLANDS 1892

FIJI 1874

NEW ZEALAND

SOLOMON ISLANDS 1893

NORFOLK ISLAND 1853

LORD HOWE ISLAND 1788

Botany Bay 1788

QUEENSLAND

NORTHERN TERRITORY

A U S T R A L I A

NEW SOUTH WALES

VICTORIA

Port Philip 1835

TASMANIA 1803

PAPUA 1884

SOUTH AUSTRALIA

WESTERN AUSTRALIA

HONG KONG 1842

NTH. BORNEO 1888

LABUAN 1846

SINGAPORE 1819

SARAWAK 1888

MALAYA 1874-96

COCOS ISLANDS 1857

BURMA 1886

ANDAMAN ISLANDS 1858

NICOBAR ISLANDS 1869

1901 Australia becomes a Commonwealth in British Empire
1907 New Zealand becomes a self-governing Dominion

0   Miles   1000

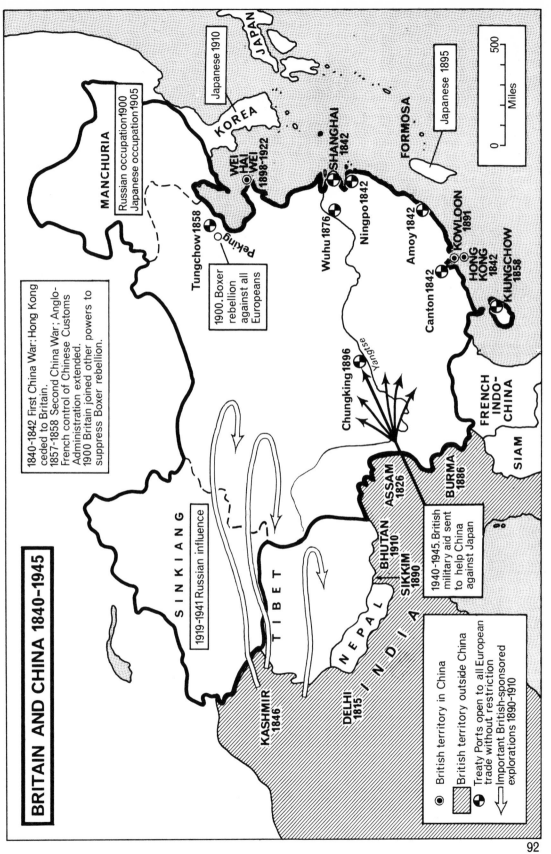

BRITAIN AND CHINA 1840-1945

Japanese 1910

Japanese 1895

MANCHURIA
Russian occupation 1900
Japanese occupation 1905

KOREA

JAPAN

WEI HAI WEI
1898-1922

SHANGHAI
1842

FORMOSA

Tungchow 1858

Wuhu 1876

Ningpo 1842

Amoy 1842

Peking

1900. Boxer
rebellion
against all
Europeans

KOWLOON
1891

Canton 1842

HONG KONG
1842

KIUNGCHOW
1858

1840-1842 First China War: Hong Kong
ceded to Britain.
1857-1858 Second China War.; Anglo-
French control of Chinese Customs
Administration extended.
1900 Britain joined other powers to
suppress Boxer rebellion.

SINKIANG

1919-1941 Russian influence

Yangtse

Chungking 1896

FRENCH
INDO-
CHINA

SIAM

TIBET

BURMA
1886

ASSAM
1826

BHUTAN
1910

1940-1945. British
military aid sent
to help China
against Japan

NEPAL

SIKKIM
1890

INDIA

KASHMIR
1846

DELHI
1815

500

Miles

0

● British territory in China

▧ British territory outside China

◉ Treaty Ports open to all European
trade without restriction

⇨ Important British-sponsored
explorations 1890-1910

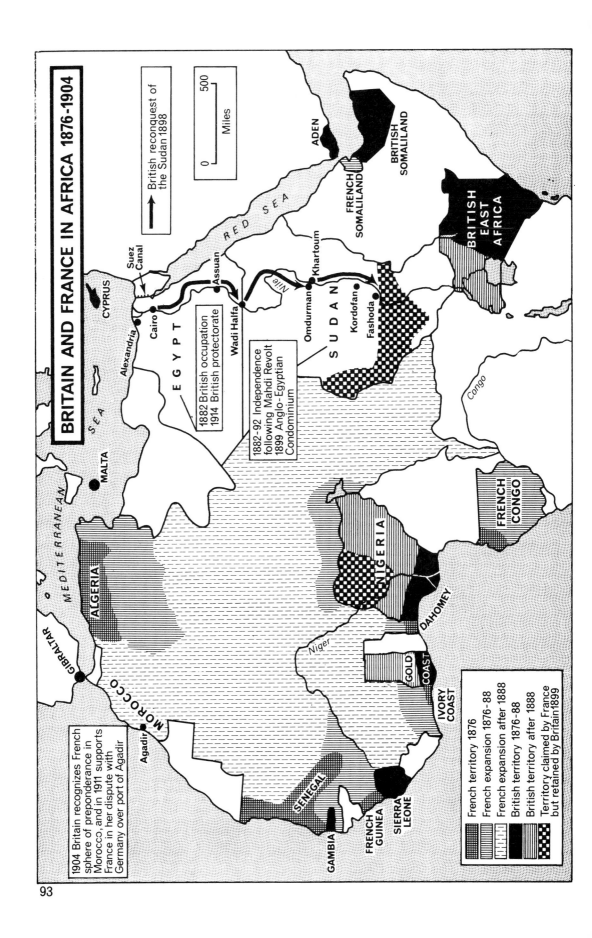

BRITAIN AND FRANCE IN AFRICA 1876-1904

British reconquest of the Sudan 1898

500 Miles

1904 Britain recognizes French sphere of preponderance in Morocco, and in 1911 supports France in her dispute with Germany over port of Agadir

1882 British occupation
1914 British protectorate

1882-92 Independence following Mahdi Revolt
1899 Anglo-Egyptian Condominium

RED SEA

ADEN

BRITISH SOMALILAND

FRENCH SOMALILAND

BRITISH EAST AFRICA

Suez Canal

Assuan

Khartoum

Omdurman

Kordofan

Fashoda

SUDAN

Cairo

Alexandria

CYPRUS

Wadi Halfa

E G Y P T

Nile

Congo

MALTA

MEDITERRANEAN SEA

ALGERIA

GIBRALTAR

MOROCCO

Agadir

Niger

NIGERIA

FRENCH CONGO

DAHOMEY

GOLD COAST

IVORY COAST

SENEGAL

FRENCH GUINEA

GAMBIA

SIERRA LEONE

French territory 1876
French expansion 1876-88
French expansion after 1888
British territory 1876-88
British territory after 1888
Territory claimed by France but retained by Britain 1899

93

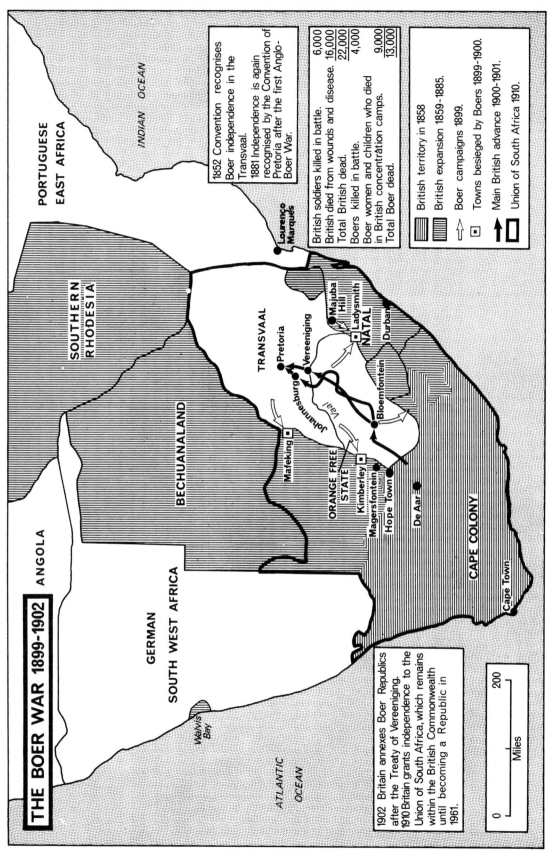

THE BOER WAR 1899-1902

PORTUGUESE EAST AFRICA

INDIAN OCEAN

ANGOLA

GERMAN SOUTH WEST AFRICA

Walvis Bay

ATLANTIC OCEAN

SOUTHERN RHODESIA

BECHUANALAND

Lourenço Marques

Mafeking

TRANSVAAL

Pretoria
Johannesburg
Vereeniging
Majuba Hill
Ladysmith
NATAL
Durban

Vaal

ORANGE FREE STATE

Bloemfontein
Kimberley
Magersfontein
Hope Town
De Aar

CAPE COLONY

Cape Town

1852 Convention recognises Boer independence in the Transvaal.
1881 Independence is again recognised by the Convention of Pretoria after the first Anglo-Boer War.

British soldiers killed in battle.	6,000
British died from wounds and disease.	16,000
Total British dead.	22,000
Boers killed in battle.	4,000
Boer women and children who died in British concentration camps.	9,000
Total Boer dead.	13,000

British territory in 1858

British expansion 1859-1885.

→ Boer campaigns 1899.

□ Towns besieged by Boers 1899-1900.

➡ Main British advance 1900-1901.

□ Union of South Africa 1910.

1902 Britain annexes Boer Republics after the Treaty of Vereeniging.
1910 Britain grants independence to the Union of South Africa, which remains within the British Commonwealth until becoming a Republic in 1961.

Miles
0   200

94

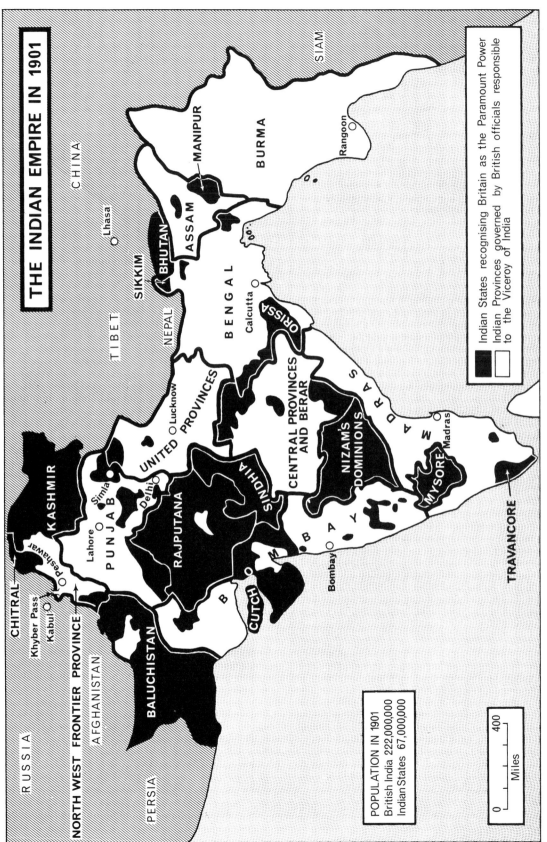

THE INDIAN EMPIRE IN 1901

RUSSIA

PERSIA

AFGHANISTAN

Kabul
Khyber Pass
CHITRAL
NORTH WEST FRONTIER PROVINCE
Peshawar

BALUCHISTAN

KASHMIR

CHINA

TIBET

Lhasa

SIKKIM

NEPAL

BHUTAN

ASSAM

MANIPUR

SIAM

BURMA

Rangoon

PUNJAB
Lahore
Simla
Delhi

UNITED PROVINCES
Lucknow

RAJPUTANA

SINDHIA

BENGAL
Calcutta

ORISSA

CUTCH

B

CENTRAL PROVINCES AND BERAR

NIZAM'S DOMINIONS

MADRAS

Bombay

M B A Y

Madras

MYSORE

TRAVANCORE

■ Indian States recognising Britain as the Paramount Power
□ Indian Provinces governed by British officials responsible to the Viceroy of India

POPULATION IN 1901
British India 222,000,000
Indian States 67,000,000

0   400
Miles

95

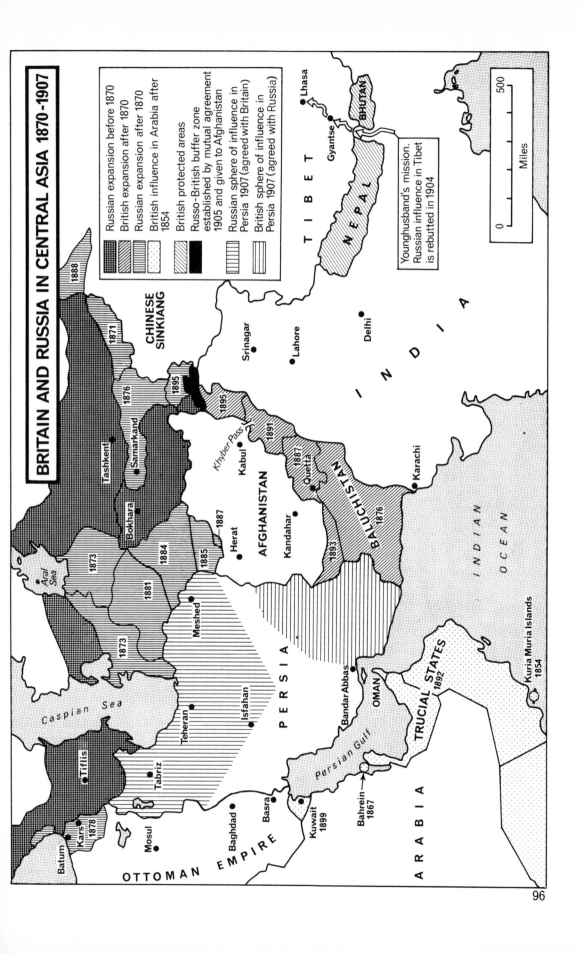

BRITAIN AND RUSSIA IN CENTRAL ASIA 1870-1907

Legend:
- Russian expansion before 1870
- British expansion after 1870
- Russian expansion after 1870
- British influence in Arabia after 1854
- British protected areas
- Russo-British buffer zone established by mutual agreement 1905 and given to Afghanistan
- Russian sphere of influence in Persia 1907 (agreed with Britain)
- British sphere of influence in Persia 1907 (agreed with Russia)

Younghusband's mission. Russian influence in Tibet is rebutted in 1904

500

0 Miles

CHINESE SINKIANG

TIBET

NEPAL

BHUTAN

1888

1871

1876

1895

1895

1891

1887

1887

1893

1876

Khyber Pass

Kabul

Quetta

AFGHANISTAN

BALUCHISTAN

Herat

Kandahar

Srinagar

Lahore

Delhi

Karachi

INDIA

Lhasa

Gyantse

Tashkent

Samarkand

Bokhara

1873

1884

1881

1885

1873

Aral Sea

Meshed

PERSIA

INDIAN OCEAN

Caspian Sea

Isfahan

Teheran

Tabriz

Tiflis

Kars 1878

Batum

Mosul

Baghdad

Basra

Kuwait 1899

Bahrein 1867

Bandar Abbas

Persian Gulf

OMAN

TRUCIAL STATES 1892

Kuria Muria Islands 1854

ARABIA

OTTOMAN EMPIRE

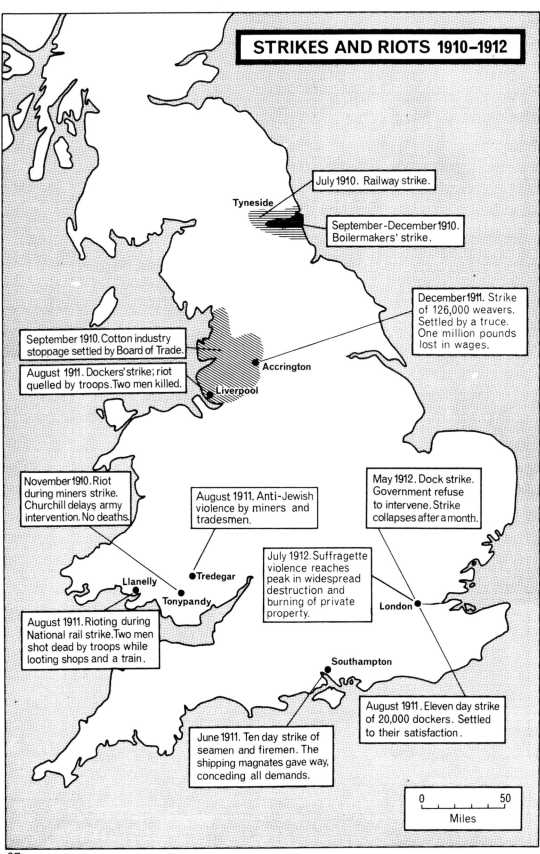

STRIKES AND RIOTS 1910–1912

July 1910. Railway strike.

Tyneside

September–December 1910.
Boilermakers' strike.

December 1911. Strike
of 126,000 weavers.
Settled by a truce.
One million pounds
lost in wages.

September 1910. Cotton industry
stoppage settled by Board of Trade.

August 1911. Dockers' strike; riot
quelled by troops. Two men killed.

●**Accrington**

Liverpool

May 1912. Dock strike.
Government refuse
to intervene. Strike
collapses after a month.

November 1910. Riot
during miners strike.
Churchill delays army
intervention. No deaths.

August 1911. Anti-Jewish
violence by miners and
tradesmen.

July 1912. Suffragette
violence reaches
peak in widespread
destruction and
burning of private
property.

Llanelly

●**Tredegar**

Tonypandy

London ●

August 1911. Rioting during
National rail strike. Two men
shot dead by troops while
looting shops and a train.

Southampton
●

June 1911. Ten day strike of
seamen and firemen. The
shipping magnates gave way,
conceding all demands.

August 1911. Eleven day strike
of 20,000 dockers. Settled
to their satisfaction.

0   50
Miles

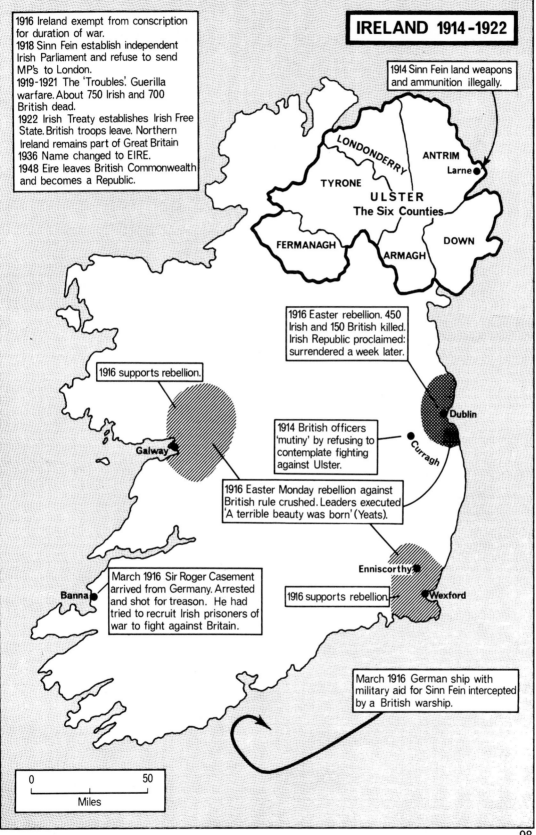

IRELAND 1914-1922

1916 Ireland exempt from conscription for duration of war.
1918 Sinn Fein establish independent Irish Parliament and refuse to send MP's to London.
1919-1921 The 'Troubles'. Guerilla warfare. About 750 Irish and 700 British dead.
1922 Irish Treaty establishes Irish Free State. British troops leave. Northern Ireland remains part of Great Britain
1936 Name changed to EIRE.
1948 Eire leaves British Commonwealth and becomes a Republic.

1914 Sinn Fein land weapons and ammunition illegally.

LONDONDERRY

ANTRIM
Larne

TYRONE

ULSTER
The Six Counties

FERMANAGH

ARMAGH

DOWN

1916 Easter rebellion. 450 Irish and 150 British killed. Irish Republic proclaimed: surrendered a week later.

1916 supports rebellion.

Galway

Dublin

1914 British officers 'mutiny' by refusing to contemplate fighting against Ulster.

Curragh

1916 Easter Monday rebellion against British rule crushed. Leaders executed 'A terrible beauty was born' (Yeats).

March 1916 Sir Roger Casement arrived from Germany. Arrested and shot for treason. He had tried to recruit Irish prisoners of war to fight against Britain.

Banna

Enniscorthy

1916 supports rebellion.

Wexford

March 1916 German ship with military aid for Sinn Fein intercepted by a British warship.

0   50
Miles

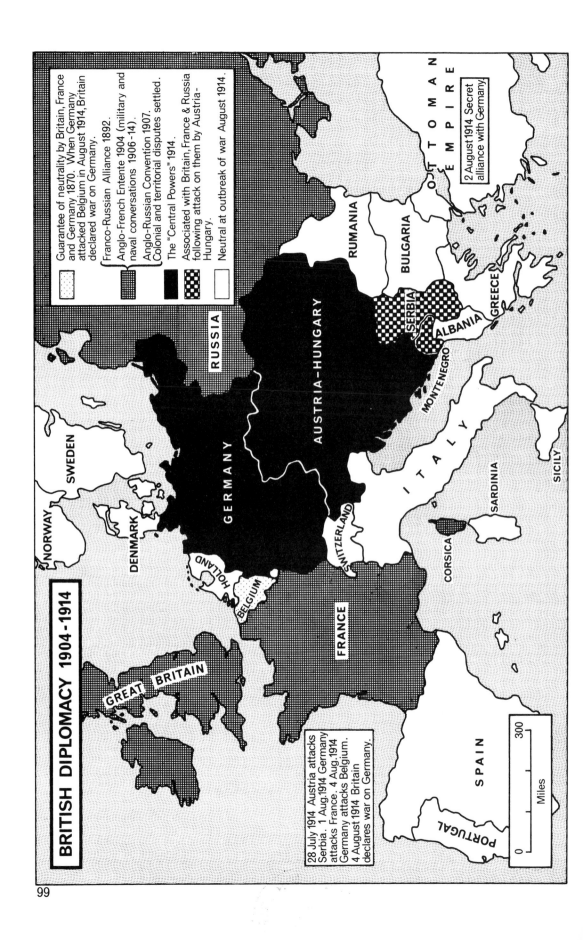

BRITISH DIPLOMACY 1904-1914

Legend:

Guarantee of neutrality by Britain, France and Germany 1870. When Germany attacked Belgium in August 1914, Britain declared war on Germany.

Franco-Russian Alliance 1892.

Anglo-French Entente 1904 (military and naval conversations 1906-14).

Anglo-Russian Convention 1907. Colonial and territorial disputes settled.

The "Central Powers" 1914.

Associated with Britain, France & Russia following attack on them by Austria-Hungary.

Neutral at outbreak of war August 1914.

2 August 1914 Secret alliance with Germany.

28 July 1914 Austria attacks Serbia. 1 Aug.1914 Germany attacks France. 4 Aug.1914 Germany attacks Belgium. 4 August 1914 Britain declares war on Germany.

NORWAY

SWEDEN

DENMARK

HOLLAND

BELGIUM

GREAT BRITAIN

FRANCE

SWITZERLAND

GERMANY

RUSSIA

AUSTRIA-HUNGARY

ITALY

CORSICA

SARDINIA

SICILY

SPAIN

PORTUGAL

RUMANIA

BULGARIA

SERBIA

MONTENEGRO

ALBANIA

GREECE

OTTOMAN EMPIRE

0   300

Miles

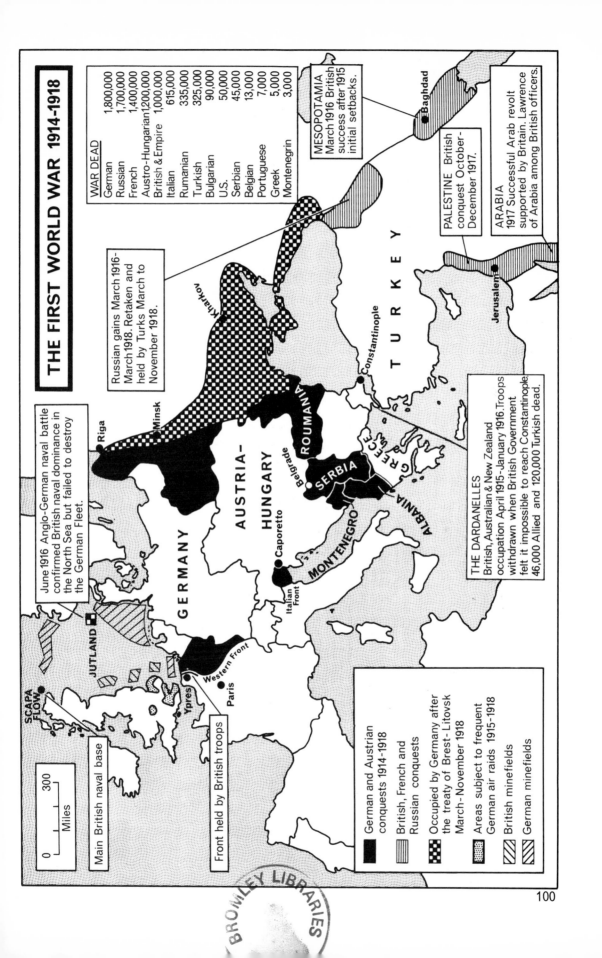

THE FIRST WORLD WAR 1914-1918

WAR DEAD
German	1,800,000
Russian	1,700,000
French	1,400,000
Austro-Hungarian	1,200,000
British & Empire	1,000,000
Italian	615,000
Rumanian	335,000
Turkish	325,000
Bulgarian	90,000
U.S.	50,000
Serbian	45,000
Belgian	13,000
Portuguese	7,000
Greek	5,000
Montenegrin	3,000

MESOPOTAMIA
March 1916 British success after 1915 initial setbacks.

PALESTINE British conquest October-December 1917.

ARABIA
1917 Successful Arab revolt supported by Britain. Lawrence of Arabia among British officers.

Russian gains March 1916-March 1918. Retaken and held by Turks March to November 1918.

June 1916 Anglo-German naval battle confirmed British naval dominance in the North Sea but failed to destroy the German Fleet.

THE DARDANELLES
British, Australian & New Zealand occupation April 1915-January 1916. Troops withdrawn when British Government felt it impossible to reach Constantinople. 46,000 Allied and 120,000 Turkish dead.

Kharkov

Riga

Minsk

Constantinople

Jerusalem

Baghdad

GERMANY

AUSTRIA–HUNGARY

ROUMANIA

SERBIA

MONTENEGRO

ALBANIA

GREECE

TURKEY

Belgrade

Caporetto

Italian Front

Western Front

Ypres

Paris

JUTLAND

SCAPA FLOW

0	300

Miles

Main British naval base

Front held by British troops

German and Austrian conquests 1914-1918

British, French and Russian conquests

Occupied by Germany after the treaty of Brest-Litovsk March-November 1918

Areas subject to frequent German air raids 1915-1918

British minefields

German minefields

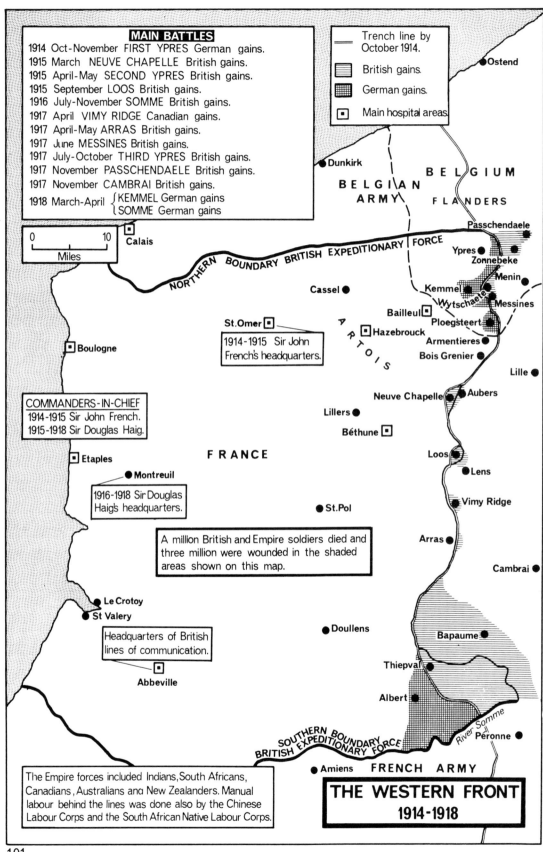

MAIN BATTLES

1914 Oct-November FIRST YPRES German gains.
1915 March NEUVE CHAPELLE British gains.
1915 April-May SECOND YPRES British gains.
1915 September LOOS British gains.
1916 July-November SOMME British gains.
1917 April VIMY RIDGE Canadian gains.
1917 April-May ARRAS British gains.
1917 June MESSINES British gains.
1917 July-October THIRD YPRES British gains.
1917 November PASSCHENDAELE British gains.
1917 November CAMBRAI British gains.
1918 March-April { KEMMEL German gains
                  { SOMME German gains

Trench line by October 1914.
British gains.
German gains.
Main hospital areas.

0   10
    Miles

St.Omer
1914-1915 Sir John French's headquarters.

COMMANDERS-IN-CHIEF
1914-1915 Sir John French.
1915-1918 Sir Douglas Haig.

1916-1918 Sir Douglas Haig's headquarters.

A million British and Empire soldiers died and three million were wounded in the shaded areas shown on this map.

Headquarters of British lines of communication.

The Empire forces included Indians, South Africans, Canadians, Australians and New Zealanders. Manual labour behind the lines was done also by the Chinese Labour Corps and the South African Native Labour Corps.

Ostend
Dunkirk
BELGIUM
BELGIAN ARMY
FLANDERS
Passchendaele
Ypres
Zonnebeke
Menin
Kemmel
Wytschaete
Messines
Bailleul
Ploegsteert
Armentieres
Bois Grenier
Lille
Neuve Chapelle
Aubers
Lillers
Béthune
Loos
Lens
Vimy Ridge
Arras
Cambrai
Calais
NORTHERN BOUNDARY BRITISH EXPEDITIONARY FORCE
Cassel
ARTOIS
Hazebrouck
Boulogne
FRANCE
Etaples
Montreuil
St.Pol
Le Crotoy
St Valery
Doullens
Bapaume
Thiepval
Albert
River Somme
Péronne
Abbeville
SOUTHERN BOUNDARY BRITISH EXPEDITIONARY FORCE
Amiens
FRENCH ARMY

THE WESTERN FRONT 1914-1918

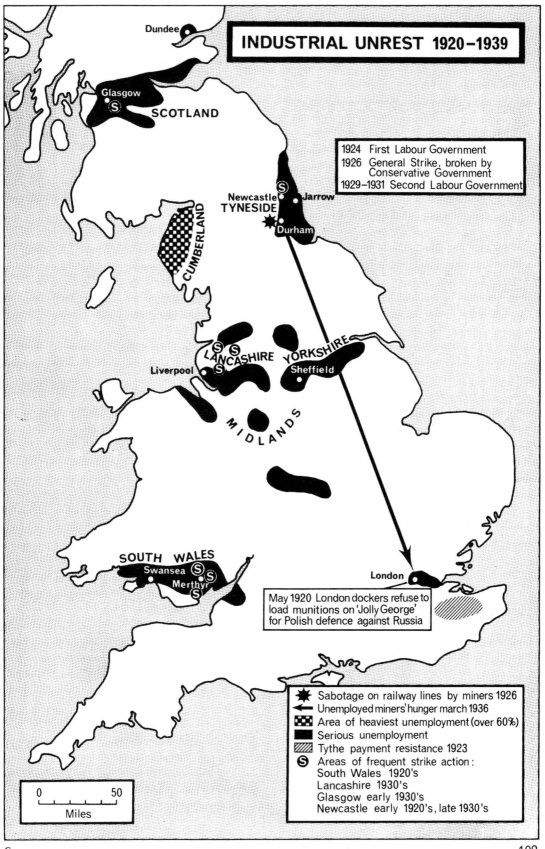

INDUSTRIAL UNREST 1920–1939

Dundee

Glasgow ⓢ

SCOTLAND

1924   First Labour Government
1926   General Strike, broken by
          Conservative Government
1929–1931 Second Labour Government

Newcastle ⓢ Jarrow
TYNESIDE
Durham

CUMBERLAND

ⓢ LANCASHIRE YORKSHIRE
Liverpool ⓢ   Sheffield

M I D L A N D S

SOUTH WALES
Swansea ⓢⓢ
Merthyr
ⓢ

London

May 1920 London dockers refuse to
load munitions on 'Jolly George'
for Polish defence against Russia

✴ Sabotage on railway lines by miners 1926
← Unemployed miners' hunger march 1936
▨ Area of heaviest unemployment (over 60%)
■ Serious unemployment
▨ Tythe payment resistance 1923
ⓢ Areas of frequent strike action:
South Wales 1920's
Lancashire 1930's
Glasgow early 1930's
Newcastle early 1920's, late 1930's

0   50
Miles

G

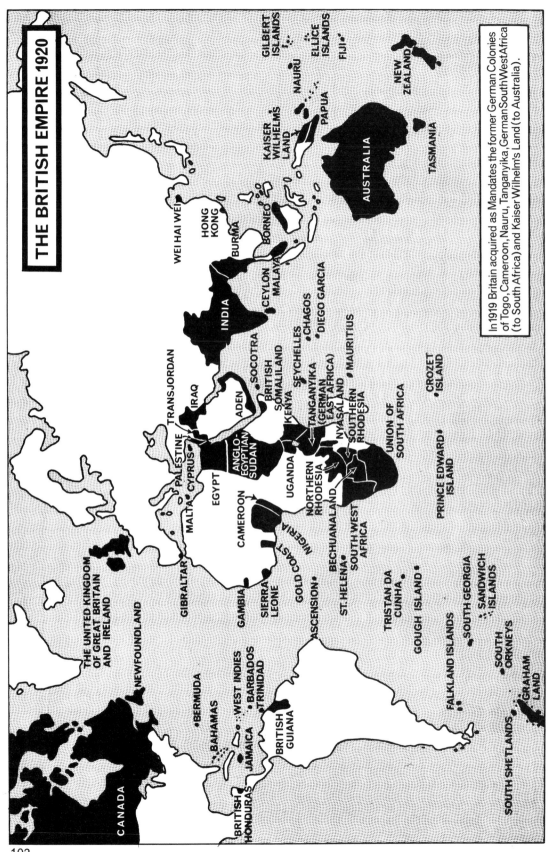

THE BRITISH EMPIRE 1920

In 1919 Britain acquired as Mandates the former German Colonies of Togo, Cameroon, Nauru, Tanganyika, German South West Africa (to South Africa) and Kaiser Wilhelm's Land (to Australia).

GILBERT ISLANDS

ELLICE ISLANDS

FIJI

KAISER WILHELMS LAND

NAURU

PAPUA

NEW ZEALAND

AUSTRALIA

TASMANIA

WEI HAI WEI

HONG KONG

BURMA

BORNEO

CEYLON

MALAYA

INDIA

SOCOTRA

SEYCHELLES

CHAGOS

DIEGO GARCIA

TRANSJORDAN

IRAQ

ADEN

BRITISH SOMALILAND

KENYA

TANGANYIKA (GERMAN EAST AFRICA)

MAURITIUS

PALESTINE

MALTA

CYPRUS

NYASALAND

SOUTHERN RHODESIA

CROZET ISLAND

EGYPT

ANGLO-EGYPTIAN SUDAN

UGANDA

UNION OF SOUTH AFRICA

NORTHERN RHODESIA

CAMEROON

NIGERIA

PRINCE EDWARD ISLAND

GIBRALTAR

GAMBIA

SIERRA LEONE

GOLD COAST

BECHUANALAND

SOUTH WEST AFRICA

THE UNITED KINGDOM OF GREAT BRITAIN AND IRELAND

ASCENSION

ST. HELENA

TRISTAN DA CUNHA

GOUGH ISLAND

NEWFOUNDLAND

BERMUDA

BAHAMAS

WEST INDIES

BARBADOS

TRINIDAD

JAMAICA

SOUTH GEORGIA

SANDWICH ISLANDS

BRITISH HONDURAS

BRITISH GUIANA

FALKLAND ISLANDS

SOUTH ORKNEYS

CANADA

SOUTH SHETLANDS

GRAHAM LAND

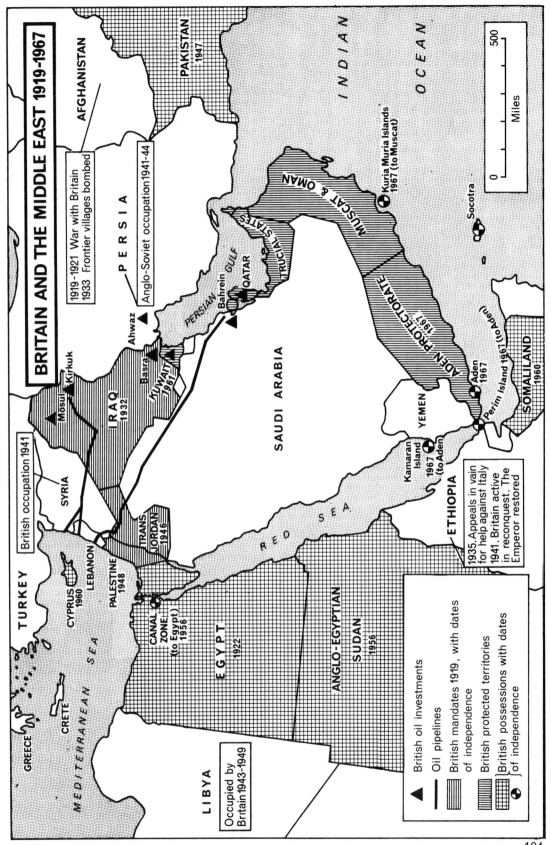

BRITAIN AND THE MIDDLE EAST 1919-1967

AFGHANISTAN

1919-1921 War with Britain
1933 Frontier villages bombed

Anglo-Soviet occupation 1941-44

P E R S I A

PAKISTAN
1947

PERSIAN GULF

Ahwaz

Bahrein
QATAR

Kirkuk

Mosul

TRUCIAL STATES

MUSCAT & OMAN

I N D I A N   O C E A N

500

Miles

0

Kuria Muria Islands
1967 (to Muscat)

Socotra

British occupation 1941

SYRIA

Basra

KUWAIT
1961

IRAQ
1932

SAUDI ARABIA

ADEN PROTECTORATE
1967

Perim Island 1967 (to Aden)

SOMALILAND
1960

TURKEY

CYPRUS
1960

LEBANON

PALESTINE
1948

TRANS-
JORDAN
1946

RED SEA

YEMEN

Aden
1967

Kamaran
Island
1967
(to Aden)

ETHIOPIA

1935. Appeals in vain
for help against Italy
1941. Britain active
in reconquest. The
Emperor restored

GREECE

CRETE

M E D I T E R R A N E A N   S E A

CANAL
ZONE
(to Egypt) 1956

E G Y P T
1922

ANGLO-EGYPTIAN
SUDAN
1956

L I B Y A

Occupied by
Britain 1943-1949

British oil investments

Oil pipelines

British mandates 1919, with dates
of independence

British protected territories

British possessions with dates
of independence

104

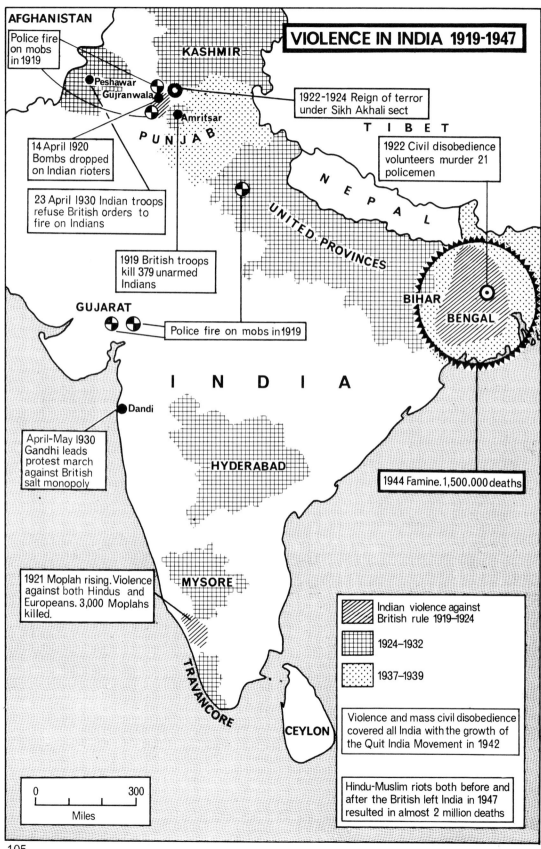

VIOLENCE IN INDIA 1919-1947

AFGHANISTAN

Police fire on mobs in 1919

KASHMIR

Peshawar
Gujranwala

Amritsar

PUNJAB

14 April 1920 Bombs dropped on Indian rioters

23 April 1930 Indian troops refuse British orders to fire on Indians

1922-1924 Reign of terror under Sikh Akhali sect

T I B E T

1922 Civil disobedience volunteers murder 21 policemen

N E P A L

UNITED PROVINCES

1919 British troops kill 379 unarmed Indians

GUJARAT

Police fire on mobs in 1919

BIHAR

BENGAL

I N D I A

Dandi

April-May 1930 Gandhi leads protest march against British salt monopoly

1944 Famine. 1,500,000 deaths

HYDERABAD

1921 Moplah rising. Violence against both Hindus and Europeans. 3,000 Moplahs killed.

MYSORE

TRAVANCORE

CEYLON

Indian violence against British rule 1919–1924

1924–1932

1937–1939

Violence and mass civil disobedience covered all India with the growth of the Quit India Movement in 1942

Hindu-Muslim riots both before and after the British left India in 1947 resulted in almost 2 million deaths

0   300
Miles

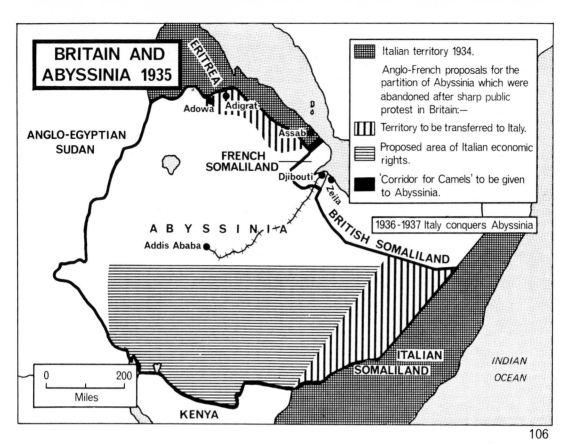

BRITAIN AND ABYSSINIA 1935

ERITREA

ANGLO-EGYPTIAN SUDAN

Adowa Adigrat

Assab

FRENCH SOMALILAND

Djibouti

Zeila

BRITISH SOMALILAND

A B Y S S I N I A

Addis Ababa

INDIAN OCEAN

ITALIAN SOMALILAND

KENYA

	Italian territory 1934.
	Anglo-French proposals for the partition of Abyssinia which were abandoned after sharp public protest in Britain:—
	Territory to be transferred to Italy.
	Proposed area of Italian economic rights.
	'Corridor for Camels' to be given to Abyssinia.

1936-1937 Italy conquers Abyssinia

0   200
Miles

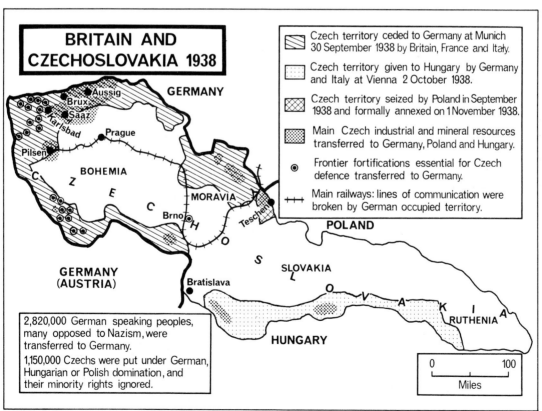

BRITAIN AND CZECHOSLOVAKIA 1938

GERMANY

Aussig
Brux
Karlsbad Saaz
Pilsen
Prague

BOHEMIA

C   Z   E

C

Brno

MORAVIA

Teschen

POLAND

GERMANY (AUSTRIA)

Bratislava

H   O   S

L

SLOVAKIA

O   V   A   K   I   A

RUTHENIA

HUNGARY

	Czech territory ceded to Germany at Munich 30 September 1938 by Britain, France and Italy.
	Czech territory given to Hungary by Germany and Italy at Vienna 2 October 1938.
	Czech territory seized by Poland in September 1938 and formally annexed on 1 November 1938.
	Main Czech industrial and mineral resources transferred to Germany, Poland and Hungary.
⊙	Frontier fortifications essential for Czech defence transferred to Germany.
+++	Main railways: lines of communication were broken by German occupied territory.

2,820,000 German speaking peoples, many opposed to Nazism, were transferred to Germany.

1,150,000 Czechs were put under German, Hungarian or Polish domination, and their minority rights ignored.

0   100
Miles

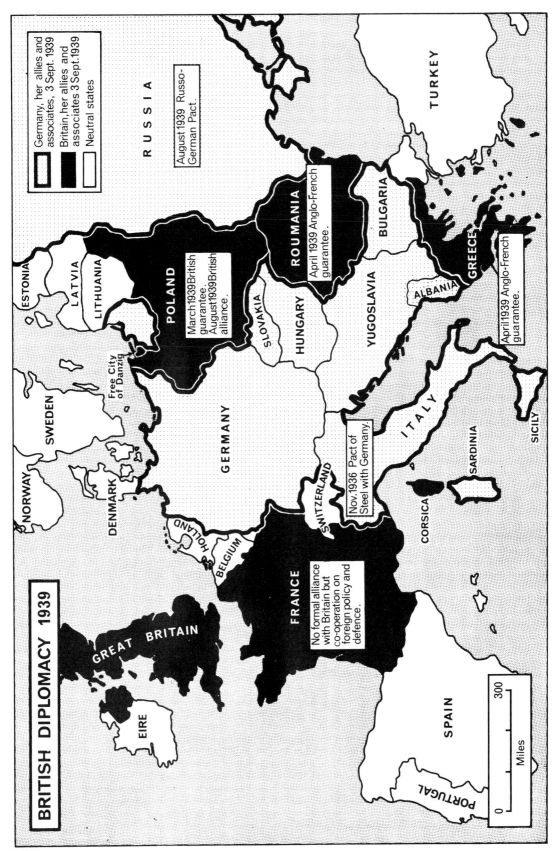

BRITISH DIPLOMACY 1939

Legend:
- Germany, her allies and associates, 3 Sept. 1939
- Britain, her allies and associates 3 Sept.1939
- Neutral states

August 1939 Russo-German Pact.

GREAT BRITAIN

EIRE

NORWAY

SWEDEN

DENMARK

HOLLAND

BELGIUM

ESTONIA

LATVIA

LITHUANIA

Free City of Danzig

POLAND

March1939British guarantee. August1939British alliance.

GERMANY

SLOVAKIA

HUNGARY

ROUMANIA

April 1939 Anglo-French guarantee.

BULGARIA

YUGOSLAVIA

ALBANIA

GREECE

April1939 Anglo-French guarantee.

R U S S I A

TURKEY

SWITZERLAND

Nov.1936 Pact of Steel with Germany.

FRANCE

No formal alliance with Britain but co-operation on foreign policy and defence.

I T A L Y

CORSICA

SARDINIA

SICILY

SPAIN

PORTUGAL

0   300

Miles

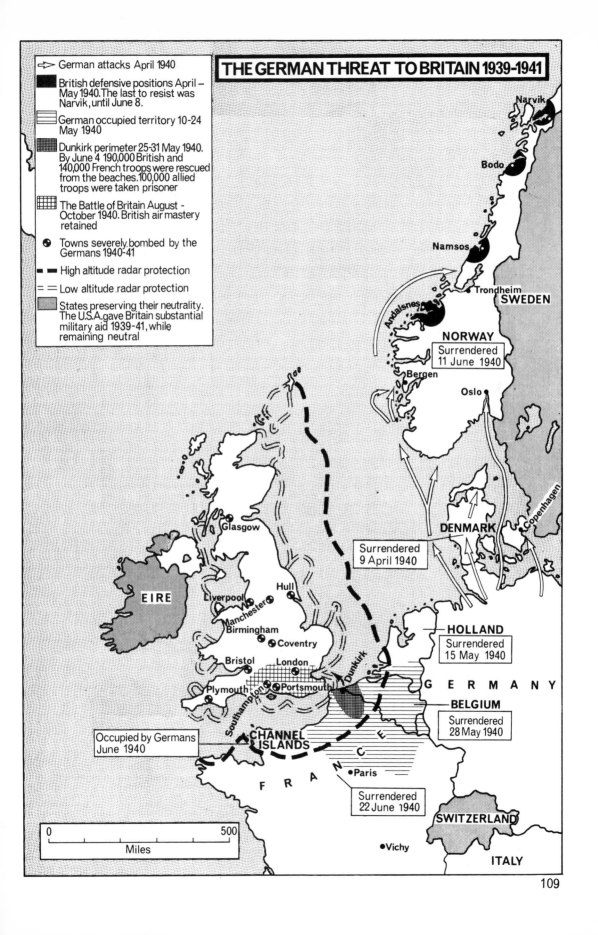

THE GERMAN THREAT TO BRITAIN 1939-1941

Legend:

- ⟹ German attacks April 1940
- British defensive positions April – May 1940. The last to resist was Narvik, until June 8.
- German occupied territory 10-24 May 1940
- Dunkirk perimeter 25-31 May 1940. By June 4 190,000 British and 140,000 French troops were rescued from the beaches. 100,000 allied troops were taken prisoner
- The Battle of Britain August – October 1940. British air mastery retained
- ⊛ Towns severely bombed by the Germans 1940-41
- ▬ ▬ High altitude radar protection
- = = Low altitude radar protection
- States preserving their neutrality. The U.S.A. gave Britain substantial military aid 1939-41, while remaining neutral

Narvik

Bodo

Namsos

Trondheim

SWEDEN

Andalsnes

NORWAY
Surrendered 11 June 1940

Bergen

Oslo

Copenhagen

DENMARK
Surrendered 9 April 1940

Glasgow

EIRE

Liverpool

Hull

Manchester

Birmingham

⊛ Coventry

HOLLAND
Surrendered 15 May 1940

Bristol

London

Dunkirk

G E R M A N Y

Plymouth

Southampton

Portsmouth

BELGIUM
Surrendered 28 May 1940

CHANNEL ISLANDS

Occupied by Germans June 1940

F R A N C E

Paris

Surrendered 22 June 1940

SWITZERLAND

Vichy

ITALY

0   500
Miles

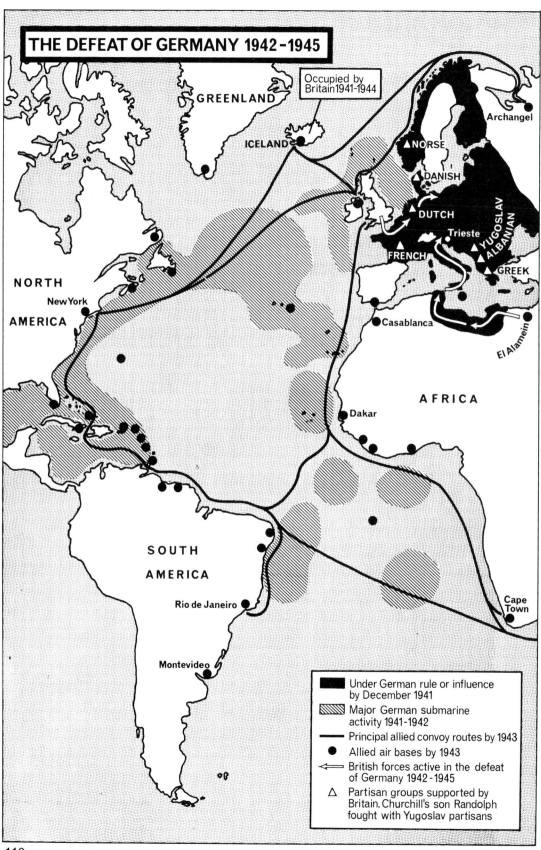

THE DEFEAT OF GERMANY 1942-1945

GREENLAND

Occupied by
Britain 1941-1944

ICELAND

Archangel

▲ NORSE

▲ DANISH

DUTCH

Trieste

▲ YUGOSLAV

▲ ALBANIAN

FRENCH ▲

▲ GREEK

NORTH

New York

AMERICA

Casablanca

AFRICA

El Alamein

Dakar

SOUTH

AMERICA

Rio de Janeiro

Cape
Town

Montevideo

Under German rule or influence
by December 1941

Major German submarine
activity 1941-1942

Principal allied convoy routes by 1943

● Allied air bases by 1943

⇐ British forces active in the defeat
of Germany 1942-1945

△ Partisan groups supported by
Britain. Churchill's son Randolph
fought with Yugoslav partisans

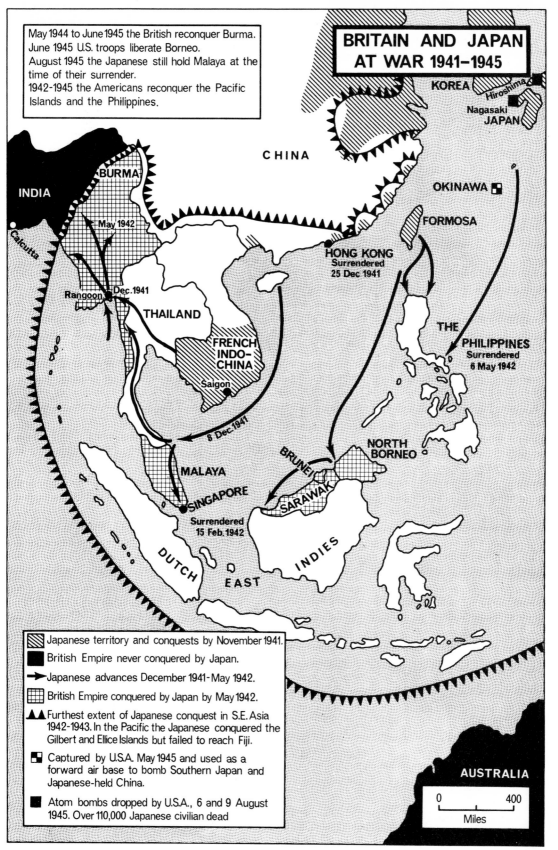

May 1944 to June 1945 the British reconquer Burma.
June 1945 U.S. troops liberate Borneo.
August 1945 the Japanese still hold Malaya at the time of their surrender.
1942-1945 the Americans reconquer the Pacific Islands and the Philippines.

BRITAIN AND JAPAN AT WAR 1941–1945

KOREA

Hiroshima

Nagasaki

JAPAN

CHINA

OKINAWA

FORMOSA

BURMA

INDIA

May 1942

Calcutta

Rangoon   Dec.1941

THAILAND

HONG KONG
Surrendered
25 Dec 1941

THE
PHILIPPINES
Surrendered
6 May 1942

FRENCH
INDO–
CHINA

Saigon

8 Dec.1941

NORTH
BORNEO

BRUNEI

SARAWAK

MALAYA

SINGAPORE
Surrendered
15 Feb.1942

DUTCH   EAST   INDIES

AUSTRALIA

Japanese territory and conquests by November 1941.

British Empire never conquered by Japan.

Japanese advances December 1941-May 1942.

British Empire conquered by Japan by May 1942.

Furthest extent of Japanese conquest in S.E. Asia 1942-1943. In the Pacific the Japanese conquered the Gilbert and Ellice Islands but failed to reach Fiji.

Captured by U.S.A. May 1945 and used as a forward air base to bomb Southern Japan and Japanese-held China.

Atom bombs dropped by U.S.A., 6 and 9 August 1945. Over 110,000 Japanese civilian dead

0   400
Miles

111

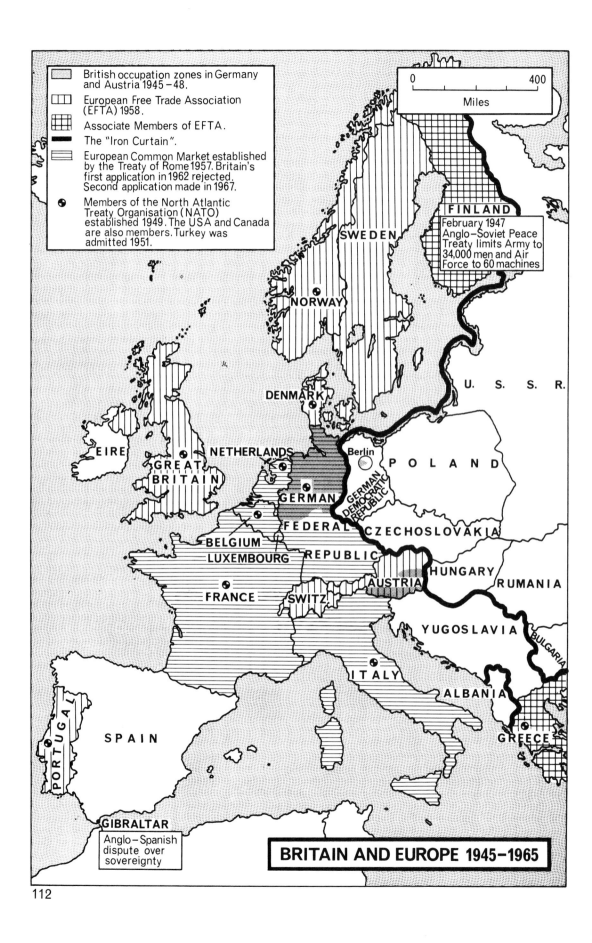

BRITAIN AND EUROPE 1945–1965

Legend:

- British occupation zones in Germany and Austria 1945–48.
- European Free Trade Association (EFTA) 1958.
- Associate Members of EFTA.
- The "Iron Curtain".
- European Common Market established by the Treaty of Rome 1957. Britain's first application in 1962 rejected. Second application made in 1967.
- Members of the North Atlantic Treaty Organisation (NATO) established 1949. The USA and Canada are also members. Turkey was admitted 1951.

Scale: 0 — 400 Miles

FINLAND
February 1947 Anglo–Soviet Peace Treaty limits Army to 34,000 men and Air Force to 60 machines

SWEDEN

NORWAY

DENMARK

U. S. S. R.

Berlin

POLAND

EIRE

GREAT BRITAIN

NETHERLANDS

GERMAN DEMOCRATIC REPUBLIC

GERMAN FEDERAL REPUBLIC

CZECHOSLOVAKIA

BELGIUM

LUXEMBOURG

HUNGARY

AUSTRIA

RUMANIA

FRANCE

SWITZ.

YUGOSLAVIA

BULGARIA

ITALY

ALBANIA

PORTUGAL

SPAIN

GREECE

GIBRALTAR
Anglo–Spanish dispute over sovereignty

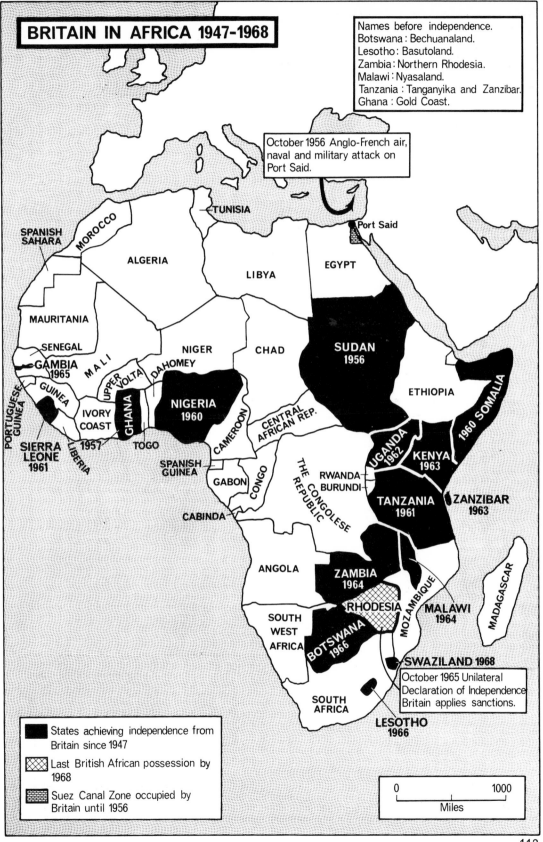

BRITAIN IN AFRICA 1947-1968

Names before independence.
Botswana : Bechuanaland.
Lesotho : Basutoland.
Zambia : Northern Rhodesia.
Malawi : Nyasaland.
Tanzania : Tanganyika and Zanzibar.
Ghana : Gold Coast.

October 1956 Anglo-French air, naval and military attack on Port Said.

SPANISH SAHARA
MOROCCO
TUNISIA
ALGERIA
LIBYA
EGYPT
Port Said
MAURITANIA
SENEGAL
GAMBIA 1965
MALI
NIGER
CHAD
SUDAN 1956
PORTUGUESE GUINEA
GUINEA
UPPER VOLTA
DAHOMEY
GHANA 1957
IVORY COAST
LIBERIA
TOGO
NIGERIA 1960
CAMEROON
CENTRAL AFRICAN REP.
ETHIOPIA
1960 SOMALIA
SIERRA LEONE 1961
SPANISH GUINEA
GABON
CONGO
THE CONGOLESE REPUBLIC
RWANDA
BURUNDI
UGANDA 1962
KENYA 1963
CABINDA
TANZANIA 1961
ZANZIBAR 1963
ANGOLA
ZAMBIA 1964
RHODESIA
MOZAMBIQUE
MALAWI 1964
MADAGASCAR
SOUTH WEST AFRICA
BOTSWANA 1966
SWAZILAND 1968
SOUTH AFRICA
LESOTHO 1966

October 1965 Unilateral Declaration of Independence Britain applies sanctions.

States achieving independence from Britain since 1947

Last British African possession by 1968

Suez Canal Zone occupied by Britain until 1956

0   1000
Miles

UNIVERSITY FOUNDATIONS 1264–1967

Miles
0   50

Aberdeen 1495
Dundee 1967
St. Andrews 1410
1967 Stirling
Glasgow 1451
Strathclyde 1964
Edinburgh 1583
Heriot-Watt 1966

Newcastle 1963
Durham 1832

Lancaster 1964
York 1963
Leeds 1904
Hull 1954
Bradford 1966
Liverpool 1903
Manchester 1851
Sheffield 1905
Salford 1967

Bangor

Keele 1962
Nottingham 1938
1966 Loughborough
Leicester 1957
East Anglia 1964

University of
Wales 1893

Aberystwyth

Aston 1966
Birmingham 1900
Warwick 1965
Cambridge 1284

Swansea
Cardiff

Essex 1965

Oxford 1264
Brunel 1966
Reading 1926
Surrey 1966
London 1836
The City University 1966
Kent 1965

Bristol 1909
Bath 1966
Southampton 1952
Sussex 1961

Exeter 1955

● Founded 1264–1583
◉ Nineteenth century foundations
⊕ Founded 1900–1938
◎ Founded 1952–1967

114

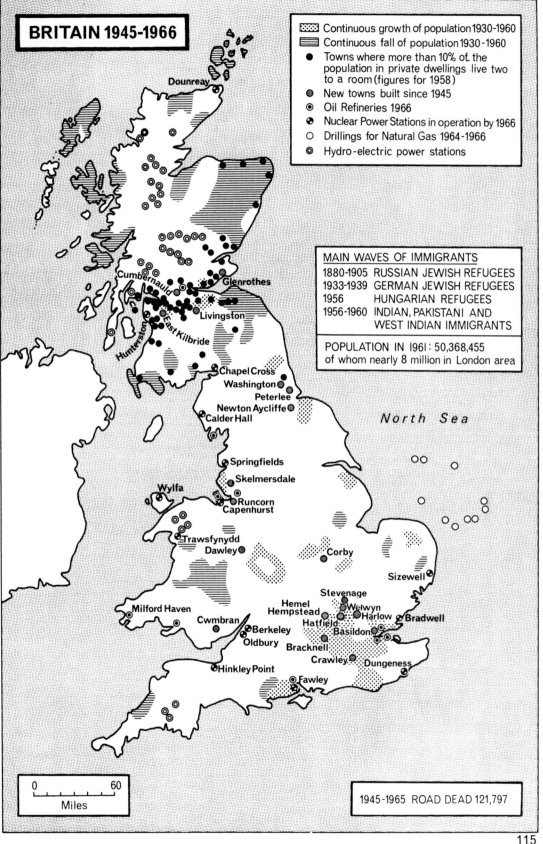

BRITAIN 1945-1966

Continuous growth of population 1930-1960
Continuous fall of population 1930-1960
● Towns where more than 10% of the population in private dwellings live two to a room (figures for 1958)
⊖ New towns built since 1945
⊙ Oil Refineries 1966
⊗ Nuclear Power Stations in operation by 1966
○ Drillings for Natural Gas 1964-1966
⊙ Hydro-electric power stations

MAIN WAVES OF IMMIGRANTS
1880-1905 RUSSIAN JEWISH REFUGEES
1933-1939 GERMAN JEWISH REFUGEES
1956   HUNGARIAN REFUGEES
1956-1960 INDIAN, PAKISTANI AND WEST INDIAN IMMIGRANTS

POPULATION IN 1961: 50,368,455
of whom nearly 8 million in London area

North Sea

Dounreay

Cumbernauld
Glenrothes
Livingston
East Kilbride
Hunterston

Chapel Cross
Washington
Peterlee
Newton Aycliffe
Calder Hall

Springfields
Skelmersdale
Wylfa
Runcorn
Capenhurst
Trawsfynydd
Dawley
Corby
Sizewell
Stevenage
Hemel Hempstead
Welwyn
Harlow
Hatfield
Bradwell
Basildon
Milford Haven
Cwmbran
Berkeley
Oldbury
Bracknell
Crawley
Dungeness
Hinkley Point
Fawley

0 ——— 60
Miles

1945-1965 ROAD DEAD 121,797

115

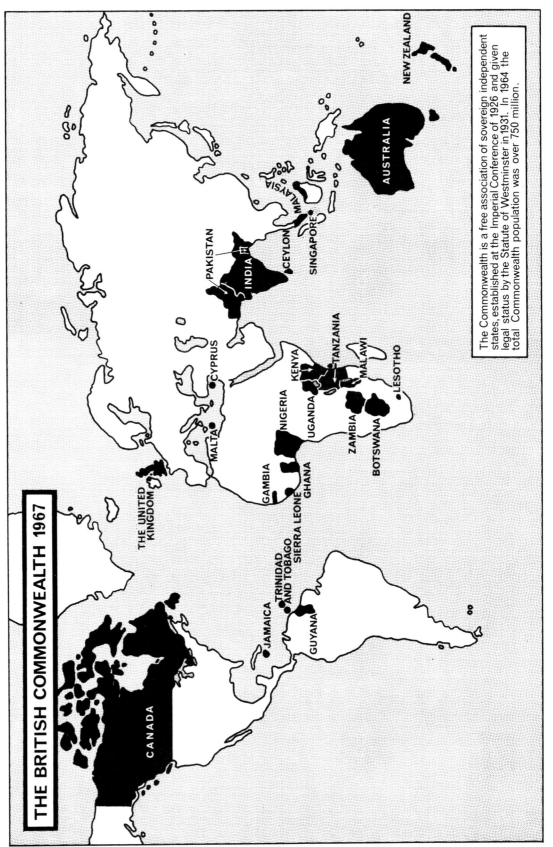

THE BRITISH COMMONWEALTH 1967

The Commonwealth is a free association of sovereign independent states, established at the Imperial Conference of 1926 and given legal status by the Statute of Westminster in 1931. In 1964 the total Commonwealth population was over 750 million.

CANADA

THE UNITED KINGDOM

JAMAICA

TRINIDAD AND TOBAGO

GUYANA

SIERRA LEONE

GHANA

GAMBIA

NIGERIA

MALTA

CYPRUS

PAKISTAN

INDIA

CEYLON

SINGAPORE

MALAYSIA

AUSTRALIA

NEW ZEALAND

KENYA

UGANDA

TANZANIA

MALAWI

ZAMBIA

BOTSWANA

LESOTHO

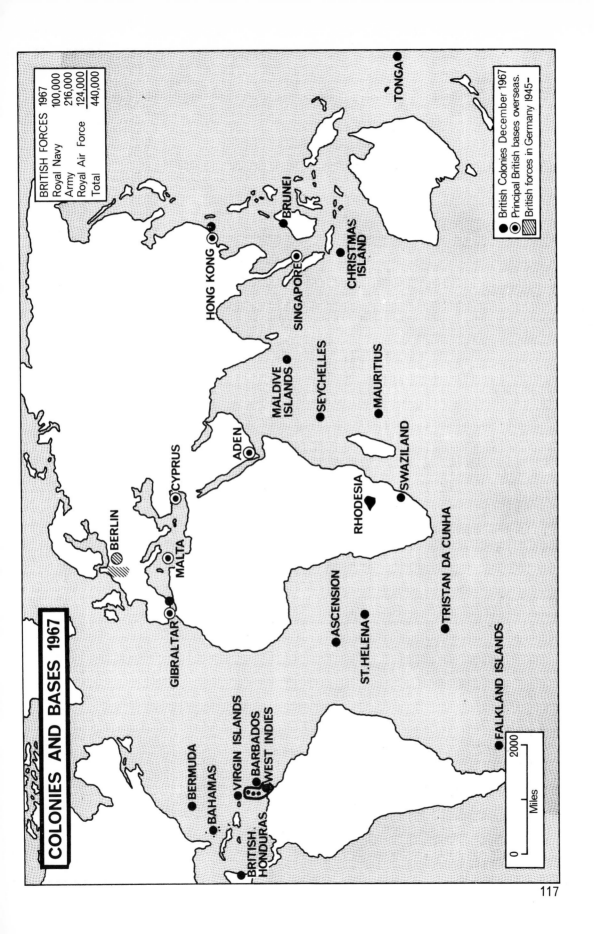

COLONIES AND BASES 1967

BRITISH FORCES 1967
Royal Navy   100,000
Army   216,000
Royal Air Force   124,000
Total   440,000

TONGA

HONG KONG

BRUNEI

CHRISTMAS ISLAND

SINGAPORE

MALDIVE ISLANDS

SEYCHELLES

MAURITIUS

ADEN

CYPRUS

BERLIN

MALTA

SWAZILAND

RHODESIA

GIBRALTAR

ASCENSION

ST. HELENA

TRISTAN DA CUNHA

FALKLAND ISLANDS

BERMUDA

BAHAMAS

VIRGIN ISLANDS

BARBADOS
WEST INDIES

BRITISH HONDURAS

● British Colonies December 1967.
◉ Principal British bases overseas.
▨ British forces in Germany 1945–

0   Miles   2000

117

THE WESTERN PACIFIC SINCE 1945

ALASKA
49th U.S. STATE

U.S.S.R.

ALEUTIAN ISLANDS

50th U.S. STATE

HAWAIIAN ISLANDS

●MIDWAY

JAPAN

●JOHNSTON

CHINA

U.S. MILITARY ADMINISTRATION

●BONIN
●DAITO
OKINAWA ●VOLCANO ●MARCUS
Hong Kong

FORMOSA

PHILLIPINES

●WAKE

VIET-NAM

MARIANAS ISLANDS
●GUAM

ISLANDS

●BIKINI

U.S. TRUST TERRITORY

●YAP
●PALAU

CAROLINE

ENIWETOK
●TRUK
MARSHALL ISLANDS

Brunei

BORNEO

INDONESIA

NEW GUINEA

TO AUSTRALIA

●OCEAN ISLAND 1900

GILBERT ISLANDS
1892

●HOWLAND BAKER

CANTON ISLAND
●1939

ELLICE ISLANDS

PHOENIX ISLANDS
1937

SOLOMON ISLANDS 1893

●SANTA CRUZ ISLANDS 1898

FRENCH

AUSTRALIA

NEW HEBRIDES
1887
FRENCH

FIJI 1874

●SAMOA
●TUTUILA

NEW CALEDONIA

TONGA 1900

TO NEW ZEALAND

●KERMADEC
TO NEW ZEALAND

COOK

NEW ZEALAND

TO NEW ZEALAND
CHATHAM

British possessions with date of acquisition.

Anglo-French Condominium.

Anglo-American joint sovereignty.

United States possessions.

Commonwealth possessions.

0   500

Miles approx.

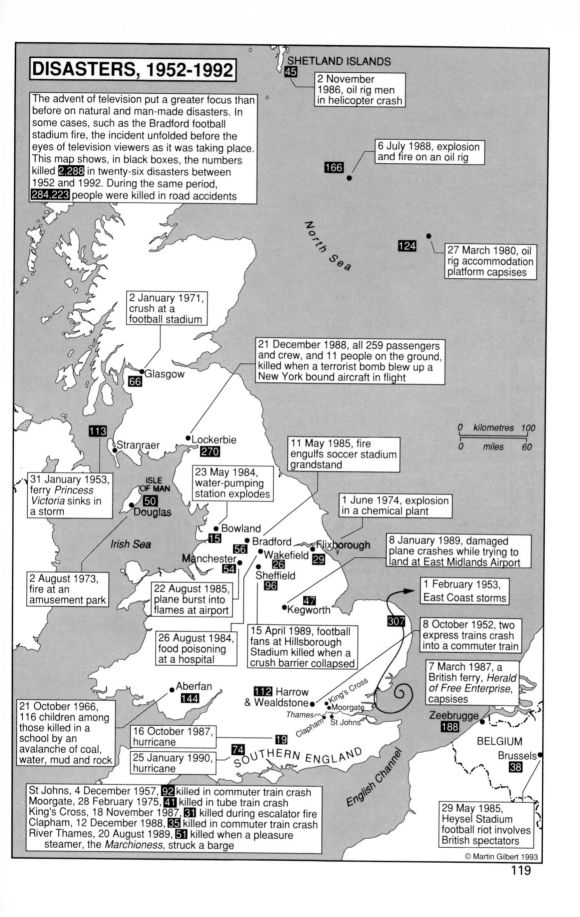

DISASTERS, 1952-1992

The advent of television put a greater focus than before on natural and man-made disasters. In some cases, such as the Bradford football stadium fire, the incident unfolded before the eyes of television viewers as it was taking place. This map shows, in black boxes, the numbers killed **2,288** in twenty-six disasters between 1952 and 1992. During the same period, **284,223** people were killed in road accidents

SHETLAND ISLANDS
45
2 November 1986, oil rig men in helicopter crash

6 July 1988, explosion and fire on an oil rig
166

124 27 March 1980, oil rig accommodation platform capsises

North Sea

2 January 1971, crush at a football stadium

21 December 1988, all 259 passengers and crew, and 11 people on the ground, killed when a terrorist bomb blew up a New York bound aircraft in flight

●Glasgow
66

113
Stranraer

●Lockerbie
270

11 May 1985, fire engulfs soccer stadium grandstand

1 June 1974, explosion in a chemical plant

31 January 1953, ferry *Princess Victoria* sinks in a storm

ISLE OF MAN
50
●Douglas

23 May 1984, water-pumping station explodes

Irish Sea

●Bowland
15
●Bradford
56
Manchester●
54
●Wakefield
26
●Flixborough
29

Sheffield
96

8 January 1989, damaged plane crashes while trying to land at East Midlands Airport

2 August 1973, fire at an amusement park

22 August 1985, plane burst into flames at airport

47
●Kegworth
307

1 February 1953, East Coast storms

8 October 1952, two express trains crash into a commuter train

26 August 1984, food poisoning at a hospital

15 April 1989, football fans at Hillsborough Stadium killed when a crush barrier collapsed

●Aberfan
144

21 October 1966, 116 children among those killed in a school by an avalanche of coal, water, mud and rock

112 Harrow & Wealdstone●
Thames~
Clapham●
King's Cross
●Moorgate
St Johns

7 March 1987, a British ferry, *Herald of Free Enterprise*, capsises

Zeebrugge●
188

BELGIUM
Brussels●
38

16 October 1987, hurricane
19

25 January 1990, hurricane
74

SOUTHERN ENGLAND

English Channel

29 May 1985, Heysel Stadium football riot involves British spectators

St Johns, 4 December 1957, **92** killed in commuter train crash
Moorgate, 28 February 1975, **41** killed in tube train crash
King's Cross, 18 November 1987, **31** killed during escalator fire
Clapham, 12 December 1988, **35** killed in commuter train crash
River Thames, 20 August 1989, **51** killed when a pleasure
    steamer, the *Marchioness*, struck a barge

© Martin Gilbert 1993

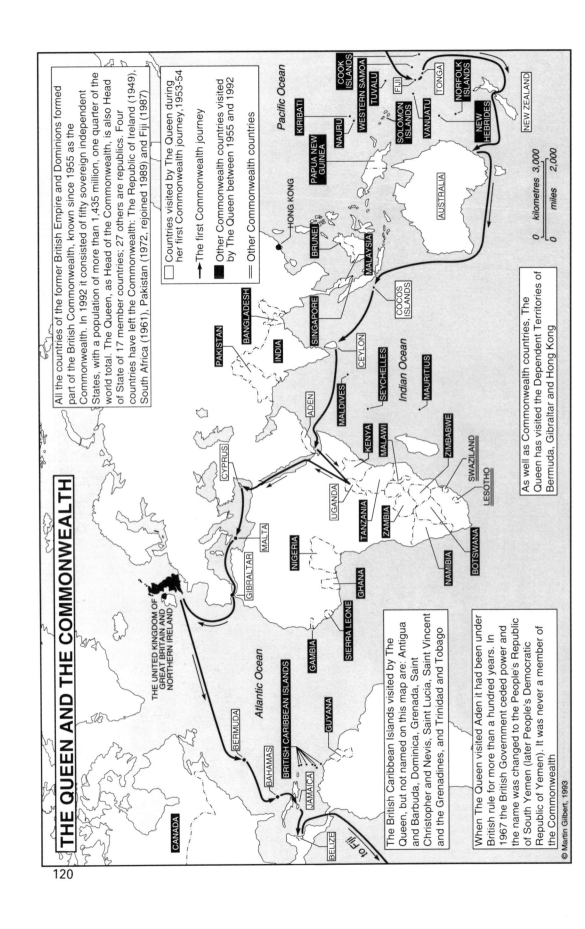

THE QUEEN AND THE COMMONWEALTH

All the countries of the former British Empire and Dominions formed part of the British Commonwealth, known since 1955 as the Commonwealth. In 1992 it consisted of fifty sovereign independent States, with a population of more than 1,435 million, one quarter of the world total. The Queen, as Head of the Commonwealth, is also Head of State of 17 member countries; 27 others are republics. Four countries have left the Commonwealth: The Republic of Ireland (1949), South Africa (1961), Pakistan (1972, rejoined 1989) and Fiji (1987)

☐ Countries visited by The Queen during her first Commonwealth journey, 1953-54

→ The first Commonwealth journey

■ Other Commonwealth countries visited by The Queen between 1955 and 1992

= Other Commonwealth countries

As well as Commonwealth countries, The Queen has visited the Dependent Territories of Bermuda, Gibraltar and Hong Kong

The British Caribbean Islands visited by The Queen, but not named on this map are: Antigua and Barbuda, Dominica, Grenada, Saint Christopher and Nevis, Saint Lucia, Saint Vincent and the Grenadines, and Trinidad and Tobago

When The Queen visited Aden it had been under British rule for more than a hundred years. In 1967 the British Government ceded power and the name was changed to the People's Republic of South Yemen (later People's Democratic Republic of Yemen). It was never a member of the Commonwealth

© Martin Gilbert, 1993

Pacific Ocean

COOK ISLANDS
WESTERN SAMOA
TUVALU
FIJI
TONGA
NORFOLK ISLANDS
KIRIBATI
SOLOMON ISLANDS
NAURU
VANUATU
NEW HEBRIDES
PAPUA NEW GUINEA
NEW ZEALAND
AUSTRALIA

0 kilometres 3,000
0 miles 2,000

HONG KONG
BRUNEI
MALAYSIA
SINGAPORE
COCOS ISLANDS
BANGLADESH
INDIA
PAKISTAN
CEYLON
SEYCHELLES
Indian Ocean
MAURITIUS
MALDIVES
ADEN
KENYA
MALAWI
ZIMBABWE
SWAZILAND
LESOTHO
TANZANIA
ZAMBIA
UGANDA
CYPRUS
MALTA
GIBRALTAR
NIGERIA
NAMIBIA
BOTSWANA
GHANA
SIERRA LEONE
GAMBIA
GUYANA

THE UNITED KINGDOM OF GREAT BRITAIN AND NORTHERN IRELAND

Atlantic Ocean

CANADA
BERMUDA
BAHAMAS
BRITISH CARIBBEAN ISLANDS
JAMAICA
BELIZE
to Fiji

OLD ENEMIES, NEW NATIONS: STATE VISITS 1955-1992

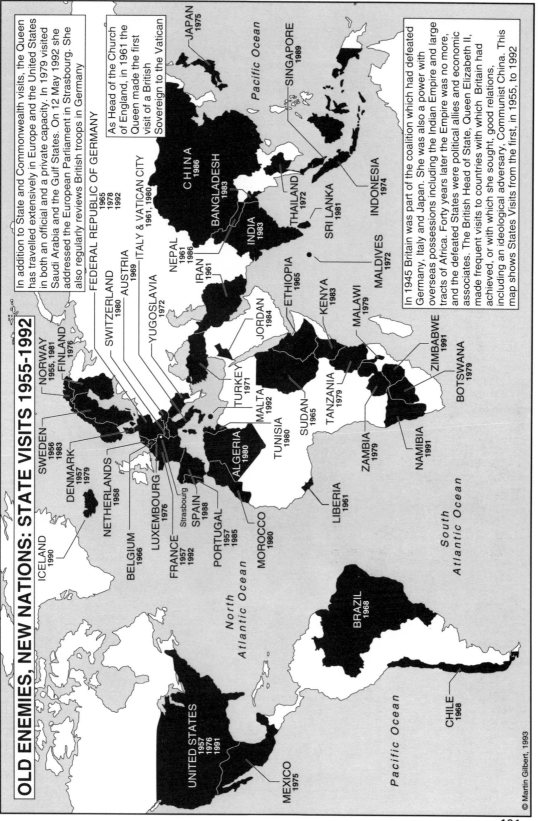

In addition to State and Commonwealth visits, the Queen has travelled extensively in Europe and the United States in both an official and a private capacity. In 1979 visited Saudi Arabia and the Gulf States. On 12 May 1992 she addressed the European Parliament in Strasbourg. She also regularly reviews British troops in Germany

As Head of the Church of England, in 1961 the Queen made the first visit of a British Sovereign to the Vatican

In 1945 Britain was part of the coalition which had defeated Germany, Italy and Japan. She was also a power with overseas possessions including the Indian Empire and large tracts of Africa. Forty years later the Empire was no more, and the defeated States were political allies and economic associates. The British Head of State, Queen Elizabeth II, made frequent visits to countries with which Britain had achieved, or with which she sought, good relations, including an ideological adversary, Communist China. This map shows States Visits from the first, in 1955, to 1992

JAPAN
1975

SINGAPORE
1989

Pacific Ocean

CHINA
1986

BANGLADESH
1983

INDONESIA
1974

THAILAND
1972

SRI LANKA
1981

MALDIVES
1972

INDIA
1983

NEPAL
1961
1986

IRAN
1961

FEDERAL REPUBLIC OF GERMANY
1965
1978
1992

AUSTRIA
1969

ITALY & VATICAN CITY
1961, 1980

SWITZERLAND
1980

YUGOSLAVIA
1972

ETHIOPIA
1965

KENYA
1983

MALAWI
1979

ZIMBABWE
1991

BOTSWANA
1979

JORDAN
1984

TURKEY
1971

SUDAN
1965

TANZANIA
1979

ZAMBIA
1979

NAMIBIA
1991

NORWAY
1955, 1981

FINLAND
1976

SWEDEN
1956
1983

DENMARK
1957
1979

ICELAND
1990

NETHERLANDS
1958

BELGIUM
1966

LUXEMBOURG
1976

Strasbourg

FRANCE
1957
1992

SPAIN
1988

PORTUGAL
1957
1985

MALTA
1992

ALGERIA
1980

TUNISIA
1980

MOROCCO
1980

LIBERIA
1961

North
Atlantic Ocean

South
Atlantic Ocean

UNITED STATES
1957
1976
1991

MEXICO
1975

BRAZIL
1968

CHILE
1968

Pacific Ocean

© Martin Gilbert, 1993

121

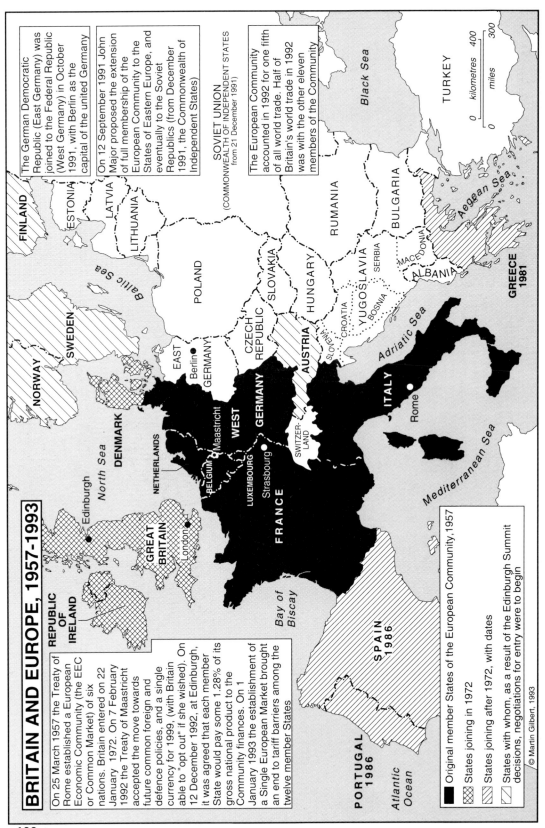

BRITAIN AND EUROPE, 1957-1993

On 25 March 1957 the Treaty of Rome established a European Economic Community (the EEC or Common Market) of six nations. Britain entered on 22 January 1972. On 7 February 1992 the Treaty of Maastricht accepted the move towards future common foreign and defence policies, and a single currency for 1999, (with Britain able to "opt out" if she wished). On 12 December 1992, at Edinburgh, it was agreed that each member State would pay some 1.28% of its gross national product to the Community finances. On 1 January 1993 the establishment of a Single European Market brought an end to tariff barriers among the twelve member States

The German Democratic Republic (East Germany) was joined to the Federal Republic (West Germany) in October 1991, with Berlin as the capital of the united Germany

On 12 September 1991 John Major proposed the extension of full membership of the European Community to the States of Eastern Europe, and eventually to the Soviet Republics (from December 1991, the Commonwealth of Independent States)

SOVIET UNION
(COMMONWEALTH OF INDEPENDENT STATES
from 21 December 1991)

The European Community accounted in 1992 for one fifth of all world trade. Half of Britain's world trade in 1992 was with the other eleven members of the Community

FINLAND

ESTONIA

LATVIA

LITHUANIA

Baltic Sea

SWEDEN

NORWAY

POLAND

EAST GERMANY

Berlin

DENMARK

North Sea

NETHERLANDS

BELGIUM

Maastricht

LUXEMBOURG

WEST GERMANY

Strasbourg

SWITZER-LAND

AUSTRIA

HUNGARY

CZECH REPUBLIC

SLOVAKIA

RUMANIA

BULGARIA

SLOVENIA

CROATIA

YUGOSLAVIA

BOSNIA

SERBIA

MACEDONIA

ALBANIA

Adriatic Sea

Aegean Sea

Black Sea

TURKEY

GREECE
1981

ITALY

Rome

Mediterranean Sea

FRANCE

Bay of Biscay

GREAT BRITAIN

London

Edinburgh

REPUBLIC OF IRELAND

SPAIN
1986

PORTUGAL
1986

Atlantic Ocean

0   *kilometres*   400

0   *miles*   300

■ Original member States of the European Community, 1957

▨ States joining in 1972

▧ States joining after 1972, with dates

▢ States with whom, as a result of the Edinburgh Summit decisions, negotiations for entry were to begin

© Martin Gilbert, 1993

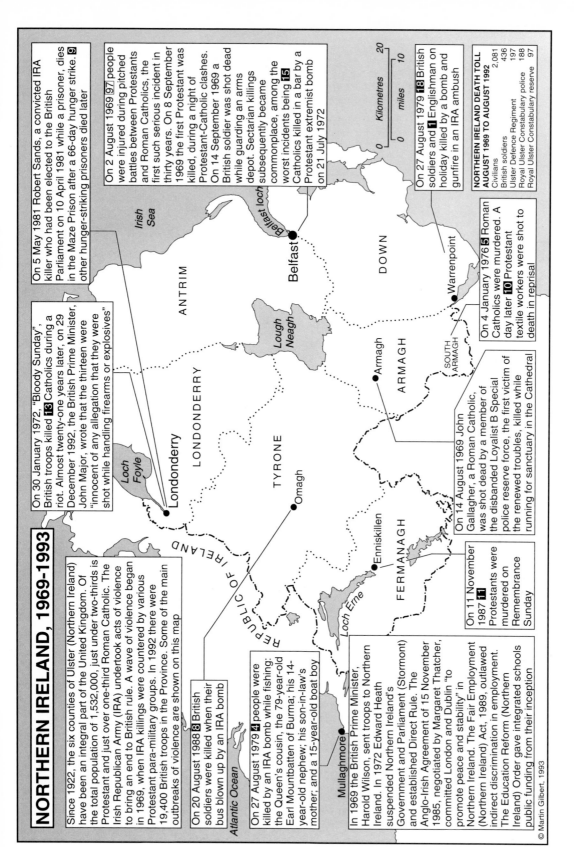

NORTHERN IRELAND, 1969-1993

Since 1922, the six counties of Ulster (Northern Ireland) have been an integral part of the United Kingdom. Of the total population of 1,532,000, just under two-thirds is Protestant and just over one-third Roman Catholic. The Irish Republican Army (IRA) undertook acts of violence to bring an end to British rule. A wave of violence began in 1969, when IRA killings were countered by various Protestant para-military groups. In 1992 there were 19,400 British troops in the Province. Some of the main outbreaks of violence are shown on this map

On 20 August 1988 **8** British soldiers were killed when their bus blown up by an IRA bomb

On 27 August 1979 **4** people were killed by an IRA bomb while fishing: the Queen's cousin, the 79-year-old Earl Mountbatten of Burma; his 14-year-old nephew; his son-in-law's mother; and a 15-year-old boat boy

In 1969 the British Prime Minister, Harold Wilson, sent troops to Northern Ireland. In 1972 Edward Heath suspended Northern Ireland's Government and Parliament (Stormont) and established Direct Rule. The Anglo-Irish Agreement of 15 November 1985, negotiated by Margaret Thatcher, committed London and Dublin "to promote peace and stability" in Northern Ireland. The Fair Employment (Northern Ireland) Act, 1989, outlawed indirect discrimination in employment. The Education Reform (Northern Ireland) Order gave integrated schools public funding from their inception

On 11 November 1987 **11** Protestants were murdered on Remembrance Sunday

On 14 August 1969 John Gallagher, a Roman Catholic, was shot dead by a member of the disbanded Loyalist B Special police reserve force, the first victim of the renewed troubles, killed while running for sanctuary in the Cathedral

On 4 January 1976 **5** Roman Catholics were murdered. A day later **10** Protestant textile workers were shot to death in reprisal

On 30 January 1972, "Bloody Sunday", British troops killed **13** Catholics during a riot. Almost twenty-one years later, on 29 December 1992, the British Prime Minister, John Major, wrote that the thirteen were "innocent of any allegation that they were shot while handling firearms or explosives"

On 5 May 1981 Robert Sands, a convicted IRA killer who had been elected to the British Parliament on 10 April 1981 while a prisoner, dies in the Maze Prison after a 66-day hunger strike. **9** other hunger-striking prisoners died later

On 2 August 1969 **97** people were injured during pitched battles between Protestants and Roman Catholics, the first such serious incident in thirty years. On 8 September 1969 the first Protestant was killed, during a night of Protestant-Catholic clashes. On 14 September 1969 a British soldier was shot dead while guarding an arms depot. Sectarian killings subsequently became commonplace, among the worst incidents being **15** Catholics killed in a bar by a Protestant extremist bomb on 21 July 1972

On 27 August 1979 **18** British soldiers and **1** Englishman on holiday killed by a bomb and gunfire in an IRA ambush

NORTHERN IRELAND DEATH TOLL AUGUST 1969 TO AUGUST 1992

Civilians	2,081
British soldiers	436
Ulster Defence Regiment	197
Royal Ulster Constabulary police	188
Royal Ulster Constabulary reserve	97

Irish Sea

Belfast loch

Belfast

DOWN

Warrenpoint

ANTRIM

Lough Neagh

Loch Foyle

Londonderry

LONDONDERRY

Armagh

ARMAGH

SOUTH ARMAGH

TYRONE

Omagh

REPUBLIC OF IRELAND

Atlantic Ocean

Mullaghmore

Enniskillen

Loch Erne

FERMANAGH

0   10   20 Kilometres
0   miles   10

© Martin Gilbert, 1993

TERRORISM ON THE BRITISH MAINLAND, 1972-1992

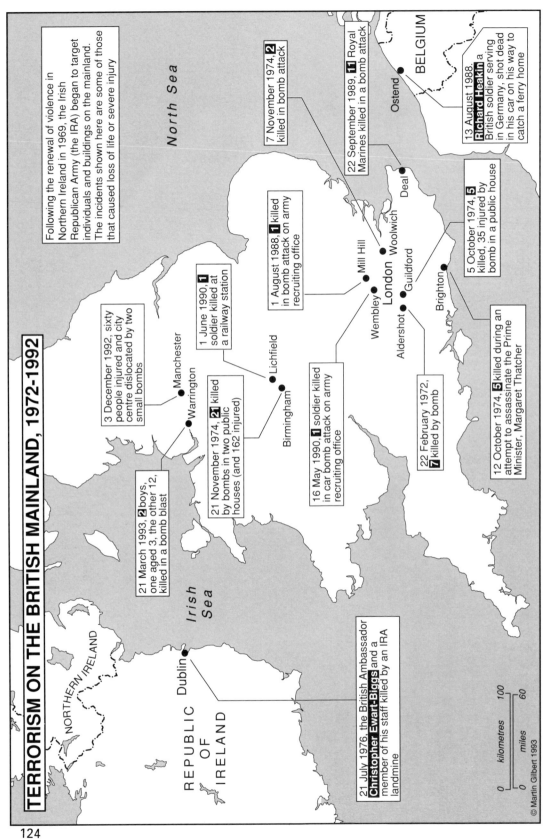

Following the renewal of violence in Northern Ireland in 1969, the Irish Republican Army (the IRA) began to target individuals and buildings on the mainland. The incidents shown here are some of those that caused loss of life or severe injury

North Sea

BELGIUM

Ostend

7 November 1974, **2** killed in bomb attack

22 September 1989, **1** Royal Marines killed in a bomb attack

13 August 1988, **Richard Heakin** a British soldier serving in Germany, shot dead in his car on his way to catch a ferry home

Deal

1 August 1988, **1** killed in bomb attack on army recruiting office

Woolwich

Mill Hill

London

5 October 1974, **5** killed, 35 injured by bomb in a public house

Wembley

Aldershot

Guildford

Brighton

3 December 1992, sixty people injured and city centre dislocated by two small bombs

1 June 1990, **1** soldier killed at a railway station

Manchester

Warrington

Lichfield

21 November 1974, **2** killed by bombs in two public houses (and 162 injured)

Birmingham

16 May 1990, **1** soldier killed in car bomb attack on army recruiting office

22 February 1972, **7** killed by bomb

12 October 1974, **5** killed during an attempt to assassinate the Prime Minister, Margaret Thatcher

21 March 1993, **2** boys, one aged 3, the other 12, killed in a bomb blast

Irish Sea

NORTHERN IRELAND

Dublin

REPUBLIC OF IRELAND

21 July 1976, the British Ambassador **Christopher Ewart-Biggs** and a member of his staff killed by an IRA landmine

0   kilometres   100

0   miles   60

© Martin Gilbert 1993

124

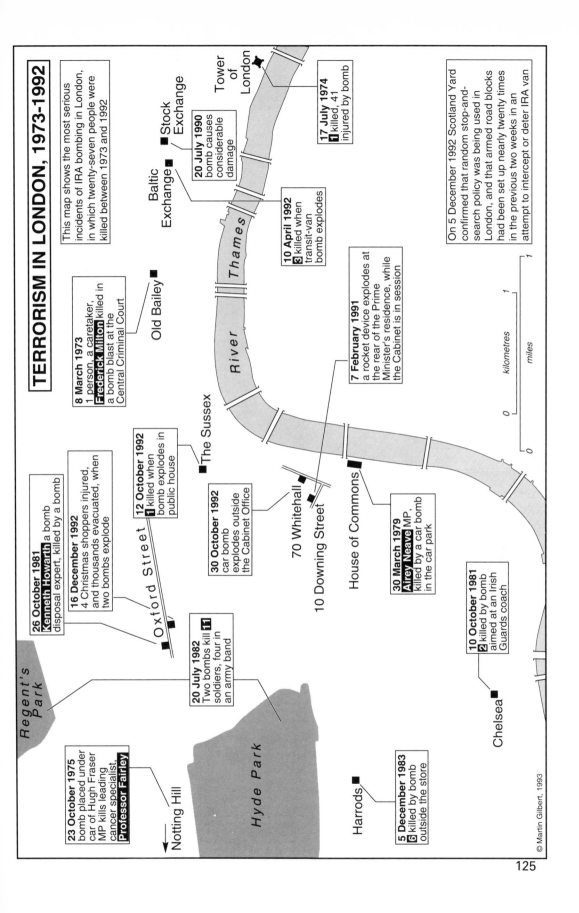

TERRORISM IN LONDON, 1973-1992

This map shows the most serious incidents of IRA bombing in London, in which twenty-seven people were killed between 1973 and 1992

8 March 1973 1 person, a caretaker, **Frederick Milton** killed in a bomb blast at the Central Criminal Court

26 October 1981 **Kenneth Howarth** a bomb disposal expert, killed by a bomb

16 December 1992 4 Christmas shoppers injured, and thousands evacuated, when two bombs explode

12 October 1992 **1** killed when bomb explodes in public house

30 October 1992 car bomb explodes outside the Cabinet Office

20 July 1982 Two bombs kill **11** soldiers, four in an army band

23 October 1975 bomb placed under car of Hugh Fraser MP kills leading cancer specialist, **Professor Fairley**

5 December 1983 **6** killed by bomb outside the store

10 October 1981 **2** killed by bomb aimed at an Irish Guards coach

30 March 1979 **Airey Neave** MP, killed by a car bomb in the car park

7 February 1991 a rocket device explodes at the rear of the Prime Minister's residence, while the Cabinet is in session

10 April 1992 **3** killed when transit-van bomb explodes

20 July 1990 bomb causes considerable damage

17 July 1974 **1** killed, 41 injured by bomb

On 5 December 1992 Scotland Yard confirmed that random stop-and-search policy was being used in London, and that armed road blocks had been set up nearly twenty times in the previous two weeks in an attempt to intercept or deter IRA van

Old Bailey

Baltic Exchange

Stock Exchange

Tower of London

The Sussex

70 Whitehall

10 Downing Street

House of Commons

Oxford Street

Regent's Park

Notting Hill

Hyde Park

Harrods

Chelsea

River Thames

0   1   kilometres
0   1   miles

© Martin Gilbert, 1993

125

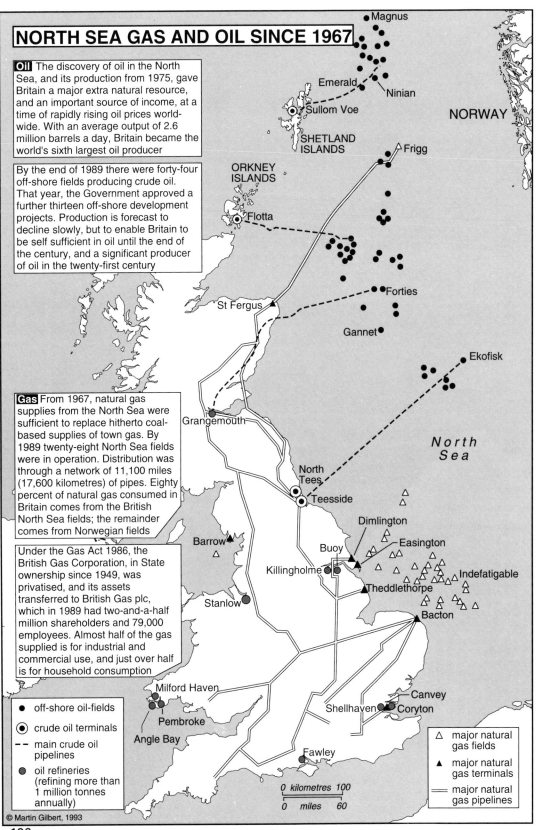

NORTH SEA GAS AND OIL SINCE 1967

Oil The discovery of oil in the North Sea, and its production from 1975, gave Britain a major extra natural resource, and an important source of income, at a time of rapidly rising oil prices worldwide. With an average output of 2.6 million barrels a day, Britain became the world's sixth largest oil producer

By the end of 1989 there were forty-four off-shore fields producing crude oil. That year, the Government approved a further thirteen off-shore development projects. Production is forecast to decline slowly, but to enable Britain to be self sufficient in oil until the end of the century, and a significant producer of oil in the twenty-first century

Gas From 1967, natural gas supplies from the North Sea were sufficient to replace hitherto coal-based supplies of town gas. By 1989 twenty-eight North Sea fields were in operation. Distribution was through a network of 11,100 miles (17,600 kilometres) of pipes. Eighty percent of natural gas consumed in Britain comes from the British North Sea fields; the remainder comes from Norwegian fields

Under the Gas Act 1986, the British Gas Corporation, in State ownership since 1949, was privatised, and its assets transferred to British Gas plc, which in 1989 had two-and-a-half million shareholders and 79,000 employees. Almost half of the gas supplied is for industrial and commercial use, and just over half is for household consumption

Magnus

Emerald
Ninian
Sullom Voe
NORWAY

SHETLAND ISLANDS
Frigg

ORKNEY ISLANDS

Flotta

St Fergus
Forties

Gannet

Ekofisk

Grangemouth

North Sea

North Tees
Teesside

Dimlington
Easington
Buoy
Killingholme
Indefatigable
Theddlethorpe
Stanlow
Bacton
Barrow

Milford Haven
Canvey
Shellhaven
Coryton
Pembroke
Angle Bay

Fawley

● off-shore oil-fields

◉ crude oil terminals

-- main crude oil pipelines

● oil refineries (refining more than 1 million tonnes annually)

△ major natural gas fields

▲ major natural gas terminals

= major natural gas pipelines

0 kilometres 100
0 miles 60

© Martin Gilbert, 1993

126

BRITAIN AND THE PACIFIC OCEAN, 1968-1980

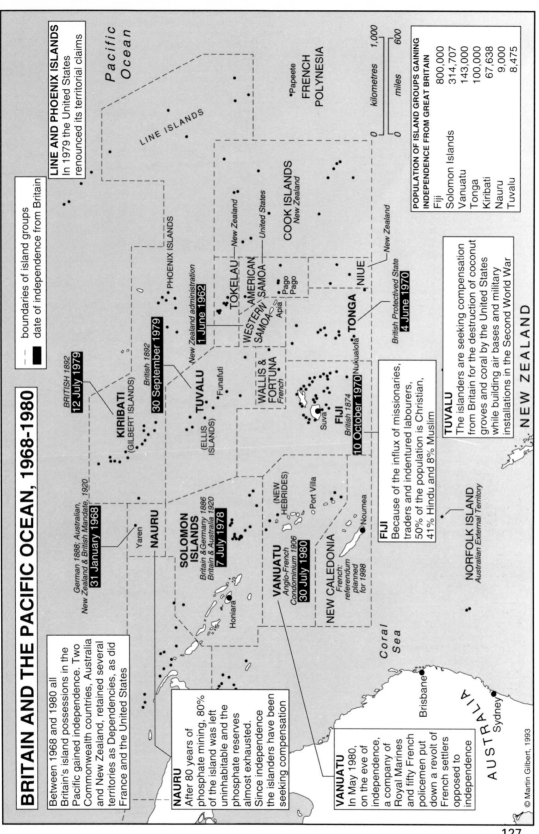

Between 1968 and 1980 all Britain's island possessions in the Pacific gained independence. Two Commonwealth countries, Australia and New Zealand, retained several territories as Dependencies, as did France and the United States

— boundaries of island groups
▬ date of independence from Britain

LINE AND PHOENIX ISLANDS
In 1979 the United States renounced its territorial claims

Pacific Ocean

POPULATION OF ISLAND GROUPS GAINING INDEPENDENCE FROM GREAT BRITAIN	
Fiji	800,000
Solomon Islands	314,707
Vanuatu	143,000
Tonga	100,000
Kiribati	67,638
Nauru	9,000
Tuvalu	8,475

kilometres 0 — 1,000
miles 0 — 600

Papeete
FRENCH POLYNESIA

LINE ISLANDS

PHOENIX ISLANDS

BRITISH 1892
12 July 1979

KIRIBATI
(GILBERT ISLANDS)

German 1888; Australian, New Zealand & British Mandate, 1920
31 January 1968

Yaren
NAURU

British 1892
30 September 1979

(ELLIS ISLANDS)
TUVALU
Funafuti

New Zealand administration
1 June 1962
TOKELAU — *New Zealand*

WESTERN SAMOA
Apia
AMERICAN SAMOA — *United States*
Pago Pago

COOK ISLANDS
New Zealand

WALLIS & FORTUNA
French

FIJI
British 1874
10 October 1970
Suva

British Protected State
4 June 1970
TONGA
Nukualofa

NIUE — *New Zealand*

SOLOMON ISLANDS
Britain & Germany 1886
Britain & Australia 1920
7 July 1978
Honiara

(NEW HEBRIDES)
Port Villa

VANUATU
Anglo-French Condominium 1906
30 July 1980

NEW CALEDONIA
French: referendum planned for 1998
Noumea

NAURU
After 80 years of phosphate mining, 80% of the island was left uninhabitable and the phosphate reserves almost exhausted. Since independence the islanders have been seeking compensation

VANUATU
In May 1980, on the eve of independence, a company of Royal Marines and fifty French policemen put down a revolt of French settlers opposed to independence

FIJI
Because of the influx of missionaries, traders and indentured labourers, 50% of the population is Christian, 41% Hindu and 8% Muslim

TUVALU
The islanders are seeking compensation from Britain for the destruction of coconut groves and coral by the United States while building air bases and military installations in the Second World War

NORFOLK ISLAND
Australian External Territory

Coral Sea

Brisbane

AUSTRALIA
Sydney

NEW ZEALAND

© Martin Gilbert, 1993

127

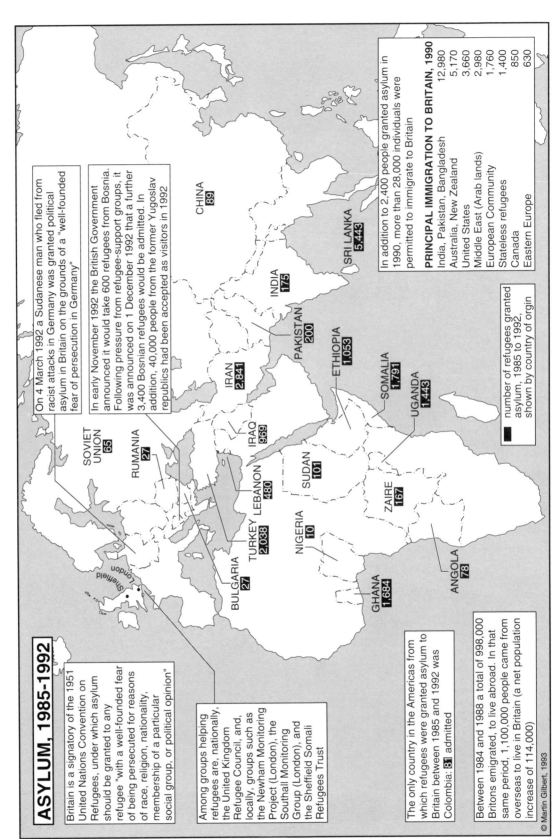

ASYLUM, 1985-1992

Britain is a signatory of the 1951 United Nations Convention on Refugees, under which asylum should be granted to any refugee "with a well-founded fear of being persecuted for reasons of race, religion, nationality, membership of a particular social group, or political opinion"

On 4 March 1992 a Sudanese man who fled from racist attacks in Germany was granted political asylum in Britain on the grounds of a "well-founded fear of persecution in Germany"

In early November 1992 the British Government announced it would take 600 refugees from Bosnia. Following pressure from refugee-support groups, it was announced on 1 December 1992 that a further 3,400 Bosnian refugees would be admitted. In addition, 40,000 people from the former Yugoslav republics had been accepted as visitors in 1992

Among groups helping refugees are, nationally, the United Kingdom Refugee Council, and, locally, groups such as the Newham Monitoring Project (London), the Southall Monitoring Group (London), and the Sheffield Somali Refugees Trust

The only country in the Americas from which refugees were granted asylum to Britain between 1985 and 1992 was Colombia: 81 admitted

Between 1984 and 1988 a total of 998,000 Britons emigrated, to live abroad. In that same period, 1,100,000 people came from overseas to live in Britain (a net population increase of 114,000)

In addition to 2,400 people granted asylum in 1990, more than 28,000 individuals were permitted to immigrate to Britain

PRINCIPAL IMMIGRATION TO BRITAIN, 1990

India, Pakistan, Bangladesh	12,980
Australia, New Zealand	5,170
United States	3,660
Middle East (Arab lands)	2,980
European Community	1,760
Stateless refugees	1,400
Canada	850
Eastern Europe	630

■ number of refugees granted asylum, 1985 to 1992, shown by country of orgin

SOVIET UNION 65

RUMANIA 27

BULGARIA 27

TURKEY 2,038

LEBANON 480

IRAQ 969

IRAN 2,841

CHINA 89

INDIA 175

PAKISTAN 200

SRI LANKA 5,443

ETHIOPIA 1,053

SOMALIA 1,791

UGANDA 1,443

SUDAN 101

NIGERIA 10

ZAIRE 167

GHANA 1,684

ANGOLA 78

Sheffield
London

© Martin Gilbert, 1993

128

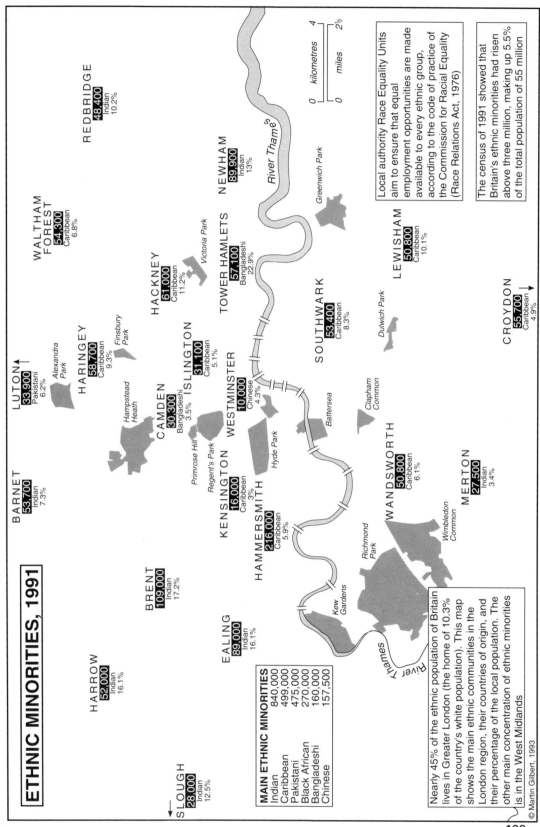

ETHNIC MINORITIES, 1991

SLOUGH
28,000
Indian
12.5%

HARROW
52,000
Indian
16.1%

BRENT
109,000
Indian
17.2%

EALING
89,000
Indian
16.1%

BARNET
53,700
Indian
7.3%

LUTON
33,900
Pakistani
6.2%

HARINGEY
58,700
Caribbean
9.3%

WALTHAM FOREST
54,300
Caribbean
6.8%

REDBRIDGE
48,400
Indian
10.2%

NEWHAM
89,900
Indian
13%

HACKNEY
61,000
Caribbean
11.2%

CAMDEN
30,300
Bangladeshi
3.5%

ISLINGTON
31,100
Caribbean
5.1%

TOWER HAMLETS
57,100
Bangladeshi
22.9%

WESTMINSTER
10,000
Chinese
4.3%

KENSINGTON
16,000
Caribbean
3%

HAMMERSMITH
216,000
Caribbean
5.9%

WANDSWORTH
50,800
Caribbean
6.1%

SOUTHWARK
53,400
Caribbean
8.3%

LEWISHAM
50,800
Caribbean
10.1%

MERTON
27,500
Indian
3.4%

CROYDON
55,700
Caribbean
4.9%

Alexandra Park
Finsbury Park
Hampstead Heath
Primrose Hill
Regent's Park
Hyde Park
Battersea
Clapham Common
Victoria Park
Greenwich Park
Dulwich Park
Wimbledon Common
Richmond Park
Kew Gardens
River Thames

MAIN ETHNIC MINORITIES	
Indian	840,000
Caribbean	499,000
Pakistani	475,000
Black African	270,000
Bangladeshi	160,000
Chinese	157,500

0 kilometres 4
0 miles 2½

Local authority Race Equality Units aim to ensure that equal employment opportunities are made available to every ethnic group, according to the code of practice of the Commission for Racial Equality (Race Relations Act, 1976)

The census of 1991 showed that Britain's ethnic minorities had risen above three million, making up 5.5% of the total population of 55 million

Nearly 45% of the ethnic population of Britain lives in Greater London (the home of 10.3% of the country's white population). This map shows the main ethnic communities in the London region, their countries of origin, and their percentage of the local population. The other main concentration of ethnic minorities is in the West Midlands

© Martin Gilbert, 1993

129

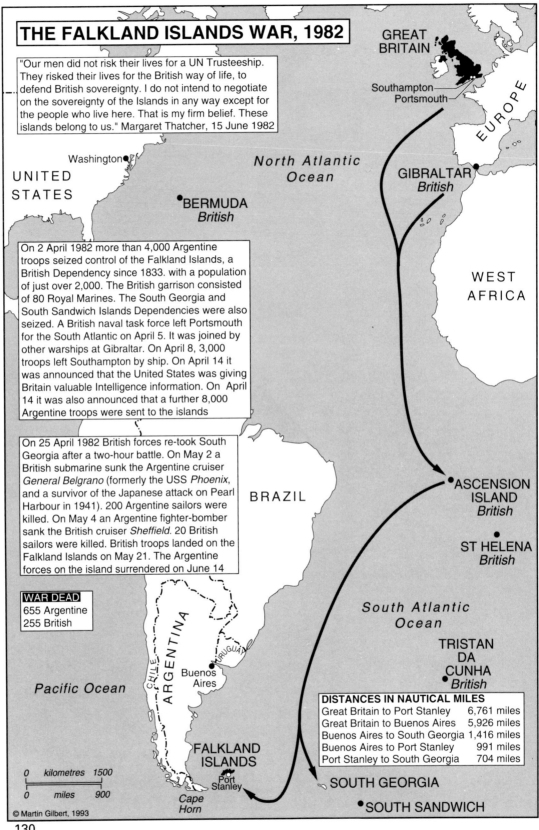

THE FALKLAND ISLANDS WAR, 1982

"Our men did not risk their lives for a UN Trusteeship. They risked their lives for the British way of life, to defend British sovereignty. I do not intend to negotiate on the sovereignty of the Islands in any way except for the people who live here. That is my firm belief. These islands belong to us." Margaret Thatcher, 15 June 1982

GREAT BRITAIN

Southampton
Portsmouth

EUROPE

Washington●

UNITED STATES

North Atlantic Ocean

GIBRALTAR
British

●BERMUDA
British

WEST AFRICA

On 2 April 1982 more than 4,000 Argentine troops seized control of the Falkland Islands, a British Dependency since 1833. with a population of just over 2,000. The British garrison consisted of 80 Royal Marines. The South Georgia and South Sandwich Islands Dependencies were also seized. A British naval task force left Portsmouth for the South Atlantic on April 5. It was joined by other warships at Gibraltar. On April 8, 3,000 troops left Southampton by ship. On April 14 it was announced that the United States was giving Britain valuable Intelligence information. On April 14 it was also announced that a further 8,000 Argentine troops were sent to the islands

On 25 April 1982 British forces re-took South Georgia after a two-hour battle. On May 2 a British submarine sunk the Argentine cruiser *General Belgrano* (formerly the USS *Phoenix*, and a survivor of the Japanese attack on Pearl Harbour in 1941). 200 Argentine sailors were killed. On May 4 an Argentine fighter-bomber sank the British cruiser *Sheffield*. 20 British sailors were killed. British troops landed on the Falkland Islands on May 21. The Argentine forces on the island surrendered on June 14

BRAZIL

●ASCENSION ISLAND
British

ST HELENA
British

WAR DEAD
655 Argentine
255 British

South Atlantic Ocean

TRISTAN DA CUNHA
●*British*

ARGENTINA

CHILE

URUGUAY

Buenos Aires

Pacific Ocean

DISTANCES IN NAUTICAL MILES
Great Britain to Port Stanley   6,761 miles
Great Britain to Buenos Aires   5,926 miles
Buenos Aires to South Georgia 1,416 miles
Buenos Aires to Port Stanley   991 miles
Port Stanley to South Georgia   704 miles

FALKLAND ISLANDS

Port Stanley

Cape Horn

0   kilometres   1500
0   miles   900

© Martin Gilbert, 1993

◇ SOUTH GEORGIA

●SOUTH SANDWICH

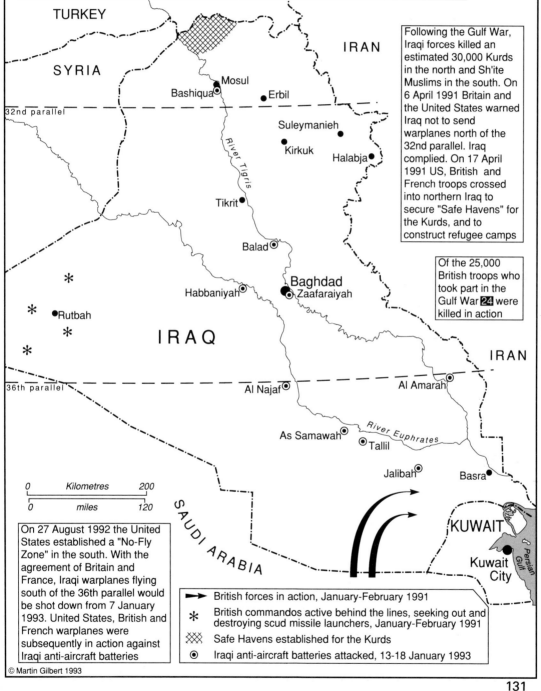

BRITAIN, THE GULF WAR AND ITS AFTERMATH, 1990-1993

On 2 August 1990 Iraqi forces occupied Kuwait. The United Nations Security Council demanded immediate withdrawal. On 29 November 1990 the Security Council authorised UN members to use force to expel Iraq from Kuwait. On 17 January 1991 Allied air forces, British among them, attacked strategic targets throughout Iraq and Iraqi-occupied Kuwait. On 24 February 1991 British forces participated in the land offensive. Four days later Iraq announced a cease-fire

TURKEY

SYRIA

IRAN

Mosul
Bashiqua
Erbil

32nd parallel

Suleymanieh
Kirkuk
Halabja

River Tigris

Tikrit

Balad

IRAQ

Habbaniyah
Baghdad
Zaafaraiyah

Rutbah

Al Najaf
Al Amarah

36th parallel

IRAN

As Samawah
Tallil
River Euphrates

Jalibah
Basra

SAUDI ARABIA

KUWAIT
Kuwait City

Persian Gulf

Following the Gulf War, Iraqi forces killed an estimated 30,000 Kurds in the north and Sh'ite Muslims in the south. On 6 April 1991 Britain and the United States warned Iraq not to send warplanes north of the 32nd parallel. Iraq complied. On 17 April 1991 US, British and French troops crossed into northern Iraq to secure "Safe Havens" for the Kurds, and to construct refugee camps

Of the 25,000 British troops who took part in the Gulf War 24 were killed in action

On 27 August 1992 the United States established a "No-Fly Zone" in the south. With the agreement of Britain and France, Iraqi warplanes flying south of the 36th parallel would be shot down from 7 January 1993. United States, British and French warplanes were subsequently in action against Iraqi anti-aircraft batteries

Kilometres 0 — 200
miles 0 — 120

➤ British forces in action, January-February 1991

✳ British commandos active behind the lines, seeking out and destroying scud missile launchers, January-February 1991

▨ Safe Havens established for the Kurds

⊙ Iraqi anti-aircraft batteries attacked, 13-18 January 1993

© Martin Gilbert 1993

131

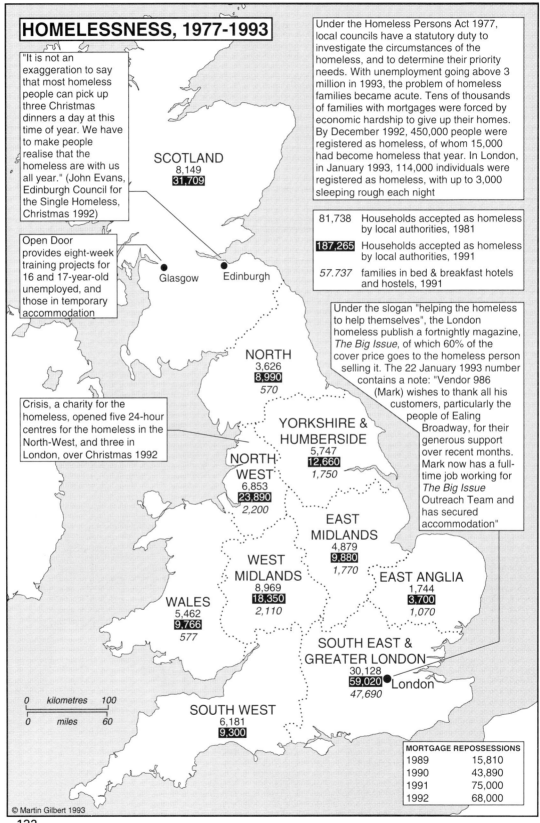

HOMELESSNESS, 1977-1993

"It is not an exaggeration to say that most homeless people can pick up three Christmas dinners a day at this time of year. We have to make people realise that the homeless are with us all year." (John Evans, Edinburgh Council for the Single Homeless, Christmas 1992)

Open Door provides eight-week training projects for 16 and 17-year-old unemployed, and those in temporary accommodation

Crisis, a charity for the homeless, opened five 24-hour centres for the homeless in the North-West, and three in London, over Christmas 1992

Under the Homeless Persons Act 1977, local councils have a statutory duty to investigate the circumstances of the homeless, and to determine their priority needs. With unemployment going above 3 million in 1993, the problem of homeless families became acute. Tens of thousands of families with mortgages were forced by economic hardship to give up their homes. By December 1992, 450,000 people were registered as homeless, of whom 15,000 had become homeless that year. In London, in January 1993, 114,000 individuals were registered as homeless, with up to 3,000 sleeping rough each night

81,738	Households accepted as homeless by local authorities, 1981
187,265	Households accepted as homeless by local authorities, 1991
57.737	families in bed & breakfast hotels and hostels, 1991

Under the slogan "helping the homeless to help themselves", the London homeless publish a fortnightly magazine, *The Big Issue*, of which 60% of the cover price goes to the homeless person selling it. The 22 January 1993 number contains a note: "Vendor 986 (Mark) wishes to thank all his customers, particularly the people of Ealing Broadway, for their generous support over recent months. Mark now has a full-time job working for *The Big Issue* Outreach Team and has secured accommodation"

SCOTLAND
8,149
31,709

Glasgow Edinburgh

NORTH
3,626
8,990
570

YORKSHIRE & HUMBERSIDE
5,747
12,660
1,750

NORTH WEST
6,853
23,890
2,200

EAST MIDLANDS
4,879
9,880
1,770

WEST MIDLANDS
8,969
18,350
2,110

EAST ANGLIA
1,744
3,700
1,070

WALES
5,462
9,766
577

SOUTH EAST & GREATER LONDON
30,128
59,020 London
47,690

SOUTH WEST
6,181
9,300

0	kilometres	100
0	miles	60

MORTGAGE REPOSSESSIONS	
1989	15,810
1990	43,890
1991	75,000
1992	68,000

© Martin Gilbert 1993

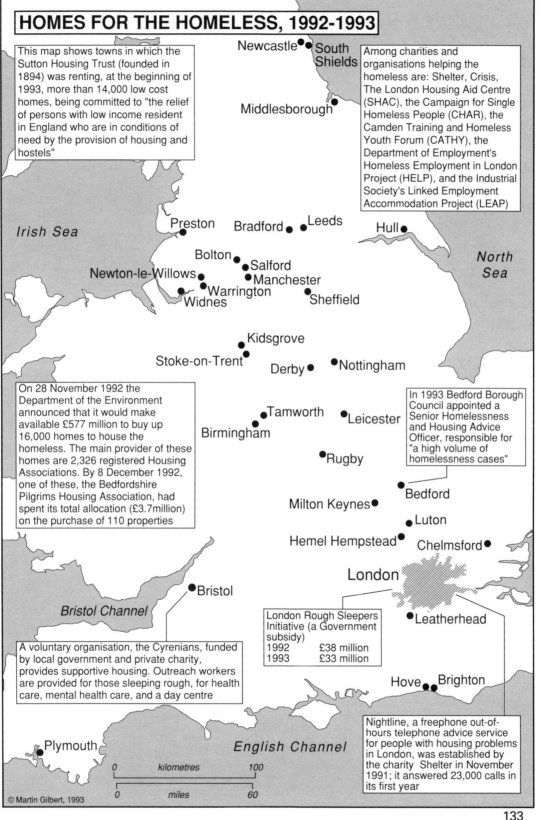

HOMES FOR THE HOMELESS, 1992-1993

This map shows towns in which the Sutton Housing Trust (founded in 1894) was renting, at the beginning of 1993, more than 14,000 low cost homes, being committed to "the relief of persons with low income resident in England who are in conditions of need by the provision of housing and hostels"

Among charities and organisations helping the homeless are: Shelter, Crisis, The London Housing Aid Centre (SHAC), the Campaign for Single Homeless People (CHAR), the Camden Training and Homeless Youth Forum (CATHY), the Department of Employment's Homeless Employment in London Project (HELP), and the Industrial Society's Linked Employment Accommodation Project (LEAP)

Newcastle • • South Shields

Middlesborough •

Irish Sea

Preston • Bradford • • Leeds Hull •

North Sea

Bolton •
Newton-le-Willows • • Salford
• • Manchester
• Warrington
Widnes

Sheffield •

Kidsgrove •

Stoke-on-Trent • Derby • • Nottingham

On 28 November 1992 the Department of the Environment announced that it would make available £577 million to buy up 16,000 homes to house the homeless. The main provider of these homes are 2,326 registered Housing Associations. By 8 December 1992, one of these, the Bedfordshire Pilgrims Housing Association, had spent its total allocation (£3.7 million) on the purchase of 110 properties

In 1993 Bedford Borough Council appointed a Senior Homelessness and Housing Advice Officer, responsible for "a high volume of homelessness cases"

Tamworth • • Leicester
Birmingham •

Rugby •

Milton Keynes • • Bedford

• Luton
Hemel Hempstead • • Chelmsford •

• Bristol

Bristol Channel

London

A voluntary organisation, the Cyrenians, funded by local government and private charity, provides supportive housing. Outreach workers are provided for those sleeping rough, for health care, mental health care, and a day centre

London Rough Sleepers Initiative (a Government subsidy)
1992   £38 million
1993   £33 million

• Leatherhead

Hove • • Brighton

Nightline, a freephone out-of-hours telephone advice service for people with housing problems in London, was established by the charity Shelter in November 1991; it answered 23,000 calls in its first year

• Plymouth

English Channel

0   kilometres   100
0   miles   60

© Martin Gilbert, 1993

PRIVATE CHARITY AND PUBLIC WELFARE

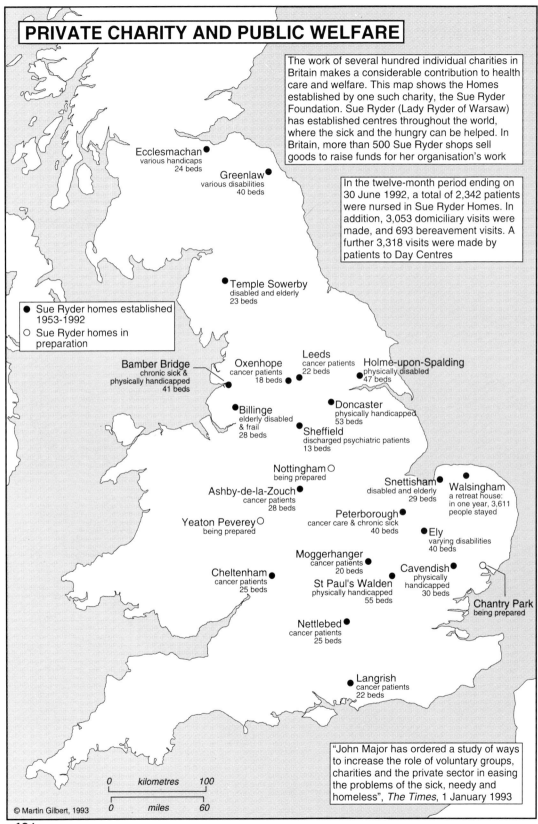

The work of several hundred individual charities in Britain makes a considerable contribution to health care and welfare. This map shows the Homes established by one such charity, the Sue Ryder Foundation. Sue Ryder (Lady Ryder of Warsaw) has established centres throughout the world, where the sick and the hungry can be helped. In Britain, more than 500 Sue Ryder shops sell goods to raise funds for her organisation's work

In the twelve-month period ending on 30 June 1992, a total of 2,342 patients were nursed in Sue Ryder Homes. In addition, 3,053 domiciliary visits were made, and 693 bereavement visits. A further 3,318 visits were made by patients to Day Centres

Ecclesmachan
various handicaps
24 beds

Greenlaw
various disabilities
40 beds

Temple Sowerby
disabled and elderly
23 beds

● Sue Ryder homes established 1953-1992
○ Sue Ryder homes in preparation

Bamber Bridge
chronic sick & physically handicapped
41 beds

Oxenhope
cancer patients
18 beds

Leeds
cancer patients
22 beds

Holme-upon-Spalding
physically disabled
47 beds

Billinge
elderly disabled & frail
28 beds

Doncaster
physically handicapped
53 beds

Sheffield
discharged psychiatric patients
13 beds

Nottingham ○
being prepared

Ashby-de-la-Zouch
cancer patients
28 beds

Snettisham
disabled and elderly
29 beds

Walsingham
a retreat house:
in one year, 3,611 people stayed

Yeaton Peverey ○
being prepared

Peterborough
cancer care & chronic sick
40 beds

Ely
varying disabilities
40 beds

Moggerhanger
cancer patients
20 beds

Cavendish
physically handicapped
30 beds

Cheltenham
cancer patients
25 beds

St Paul's Walden
physically handicapped
55 beds

Chantry Park
being prepared

Nettlebed
cancer patients
25 beds

Langrish
cancer patients
22 beds

0   kilometres   100

0   miles   60

© Martin Gilbert, 1993

"John Major has ordered a study of ways to increase the role of voluntary groups, charities and the private sector in easing the problems of the sick, needy and homeless", *The Times*, 1 January 1993

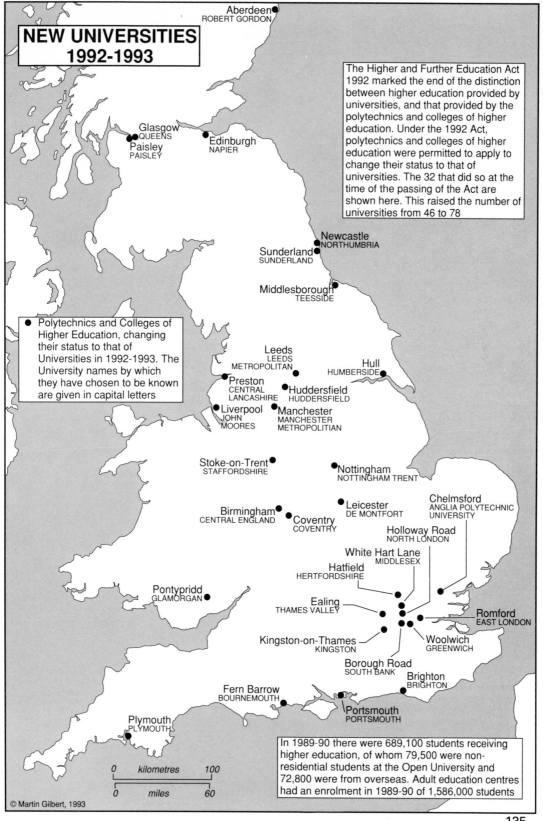

NEW UNIVERSITIES 1992-1993

Aberdeen
ROBERT GORDON

The Higher and Further Education Act 1992 marked the end of the distinction between higher education provided by universities, and that provided by the polytechnics and colleges of higher education. Under the 1992 Act, polytechnics and colleges of higher education were permitted to apply to change their status to that of universities. The 32 that did so at the time of the passing of the Act are shown here. This raised the number of universities from 46 to 78

Glasgow
QUEENS
Paisley
PAISLEY

Edinburgh
NAPIER

Newcastle
NORTHUMBRIA
Sunderland
SUNDERLAND

Middlesborough
TEESSIDE

● Polytechnics and Colleges of Higher Education, changing their status to that of Universities in 1992-1993. The University names by which they have chosen to be known are given in capital letters

Leeds
LEEDS METROPOLITAN
Hull
HUMBERSIDE
Preston
CENTRAL LANCASHIRE
Huddersfield
HUDDERSFIELD
Liverpool
JOHN MOORES
Manchester
MANCHESTER METROPOLITIAN

Stoke-on-Trent
STAFFORDSHIRE
Nottingham
NOTTINGHAM TRENT

Leicester
DE MONTFORT
Chelmsford
ANGLIA POLYTECHNIC UNIVERSITY

Birmingham
CENTRAL ENGLAND
Coventry
COVENTRY
Holloway Road
NORTH LONDON

White Hart Lane
MIDDLESEX

Hatfield
HERTFORDSHIRE

Pontypridd
GLAMORGAN
Ealing
THAMES VALLEY
Romford
EAST LONDON

Kingston-on-Thames
KINGSTON
Woolwich
GREENWICH

Borough Road
SOUTH BANK
Brighton
BRIGHTON

Fern Barrow
BOURNEMOUTH

Portsmouth
PORTSMOUTH

Plymouth
PLYMOUTH

0 kilometres 100
0 miles 60

In 1989-90 there were 689,100 students receiving higher education, of whom 79,500 were non-residential students at the Open University and 72,800 were from overseas. Adult education centres had an enrolment in 1989-90 of 1,586,000 students

© Martin Gilbert, 1993

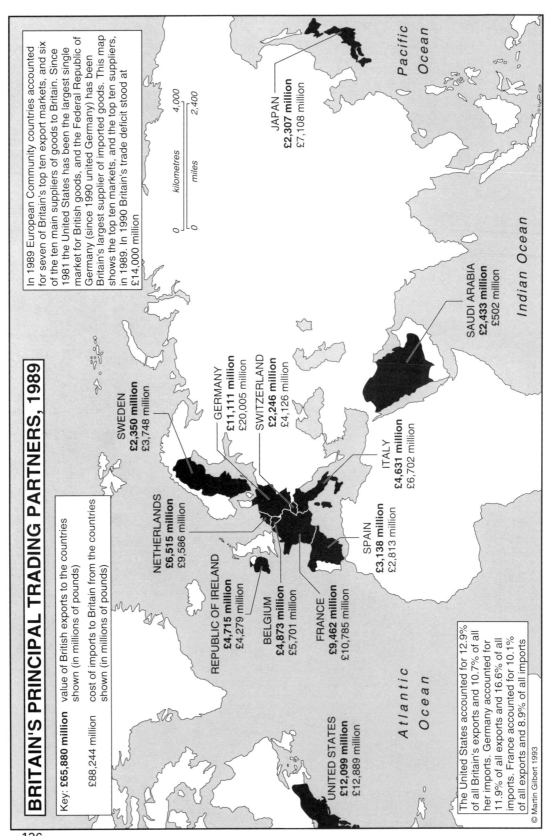

BRITAIN'S PRINCIPAL TRADING PARTNERS, 1989

Key: **£65,880 million**   value of British exports to the countries
shown (in millions of pounds)

£88,244 million   cost of imports to Britain from the countries
shown (in millions of pounds)

In 1989 European Community countries accounted for seven of Britain's top ten export markets, and six of the ten main suppliers of goods to Britain. Since 1981 the United States has been the largest single market for British goods, and the Federal Republic of Germany (since 1990 united Germany) has been Britain's largest supplier of imported goods. This map shows the top ten markets, and the top ten suppliers, in 1989. In 1990 Britain's trade deficit stood at £14,000 million

The United States accounted for 12.9% of all Britain's exports and 10.7% of all her imports. Germany accounted for 11.9% of all exports and 16.6% of all imports. France accounted for 10.1% of all exports and 8.9% of all imports

UNITED STATES
£12,099 million
£12,889 million

REPUBLIC OF IRELAND
£4,715 million
£4,279 million

BELGIUM
£4,873 million
£5,701 million

FRANCE
£9,462 million
£10,785 million

NETHERLANDS
£6,515 million
£9,586 million

SWEDEN
£2,350 million
£3,748 million

GERMANY
£11,111 million
£20,005 million

SWITZERLAND
£2,246 million
£4,126 million

ITALY
£4,631 million
£6,702 million

SPAIN
£3,138 million
£2,813 million

SAUDI ARABIA
£2,433 million
£502 million

JAPAN
£2,307 million
£7,108 million

Pacific Ocean

Indian Ocean

Atlantic Ocean

kilometres   4,000

miles   2,400

0

0

© Martin Gilbert 1993

136

BRITISH OVERSEAS DEPENDENT TERRITORIES, 1993

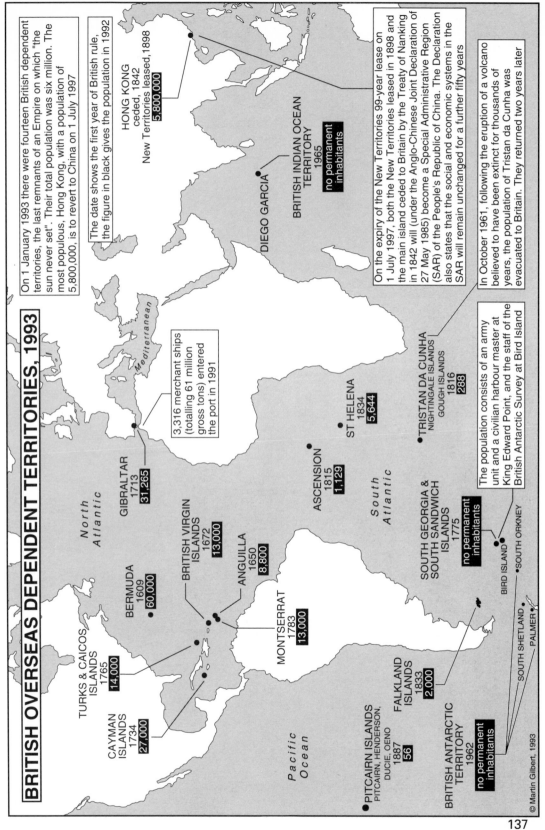

On 1 January 1993 there were fourteen British dependent territories, the last remnants of an Empire on which "the sun never set". Their total population was six million. The most populous, Hong Kong, with a population of 5,800,000, is to revert to China on 1 July 1997

The date shows the first year of British rule, the figure in black gives the population in 1992

HONG KONG
ceded, 1842
New Territories leased, 1898
5,800,000

DIEGO GARCIA

BRITISH INDIAN OCEAN TERRITORY
1965
no permanent inhabitants

On the expiry of the New Territories 99-year lease on 1 July 1997, both the New Territories leased in 1898 and the main island ceded to Britain by the Treaty of Nanking in 1842 will (under the Anglo-Chinese Joint Declaration of 27 May 1985) become a Special Administrative Region (SAR) of the People's Republic of China. The Declaration also states that the social and economic systems in the SAR will remain unchanged for a further fifty years

In October 1961, following the eruption of a volcano believed to have been extinct for thousands of years, the population of Tristan da Cunha was evacuated to Britain. They returned two years later

Mediterranean

3,316 merchant ships (totalling 61 million gross tons) entered the port in 1991

GIBRALTAR
1713
31,265

North Atlantic

BERMUDA
1609
● **60,000**

TURKS & CAICOS ISLANDS
1765
14,000

CAYMAN ISLANDS
1734
27,000

BRITISH VIRGIN ISLANDS
1672
13,000

ANGUILLA
1650
8,800

MONTSERRAT
1783
13,000

Pacific Ocean

PITCAIRN ISLANDS
PITCAIRN, HENDERSON, DUCIE, OENO
1887
56

FALKLAND ISLANDS
1833
2,000

BRITISH ANTARCTIC TERRITORY
1962
no permanent inhabitants

South Atlantic

ST HELENA
1834
5,644

ASCENSION
1815
1,129

TRISTAN DA CUNHA
NIGHTINGALE ISLANDS
GOUGH ISLANDS
1816
288

SOUTH GEORGIA & SOUTH SANDWICH ISLANDS
1775
no permanent inhabitants

The population consists of an army unit and a civilian harbour master at King Edward Point, and the staff of the British Antarctic Survey at Bird Island

BIRD ISLAND

SOUTH ORKNEY

SOUTH SHETLAND

PALMER ●

© Martin Gilbert, 1993

137

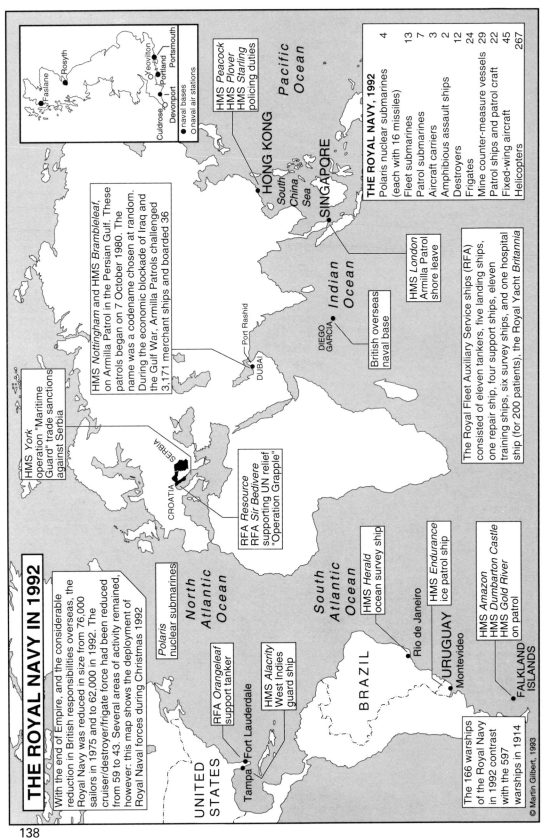

THE ROYAL NAVY IN 1992

With the end of Empire, and the considerable reduction in British responsibilities overseas, the Royal Navy was reduced in size from 76,000 sailors in 1975 and to 62,000 in 1992. The cruiser/destroyer/frigate force had been reduced from 59 to 43. Several areas of activity remained, however: this map shows the deployment of Royal Naval forces during Christmas 1992

HMS *Peacock*
HMS *Plover*
HMS *Starling*
policing duties

Pacific Ocean

HONG KONG

South China Sea

SINGAPORE

THE ROYAL NAVY, 1992	
Polaris nuclear submarines (each with 16 missiles)	4
Fleet submarines	13
Patrol submarines	7
Aircraft carriers	3
Amphibious assault ships	2
Destroyers	12
Frigates	24
Mine counter-measure vessels	29
Patrol ships and patrol craft	22
Fixed-wing aircraft	45
Helicopters	267

HMS *Nottingham* and HMS *Brambleleaf*, on Armilla Patrol in the Persian Gulf. These patrols began on 7 October 1980. The name was a codename chosen at random. During the economic blockade of Iraq and the Gulf War, Armilla Patrols challenged 3,171 merchant ships and boarded 36

HMS *London* Armilla Patrol shore leave

Indian Ocean

Port Rashid

DUBAI

DIEGO GARCIA

British overseas naval base

HMS *York* operation "Maritime Guard" trade sanctions against Serbia

SERBIA

CROATIA

RFA *Resource*
RFA *Sir Bedivere*
supporting UN relief "Operation Grapple"

The Royal Fleet Auxiliary Service ships (RFA) consisted of eleven tankers, five landing ships, one repair ship, four support ships, eleven training ships, six survey ships, and one hospital ship (for 200 patients), the Royal Yacht *Britannia*

Polaris nuclear submarines

North Atlantic Ocean

RFA *Orangeleaf* support tanker

HMS *Alacrity* West Indies guard ship

HMS *Herald* ocean survey ship

South Atlantic Ocean

HMS *Endurance* ice patrol ship

Rio de Janeiro

URUGUAY

HMS *Amazon*
HMS *Dumbarton Castle*
HMS *Gold River*
on patrol

Montevideo

FALKLAND ISLANDS

BRAZIL

UNITED STATES

Tampa   Fort Lauderdale

The 166 warships of the Royal Navy in 1992 contrast with the 597 warships in 1914

© Martin Gilbert, 1993

Rosyth

Faslane

Culdrose   Yeovilton   Portland   Portsmouth
Devonport

● naval bases
○ naval air stations

BRITISH FORCES OVERSEAS, 1992-1993

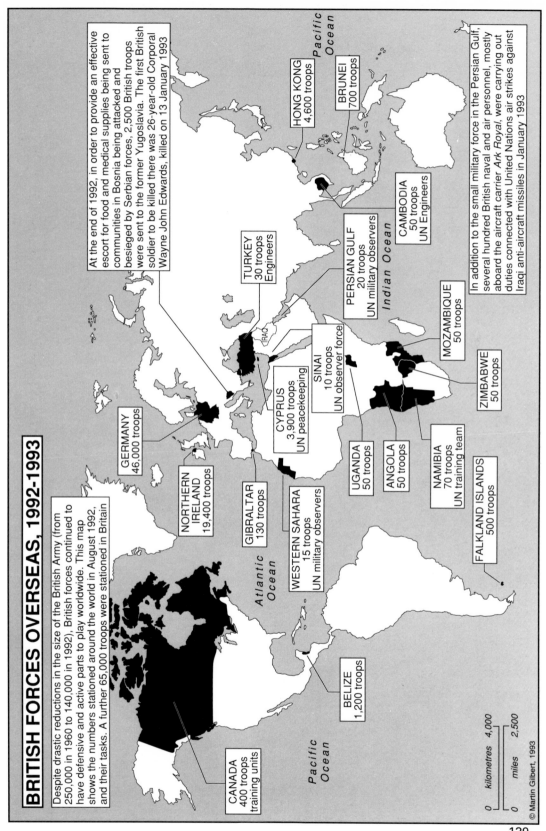

Despite drastic reductions in the size of the British Army (from 250,000 in 1960 to 140,000 in 1992), British forces continued to have defensive and active parts to play worldwide. This map shows the numbers stationed around the world in August 1992, and their tasks. A further 65,000 troops were stationed in Britain

At the end of 1992, in order to provide an effective escort for food and medical supplies being sent to communities in Bosnia being attacked and besieged by Serbian forces, 2,500 British troops were sent to the former Yugoslavia. The first British soldier to be killed there was 26-year-old Corporal Wayne John Edwards, killed on 13 January 1993

In addition to the small military force in the Persian Gulf, several hundred British naval and air personnel, mostly aboard the aircraft carrier *Ark Royal*, were carrying out duties connected with United Nations air strikes against Iraqi anti-aircraft missiles in January 1993

HONG KONG
4,600 troops

BRUNEI
700 troops

CAMBODIA
50 troops
UN Engineers

TURKEY
30 troops
Engineers

PERSIAN GULF
20 troops
UN military observers

MOZAMBIQUE
50 troops

ZIMBABWE
50 troops

IRAQ

SINAI
10 troops
UN observer force

CYPRUS
3,900 troops
UN peacekeeping

UGANDA
50 troops

ANGOLA
50 troops

NAMIBIA
70 troops
UN training team

GERMANY
46,000 troops

NORTHERN
IRELAND
19,400 troops

GIBRALTAR
130 troops

WESTERN SAHARA
15 troops
UN military observers

FALKLAND ISLANDS
500 troops

BELIZE
1,200 troops

CANADA
400 troops
training units

Pacific Ocean

Indian Ocean

Atlantic Ocean

Pacific Ocean

0   kilometres   4,000

0   miles   2,500

© Martin Gilbert, 1993

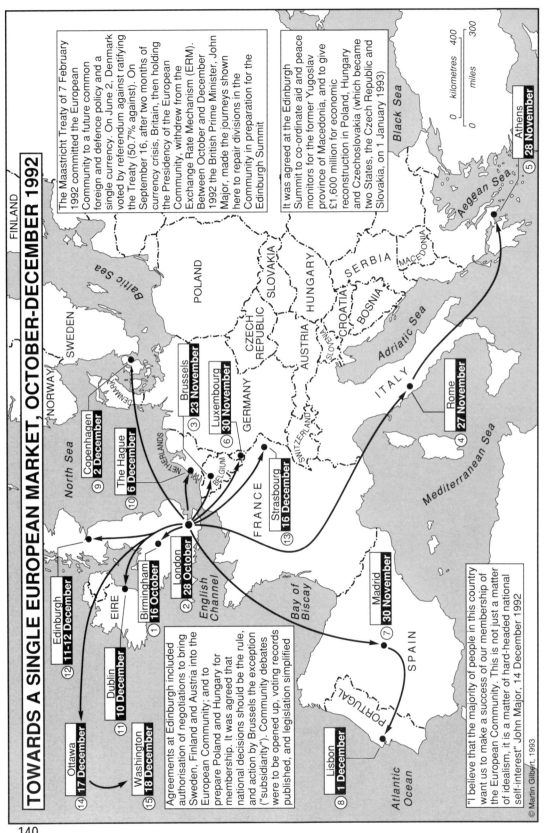

TOWARDS A SINGLE EUROPEAN MARKET, OCTOBER-DECEMBER 1992

The Maastricht Treaty of 7 February 1992 committed the European Community to a future common foreign and defence policy and a single currency. On June 2, Denmark voted by referendum against ratifying the Treaty (50.7% against). On September 16, after two months of currency crisis, Britain, then holding the Presidency of the European Community, withdrew from the Exchange Rate Mechanism (ERM). Between October and December 1992 the British Prime Minister, John Major, made the journeys shown here to repair divisions in the Community in preparation for the Edinburgh Summit

It was agreed at the Edinburgh Summit to co-ordinate aid and peace monitors for the former Yugoslav province of Macedonia, and to give £1,600 million for economic reconstruction in Poland, Hungary and Czechoslovakia (which became two States, the Czech Republic and Slovakia, on 1 January 1993)

Agreements at Edinburgh included authorisation of negotiations to bring Sweden, Finland and Austria into the European Community; and to prepare Poland and Hungary for membership. It was agreed that national decisions should be the rule, and action by Brussels the exception ("subsidiarity"). Community debates were to be opened up, voting records published, and legislation simplified

"I believe that the majority of people in this country want us to make a success of our membership of the European Community. This is not just a matter of idealism, it is a matter of hard-headed national self-interest" John Major, 14 December 1992

① London **28 October**
② Birmingham **16 October**
③ Brussels **23 November**
④ Rome **27 November**
⑤ Athens **28 November**
⑥ Luxembourg **30 November**
⑦ Madrid **30 November**
⑧ Lisbon **1 December**
⑨ Copenhagen **2 December**
⑩ The Hague **6 December**
⑪ Dublin **10 December**
⑫ Edinburgh **11-12 December**
⑬ Strasbourg **16 December**
⑭ Ottawa **17 December**
⑮ Washington **18 December**

FINLAND
NORWAY
SWEDEN
Baltic Sea
North Sea
DENMARK
NETHERLANDS
BELGIUM
POLAND
CZECH REPUBLIC
SLOVAKIA
AUSTRIA
HUNGARY
SWITZERLAND
SLOVENIA
CROATIA
BOSNIA
SERBIA
MACEDONIA
GERMANY
FRANCE
EIRE
English Channel
Bay of Biscay
SPAIN
PORTUGAL
ITALY
Adriatic Sea
Mediterranean Sea
Aegean Sea
Black Sea
Atlantic Ocean

0 400 kilometres
0 300 miles

© Martin Gilbert, 1993

140

PUBLIC SPENDING, 1993-1994

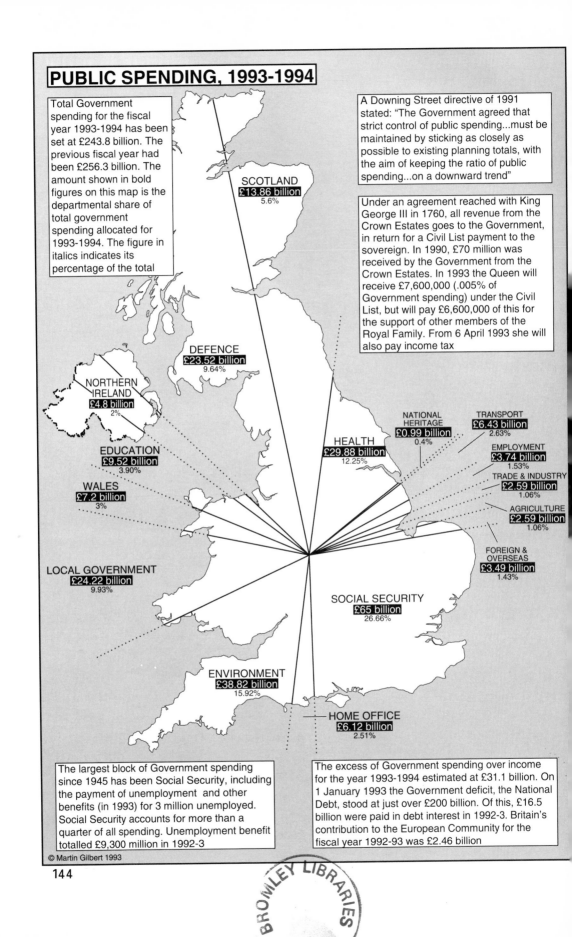

Total Government spending for the fiscal year 1993-1994 has been set at £243.8 billion. The previous fiscal year had been £256.3 billion. The amount shown in bold figures on this map is the departmental share of total government spending allocated for 1993-1994. The figure in italics indicates its percentage of the total

A Downing Street directive of 1991 stated: "The Government agreed that strict control of public spending...must be maintained by sticking as closely as possible to existing planning totals, with the aim of keeping the ratio of public spending...on a downward trend"

Under an agreement reached with King George III in 1760, all revenue from the Crown Estates goes to the Government, in return for a Civil List payment to the sovereign. In 1990, £70 million was received by the Government from the Crown Estates. In 1993 the Queen will receive £7,600,000 (.005% of Government spending) under the Civil List, but will pay £6,600,000 of this for the support of other members of the Royal Family. From 6 April 1993 she will also pay income tax

SCOTLAND
£13.86 billion
5.6%

DEFENCE
£23.52 billion
9.64%

NORTHERN IRELAND
£4.8 billion
2%

EDUCATION
£9.52 billion
3.90%

WALES
£7.2 billion
3%

LOCAL GOVERNMENT
£24.22 billion
9.93%

HEALTH
£29.88 billion
12.25%

NATIONAL HERITAGE
£0.99 billion
0.4%

TRANSPORT
£6.43 billion
2.63%

EMPLOYMENT
£3.74 billion
1.53%

TRADE & INDUSTRY
£2.59 billion
1.06%

AGRICULTURE
£2.59 billion
1.06%

FOREIGN & OVERSEAS
£3.49 billion
1.43%

SOCIAL SECURITY
£65 billion
26.66%

ENVIRONMENT
£38.82 billion
15.92%

HOME OFFICE
£6.12 billion
2.51%

The largest block of Government spending since 1945 has been Social Security, including the payment of unemployment and other benefits (in 1993) for 3 million unemployed. Social Security accounts for more than a quarter of all spending. Unemployment benefit totalled £9,300 million in 1992-3

The excess of Government spending over income for the year 1993-1994 estimated at £31.1 billion. On 1 January 1993 the Government deficit, the National Debt, stood at just over £200 billion. Of this, £16.5 billion were paid in debt interest in 1992-3. Britain's contribution to the European Community for the fiscal year 1992-93 was £2.46 billion

© Martin Gilbert 1993

144

MUSLIMS, SIKHS, HINDUS, JEWS AND BUDDHISTS, 1993

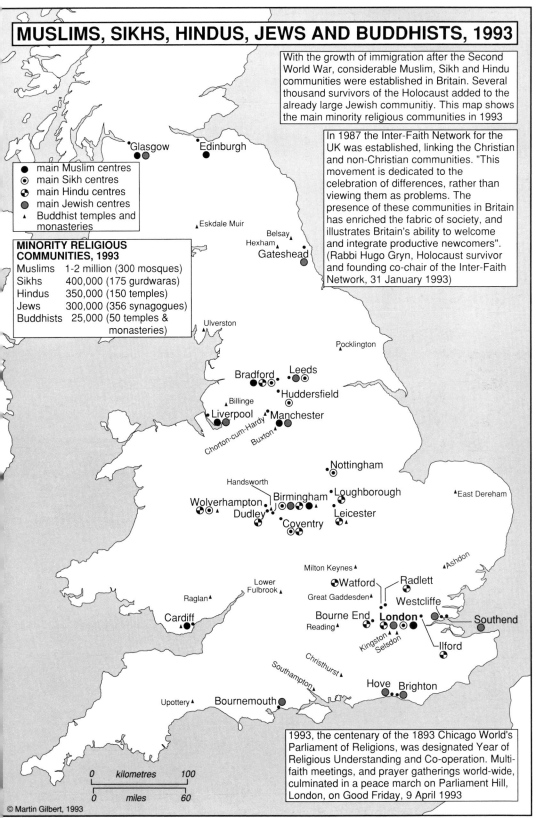

With the growth of immigration after the Second World War, considerable Muslim, Sikh and Hindu communities were established in Britain. Several thousand survivors of the Holocaust added to the already large Jewish communitiy. This map shows the main minority religious communities in 1993

In 1987 the Inter-Faith Network for the UK was established, linking the Christian and non-Christian communities. "This movement is dedicated to the celebration of differences, rather than viewing them as problems. The presence of these communities in Britain has enriched the fabric of society, and illustrates Britain's ability to welcome and integrate productive newcomers". (Rabbi Hugo Gryn, Holocaust survivor and founding co-chair of the Inter-Faith Network, 31 January 1993)

- ● main Muslim centres
- ◉ main Sikh centres
- ◕ main Hindu centres
- ● main Jewish centres
- ▲ Buddhist temples and monasteries

MINORITY RELIGIOUS COMMUNITIES, 1993

Muslims	1-2 million (300 mosques)
Sikhs	400,000 (175 gurdwaras)
Hindus	350,000 (150 temples)
Jews	300,000 (356 synagogues)
Buddhists	25,000 (50 temples & monasteries)

Glasgow
Edinburgh

Eskdale Muir
Belsay
Hexham
Gateshead

Ulverston
Pocklington

Bradford Leeds
Billinge Huddersfield
Liverpool Manchester
Chorton-cum-Hardy Buxton

Nottingham

Handsworth
Wolverhampton Birmingham Loughborough East Dereham
Dudley Leicester
Coventry

Milton Keynes Ashdon
Lower Fulbrook
Watford Radlett
Raglan Great Gaddesden Westcliffe
Cardiff Bourne End London Southend
Reading
Kingston Selsdon Ilford
Christhurst
Southampton
Hove Brighton
Upottery Bournemouth

1993, the centenary of the 1893 Chicago World's Parliament of Religions, was designated Year of Religious Understanding and Co-operation. Multi-faith meetings, and prayer gatherings world-wide, culminated in a peace march on Parliament Hill, London, on Good Friday, 9 April 1993

0 kilometres 100
0 miles 60

© Martin Gilbert, 1993

THE LONG-TERM UNEMPLOYED, 1993

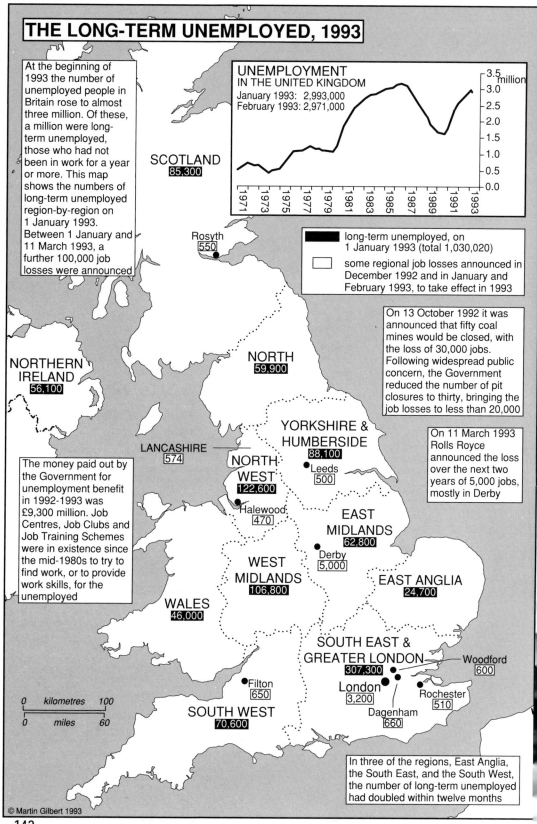

At the beginning of 1993 the number of unemployed people in Britain rose to almost three million. Of these, a million were long-term unemployed, those who had not been in work for a year or more. This map shows the numbers of long-term unemployed region-by-region on 1 January 1993. Between 1 January and 11 March 1993, a further 100,000 job losses were announced

UNEMPLOYMENT IN THE UNITED KINGDOM
January 1993: 2,993,000
February 1993: 2,971,000

long-term unemployed, on 1 January 1993 (total 1,030,020)

some regional job losses announced in December 1992 and in January and February 1993, to take effect in 1993

On 13 October 1992 it was announced that fifty coal mines would be closed, with the loss of 30,000 jobs. Following widespread public concern, the Government reduced the number of pit closures to thirty, bringing the job losses to less than 20,000

On 11 March 1993 Rolls Royce announced the loss over the next two years of 5,000 jobs, mostly in Derby

The money paid out by the Government for unemployment benefit in 1992-1993 was £9,300 million. Job Centres, Job Clubs and Job Training Schemes were in existence since the mid-1980s to try to find work, or to provide work skills, for the unemployed

SCOTLAND
85,300

Rosyth
550

NORTHERN IRELAND
56,100

NORTH
59,900

YORKSHIRE & HUMBERSIDE
88,100

LANCASHIRE
574

NORTH WEST
122,600

Leeds
500

Halewood
470

EAST MIDLANDS
62,800

WEST MIDLANDS
106,800

Derby
5,000

EAST ANGLIA
24,700

WALES
46,000

SOUTH EAST & GREATER LONDON
307,300

Woodford
600

Filton
650

London
3,200

Rochester
510

Dagenham
660

SOUTH WEST
70,600

0   kilometres   100
0   miles   60

In three of the regions, East Anglia, the South East, and the South West, the number of long-term unemployed had doubled within twelve months

© Martin Gilbert 1993

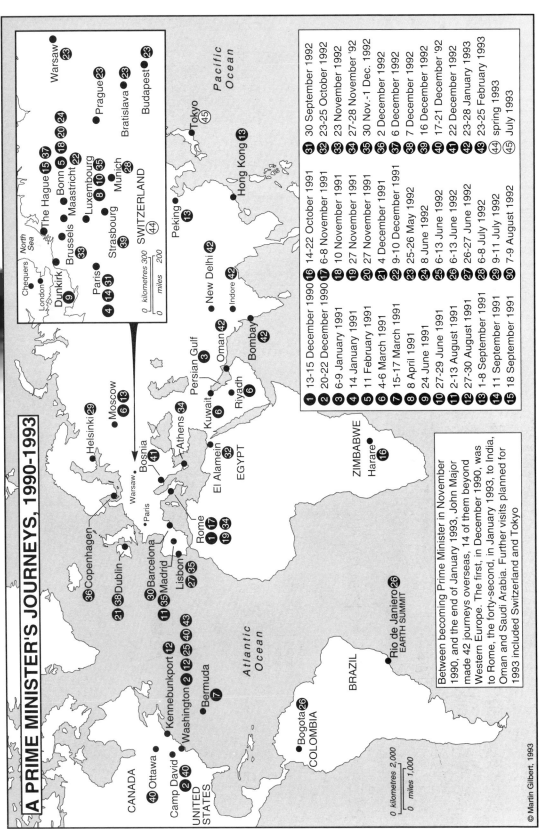

A PRIME MINISTER'S JOURNEYS, 1990-1993

© Martin Gilbert, 1993